Reasoning and Method in Economics
An Introduction to Economic Methodology

Ian M. T. Stewart
Lecturer in Economics
University of Nottingham

McGRAW-HILL Book Company (UK) Limited

London · New York · St Louis · San Francisco · Auckland · Bogotá
Guatemala · Hamburg · Johannesburg · Lisbon · Madrid · Mexico
Montreal · New Delhi · Panama · Paris · San Juan · São Paulo · Singapore
Sydney · Tokyo · Toronto

Published by
McGraw-Hill Book Company (UK) Limited
MAIDENHEAD · BERKSHIRE · ENGLAND

British Library Cataloguing in Publication Data

Stewart, Ian Marshall Thomson
  Reasoning and method in economics.
  1. Economics—Methodology
  I. Title
  330 '.01' 8   HB131   79-40446
  ISBN 0–07–084091–9

1 2 3 4 5 W.J.M. 81079

Contents

Preface   vii

Acknowledgements   x

1 Some introductory ideas   1
  1.1 Why methodology?   1
  1.2 Economics and science   4
  1.3 Reading strategy   8

2 Deduction   13
  2.1 The nature of deduction   13
  2.2 The syllogism   14
  2.3 The hypothetical syllogism   15
  2.4 Logical 'truth' v. material truth   19
  2.5 Deductive fallacies important in economics   20

3 Induction   31
  3.1 The nature of induction   31
  3.2 Proof and disproof   32
  3.3 The deductive basis of induction   35
  3.4 The logical problem of induction   36

4 Hypothetico-deductive method   39
  4.1 The stages of hypothetico-deductive method   40
  4.2 An economic illustration   42
  4.3 Hypotheses   43
  4.4 Testing   50
  4.5 Explanation v. prediction   65
  4.6 Some formal notions   70
  4.7 Postview   75

5 Distinctive features of economic data   79
  5.1 The problem of prediction   79
  5.2 Normative and positive   97
  5.3 Experimentation and control   104
  5.4 Causal v. teleological explanation   107

6 Economic theory and reality   112
6.1 The languages of economic reasoning   113
6.2 Various views   117
6.3 Economic theory: structure and testing   128
6.4 Various views revisited   150

7 The job of the applied economist   158
7.1 The economist as adviser   158
7.2 The nature of economic advice   161
7.3 The choice of investigational method   162
7.4 An overview of methods   165

8 Accuracy and error in applied economics   174
8.1 Accuracy   174
8.2 Error   177
8.3 Ignorance, error, and Statistical analysis   182

9 Sense and nonsense in econometrics   188
9.1 Basic detail   188
9.2 The epistemology of econometrics   193
9.3 Model-building as 'explanation'   196
9.4 Application   198
9.5 Summing-up   207

10 Survey method   211
10.1 Basic detail   211
10.2 Application   215
10.3 Summing-up   219

Glossary   222
References   231
Index   235

Preface

This book is intended to fill a gap in the literature: to provide a systematic *introductory* coverage of the philosophy of economic science.

When, several years ago, I began teaching a course in economic methodology, I found that there were no books available which were suitable as texts on this taught course, or indeed as supplementary reading on methodology for students in economics at an introductory or intermediate level. There is quite a substantial literature on economic methodology at an advanced level, both in books and in the journals, and this is expanding with a renewal of interest in methodological questions. But this professional literature assumes a knowledge of both philosophy and economics which puts it out of the reach of most students; indeed, the philosophical discussion may be inaccessible to the professional economist who has not first done some reading on the philosophy of science.

Excellent introductory texts do exist on the philosophy of science generally and on the philosophy of social science. Yet neither of these areas of coverage can entirely meet the needs of the student of economic methodology. Economics, in ways which are discussed in the present book, occupies a 'halfway house' position between the 'hard' sciences like physics on the one hand, and its companion social sciences on the other. While this fact is recognized in many of the existing texts, the breadth of their generalized coverage does not permit them to give more than a passing glance to the important questions raised for economic theory and practice by these special features of economic science.

Many introductory economics texts, of course, contain sections on methodology. But constraints on length must again limit the value of this coverage. More disturbingly, some texts give an account of 'economic method' which is heavily biased in favour of one particular methodological viewpoint. In this book, I try to give a balanced view of the various schools of thought in economic methodology, making it clear where controversy still exists. At the same time, in so far as students may have met a biased account of economic method, this bias can best be corrected not merely by 'sitting on the fence', but by actively explaining the nature of the bias. To this end, I have given some length to a critical discussion of the 'positivist' approach to economic reasoning, and of its empirical counterpart, econometrics.

Though this book deals with aspects of applied economics as well as with economic theory, there is no intention of giving chapter and verse on the practical detail of methods of data collection and analysis. There are many sources to which students can turn for instruction in the practice of econometrics, survey method, and data presentation, and the end-of-chapter reading guides will lead to a selection of these, together with further reading on the logic and epistemology of economics.

As regards the book's level of exposition and the knowledge which it assumes, I think it is important to point out a distinction between the economic and the philosophical sides of the coverage. On the side of economic content, it is assumed that the reader will have at least the acquaintance with basic economics which would be gained in an introductory university course or an advanced school course, or be acquiring this knowledge at the same time as reading this book.

On the philosophical side, no knowledge whatever is assumed on the part of the reader: it is a prime objective of the book to explain philosophical concepts 'from the ground up'. Starting from this zero-knowledge position, the aim is to take the reader through to the point where, if he wishes, he can comfortably embark on advanced books and the journal literature in economic methodology. Thus, although the book's economic examples and concepts are kept at an introductory level, I hope that the scope of the philosophical discussion will make the contents of interest not only to students at the beginning of their courses, but also to more advanced students and to professional economists who are seeking a lead into the methodological literature.

The book has, as I have said, been developed through some years' experience of teaching a course in economic methodology. At the same time, I am aware that relatively few institutions provide students with a separate taught course in this subject area, and that most students are therefore likely to be using the book as supplementary reading to a course in general economics, economic history, or applied social science. For this reason, I have tried above all to present the material in a *readable* style. While conventional 'scientific prose' may be appropriate in monographs and journal articles, I have studiously tried to avoid it in this book, and instead to put things in a conversational way. Another barrier to understanding of much of the advanced literature is the use by writers of unexplained technical jargon, made even more opaque by the differences in interpretation which different writers may put on a single term. Here, I have made sure that every technical term is explained when it first appears, and that students are warned of important differences in interpretation which they may find in subsequent reading; the Glossary is intended to give further help in this direction.

Citation of sources in the text has been avoided. Instead, the end-of-chapter reading guides briefly explain why each source is being recommended. The use of footnotes is minimal, and they are used for one purpose only: to alert the *advanced* reader to simplifications or points of interpretation in the main text which I have felt might call for some justification, or occasionally to make a methodological 'aside' where this seemed of interest.

Readers new to methodological discussion, i.e., the great bulk of this book's hoped-for readership, need therefore pay no attention at all to these few footnotes.

Where this book is being used as the text in a taught course on methodology, teachers will of course want to make their own directions to students as to the order and degree of detail in which the chapters and sections are to be read. For those students using the text as undirected supplementary reading, I have suggested some reading strategies in Section 1.3 of the text.

I hope that both teachers and students, if they have comments—constructive or destructive—on any aspect of this book, will accept a standing invitation to let me know of these.

My thanks go to Alex Scott, Senior Research Fellow at the Esmée Fairbairn Research Centre, Edinburgh, who read the entire text (in successive drafts) and provided comments on both detail and overall layout which were of inestimable value in dictating the final form of this book. Of my colleagues at Nottingham, Professor A. W. Coats has given me the benefit of his own interest and experience in methodology during early discussion of some of the central topics covered here. David K. Whynes likewise helped in discussion, and acted as devil's advocate in vetting the chapter on econometrics. I should also like to mention the various anonymous publishers' readers who have helped this book on its way through several draft versions.

Ian Stewart
University of Nottingham
October 1978

Acknowledgements

The quotations on the pages listed below are reproduced by permission from their respective publishers:

p. 82:   from R. G. Lipsey, *An Introduction to Positive Economics*, 4th edn, Weidenfeld and Nicolson, London, 1975, p.9.

p. 82:   from Lord Robbins, *An Essay on the Nature and Significance of Economic Science*, 2nd edn, Macmillan, London and Basingstoke, 1935, pp. 108–9.

p. 132:   from Fritz Machlup, 'Operationalism and pure theory in economics' in S. R. Krupp (ed.), *The Structure of Economic Science*, Prentice-Hall, Englewood Cliffs, 1966, p.54.

p. 151:   from R. G. Lipsey, open letter in promotional leaflet for 4th edition of *An Introduction to Positive Economics*, Weidenfeld and Nicolson, London, 1975.

p. 177:   from A. Coddington, 'Economists and policy', *National Westminster Bank Quarterly Review*, February 1973, p.61.

p. 184:   from S. Valavanis, *Econometrics*, McGraw-Hill, New York, 1959, p.6.

p. 204:   from L. R. Klein, *Econometrics*, Harper and Row, New York, p.2.

p. 215:   from M. Friedman, 'The methodology of positive economics' in *Essays in Positive Economics*, University of Chicago Press, 1953, p.31.

Some of the material in Chapter 5, especially in Section 5.1.8, was derived from my article 'Economic prediction and human action', *Futures* 7, 2, April 1975. The treatment in Chapter 8 of the question of accuracy in economic statistics follows Part I, Chapter 4, of my book *Information in the Cereals Market*, Hutchinson, London, 1970. Some of the aspects of the comparison between econometrics and survey method advanced here in Chapters 9 and 10 were originally presented in a paper 'The scope for market research techniques in economic investigations', read by me to the 1971 Annual Conference of the Market Research Society, and printed in the *Proceedings* of that Conference. I thank the respective publishers of these sources for their permission to use the material in the present book.

1

Some introductory ideas

Journal articles very often contain a section labelled 'methodology'. Usually you will find, on reading the section concerned, that what it contains is merely a description of the methods of data collection, analysis, and so on, which the author of the article has used.

This is a mistaken use of the word 'methodology', and the article-writer should have called his section simply 'methods'. In its correct sense, 'methodology' implies something much more than mere description. The ending *-logy*, here as in many other words, signifies 'study, discourse' (Greek *-logia*). Methodology, then, is the study or the discussion of methods.

The methodologist does not only set out to describe methods—though, of course, he must be able to describe them in order to discuss them. The essential part of his task is to examine the methods in question and to ask, for instance, whether the reasoning employed is logical, whether they lead to accurate results, whether they are economical in time and cost, and so on. He may compare different possible methods under these various headings, with a view to showing which methods are sound or unsound, or which is the best to use for a given purpose. Finally, he may work out new methods or make improvements to old ones.

To gain a full understanding of the methodologist's job, we need to look at the various questions he asks, and ask still further questions about those in turn. For instance, if we want to know whether or not a given method is logical, we have first to be sure what we mean by 'logical'. In examining the accuracy of a set of results, we must be sure we know what kind of 'accuracy' we are looking for. Questions like these are the main concern of this book.

1.1 Why methodology?

It may seem sensible to ask: 'Why do we need methodologists anyway? The people who *use* the methods—the applied and research economists—are best qualified to say whether their way of working is the right one or not. After all, they find out what methods are the correct ones in a very simple way: if they use the wrong methods, they will get the wrong answers.'

But, as you may suspect, this seemingly hard-headed approach is usually mistaken. Just why it is mistaken will, I hope, become clear as you read through the book. In brief, though, the fact is that wrong methods do not

1

always produce wrong answers, and right methods do not always produce right answers—the reverse is possible in either case. What is more, in economics it is not always possible to tell straight away (or ever, in some cases) whether the answers you get *are* right or wrong.

So much is simply a fact of economic life. There are other arguments which can be put forward in favour of methodology as a worthwhile study, though these are matters of opinion. First: as economics, like all sciences, becomes more and more compartmentalized into specialisms, it becomes harder and harder for the individual worker to see outside the confines of his own field and the methods used in that field. The methodologist, in his role as one who compares and appraises methods, tries to stand apart and look at the wood rather than just the trees.

Second: there is still plenty of room for disagreement, in some fields of economics, about which methods are the best to use. (Sometimes, enthusiasts for a given approach will deny that any other approach can possibly be considered by any reasonable person. In this situation, you can usually find other groups of enthusiasts saying exactly the same about the different approach they happen to favour.) What is more, there are fashions in economic method, as in everything else. Not that fashions in themselves are necessarily bad: they are merely one way in which change and development take place. But there is little doubt that on occasions, certain methods of economic investigation are used because they are fashionable rather than because they are necessarily the most suitable for the job in hand.

It is up to the methodologist to try to judge when the 'dedicated followers of fashion' are going too far, and in general to weigh the arguments and counter-arguments of various feuding schools of economic method. This is not to say for a minute that the methodologist is somehow a man apart, standing outside all controversy and immune to fashion. In fact, quite the opposite is usually true. There are very few methodologists who spend their whole time studying methodology; the great majority are active in some area of economic research or application. (Come to that, whenever any economist discusses methods, rather than just using them, he is 'putting on a methodologist's hat' for the time being.) Far from being outside controversy, the methodologist is often to be found shouting loudest in favour of the side he himself happens to be on. At the same time, if he is doing his job properly, he will be as honest and as objective as he can in appraising his own views and those of his opponents. Here as elsewhere in science, honest objectivity by no means guarantees agreement. The important thing is that economic methods should constantly be subject to scrutiny, appraisal, and discussion.

Before leaving this section, it is worth while to deal with a question which has sometimes been put to me by students on a taught course in methodology. All this about the role of the methodologist in developing economic method, they say, is fair enough. But the point is: will *they* be better at economics if they study methodology than if they do not study it?

To bring it down to specifics: what kind of economic questions might one be able to tackle better as a result of some study of methodology? To name a very few out of many possibilities:

(a) From supply-and-demand theory   We are all familiar with the supply curve, the demand curve, and the equilibrium point where the two meet. But in reality, as most of us will also be aware, equilibrium need never actually be reached; and even if it is reached, there is precious little chance of demonstrating the fact. Moreover, it is extremely difficult to find out the shapes and positions of supply and demand curves in the real world. So what is the point of supply-and-demand theory? What evidence is there for suggesting the existence of these hard-to-grasp curves and the even more problematical equilibrium between them? Can they be of any use in guiding the real-life decisions of consumers and businessmen? If so, of what use?

(b) From national-income theory   Likewise, everyone knows about the Keynesian picture of the consumption function. But where did Keynes get the consumption function from in the first place? Suppose he just dreamed it up out of his head: how can we check whether or not it is a correct picture of what really happens in the economy? Does it matter whether we check it or not? (As you will know if you have studied more than introductory macroeconomics, it has been checked, and this checking has given us several 'competing hypotheses of the consumption function'. Why are they still competing, when the hard figures are there to give evidence on the matter?)

(c) From factual economic investigation   What, if anything, do econometric methods tell us which other methods do not? Does econometric technique help in predicting the economic future, and if so, in what way?

(d) From policy application   Is it the economist's job to make policy recommendations on the basis of his personal feelings and tastes? And if not, how is he to deal with 'intangibles'—amenity, nuisance value, convenience, and so on?

These, as I have said, are just a few of the ways in which methodological study can help with the down-to-earth business of learning and practising economics. I hope, though, that at least some readers will discover an interest in the more fundamental ideas which the methodologist deals in—ideas that at first sight are far from the everyday practice of economists, but which in reality underlie the answers to practical questions like those posed above. What is 'theory'? How is it derived and developed, and how does it relate to what we see happening in the real world? Is economic theory the same kind of thing as theory in other areas of study, or is it different in important respects? Does the economist have any kind of 'crystal ball'? Is economics a matter of common sense? Or is common sense long out of date, and computerized calculation our only hope for progress?

1.2 Economics and science

1.2.1 Science: a non-definition

'Science' is a word for which many definitions have been suggested, but none universally accepted. I have no intention of adding another possible definition to the list. More important for our purpose is to note a few features of a 'science' which would be common to pretty well all suggested definitions.

First, a science (as opposed, say, to an art) bases its findings on the establishment of *facts*, rather than on other standards of judgement such as tastes, feelings, opinions, or superstitions. You can put the same idea in many other forms of words: a science is objective rather than subjective; it is positive rather than normative. Or we can use a technical term which may already be familiar to you, even if you have just begun to study economics: the term *empirical*. In the way I have already mentioned, philosophers squabble over the exact meaning that should be attached to this word; but for now we will leave them to it, and simply give 'empirical' an all-purpose definition: 'relying on, derived from, factual observation'. Thus we can say that a science must be empirically based; by this we mean that, somewhere along the line, the scientist must set his ideas against the facts. And if these ideas turn out to disagree with the facts, it is the ideas—not the facts—which have to admit defeat.

The general idea is an easy one to grasp. But, as usual with ideas, when we get down to the detail and the application, things become much less simple. What exactly do we mean by 'facts'? And how do we go about establishing whether something is a fact or not?

Arguments about this question make up a large part of what has been written by philosophers of science, economic methodologists among them. Later chapters of this book will introduce some of these controversies.

A second widely-agreed feature of a 'science' is this: the people who practise a science do not spend their time simply piling up masses of disorganized data. The distinguishing mark of an established field of science is that the data collected are organized in accordance with certain patterns of thought which are peculiar to that field of science, and indeed serve to identify it and distinguish it from all other fields. These patterns of thought, taken together, make up the *theory* of that particular scientific discipline. We shall later be looking in detail at the ways in which theories, in economics and in science generally, are constructed and tested.

One incidental point (which you will not always find in the textbooks) is that in everyday usage, 'scientific' quite often carries a meaning of 'relying not just on human senses, but on the use of instrumentation'. For instance,

4

to measure the temperature of a liquid 'scientifically', you do not just stick your finger into it; you use a thermometer. Similar meanings are quite familiar in economics: if, say, you wanted to find out businessmen's investment intentions, it might be thought 'scientific' to do it by running a properly designed sample survey, and 'unscientific' to do it by asking two or three businessmen with whom you happened to be friendly. And when it comes to instrumentation, the computer is the 'scientific' instrument *par excellence*. Whether its use, or for that matter the use of any 'scientific' device in this sense, need necessarily lead to better results is another question we will touch on in our discussion.

1.2.2 Social v. physical sciences

An important distinction, which will turn up at many points throughout this book, is that between the *social sciences* and the *physical sciences*. The reasons for the importance of the distinction will, I hope, become clear as the discussion goes on. For now, we need only note the nature of each of these subdivisions of science.

The social sciences are concerned with people, rather than with things. Our own study, economics, is a social science (despite the fact that it takes account of some non-human factors, e.g., technology, as well as of human behaviour). Sociology, social administration, and criminology are likewise parts of social science, to name only three out of a rapidly expanding number of separately recognized fields of study.

The physical sciences—very often called the 'natural sciences' (or less often, the 'exact sciences')—are concerned with things rather than with people. Physics, chemistry, and engineering are three obvious examples.

The boundary between social and physical sciences is not strictly defined. For instance, is medicine a social or a physical science? In fact, though medical studies are undoubtedly concerned with people, the procedures of most medical research are more akin to those of the physical sciences than to those of the social sciences. (A clue to the reason for this is that while medicine is certainly a study of people, it is not usually concerned with how people behave.) Then again, is geography a social or a physical science? The answer is probably that, like medicine, it can be regarded as either or both, depending on what particular lines of study you are talking about within the science in question.

As a tailpiece to this section, it is worth mentioning a distinction that is sometimes suggested within social science itself, by which certain branches of study are referred to as 'soft' social sciences—leaving the others, of course, to be considered as 'hard' social sciences, though the latter term is not often used explicitly. When we come down to it, it turns out that economics is the only social science that is implied to be 'hard' (possibly with the addition of some aspects of geography, if you consider that to be a social science at all), leaving all the rest to be regarded as 'soft'. Needless to say,

5

this distinction is seldom received too well by sociologists or anthropologists, who understandably resent the implied hint that they are soft in the head. (Or that they are soft-hearted, which, to a social scientist, is possibly even worse.) The basic idea of the distinction, though, is quite a reasonable one: it derives from the undoubted fact that economists have far more real-world data at their disposal than do other social scientists; and that the study of economics has progressed far further in developing agreed methods of objective analysis of its data than have the other social disciplines.

At the same time, there are important cautions to be sounded against carrying this notion too far. Economics may well be relatively 'hard', as social sciences go. But it is far from approaching the rock-like 'hardness' of a science like physics.

There are disagreements on this issue among economic methodologists. Some feel that it is correct to follow a procedure in economics which is as close as possible to that of physical science, and that progress in economics will come about by approaching closer and closer to the physical scientist's practice. At the other end of the spectrum are methodologists who argue that economic problems and economic data are vastly different from those of physical science, and that economics should therefore follow its own methodological trail, with little reference to the example of physical science. In the chapters to come, we shall be looking again at this important controversy.

1.2.3 Economics: a non-definition

There is no lack of suggested definitions of 'economics': hardly a self-respecting textbook is without one. Economics is 'the study of wealth' or of 'material welfare'; it is the study of 'the general methods by which men co-operate to meet their material needs'; it deals with 'that part of welfare which can be brought directly or indirectly into relation with the measuring-rod of money'; or with 'those activities which, with or without money, involve exchange transactions among people'; it is the study of human action in all fields of choice; or the study of a communication system corresponding to the 'economy'.

A striking point about this list—and it would become more striking if the list were extended, as it well could be—is that while some of the suggested definitions agree with each other, some disagree, while other pairs of definitions neither agree nor disagree, but are simply based on totally different criteria which cannot be directly compared. As with the word 'science', so with 'economics': there is no one definition that can be called the 'right' one, and so here again you may make your own choice. In any case, as we shall see, any one economist's definition of his subject may well be bound up with his methodological views.

One definition which, with minor variations, would probably be accepted by most present-day economists is that suggested by Robbins: 'Economics is

6

the science which studies human behaviour as a relationship between ends and scarce means which have alternative uses.'

For the reasoning by which Robbins arrived at this famous definition, you should turn to the first chapter of his *Essay on the Nature and Significance of Economic Science,* one of the classics of methodological writing.

We run into trouble, though, if we try to use even such a widely accepted definition as Robbins's to draw strict limits round the study we call 'economics'. For instance: one of Robbins's main reasons for choosing this form of words was that he wanted to emphasize that economics was not simply concerned with material welfare—that it was not just a matter of goods and money—but dealt with problems of choice over a much wider range of human activity. Most economists nowadays (though not all) would accept Robbins's view on this point, at least in principle. Nevertheless, it is a fact that the great bulk of economic studies *are* concerned with material things. And it is certainly true to say, in the words of one of the suggested definitions that pre-dated Robbins's, that economics in practice seems to be concerned very much with things that can be related to the 'measuring-rod of money'.

Then again, given that we accept Robbins's definition as a reasonable starting-point, where does that leave some of the various kinds of study which in practice are usually held to be part of 'economics'? The situation is clear enough when we talk, for instance, about investigations into consumer preferences, national income trends, or trade theory, all beyond a doubt qualifying as economic studies. But what about what is usually known as 'industrial economics'? If we spend some of our time studying the reasons for industrial disputes, for instance, are we studying 'human behaviour as a relationship between ends and scarce means . . .'? Or are we studying group psychology? Then again, returning to what might be called 'main-stream economics', think of the process known as 'cost-benefit analysis'. Does that draw on the field of economic knowledge? Or is it better regarded as a branch of planning, or of accountancy? As a final example: considering some of the more remote reaches of present-day theorizing in such fields as welfare economics, we may wonder how far they are concerned with 'human behaviour' in any shape or form, and how far they are simply abstract mathematics.

Opinions differ on these and other borderline cases. And it is unlikely that Robbins's definition, or any other definition one cares to adopt, could ever make it easier to delimit the boundaries of economics in practice; even if everyone were agreed on the definition itself, there would still be the problem of reaching agreement on whether 'borderline cases' fell within the terms of the definition or not.

All this brings us to the shortest and probably the most famous definition of economics (coined, some say, by Jacob Viner, but by now a part of economic folklore): 'Economics is what economists do.' There's more to this witticism, obviously, than meets the eye at first.

As an alternative suggestion—a great deal less stylish, but perhaps more useful to the new student of the subject—one could say: 'Economics is what you find in any decent general economics textbook.' This suggestion, in common with the previous one, has the advantage that it allows for the continual change that takes place in the content of economic studies. The change itself results not only from development in theory and investigational methods, but from changes in the economic environment and consequently in the problems which the economist is called on to deal with.

From all that has been said so far, it should be obvious that to spend a lot of time trying to answer the question 'is economics a science?' is an unrewarding exercise. The only watertight answer would be: 'It depends what you mean by "science"—and it depends what you mean by "economics".' For what it is worth, most people would probably credit economics with being a science, on both the main counts already mentioned—that it is concerned with facts rather than fancies, and that it does have an underpinning of theory. In any event, it does not much matter whether we choose to label economics a 'science' or not, so long as we are aware of the kinds of reasoning and investigational method that are actually used in the discipline.

1.3 Reading strategy

The contents of this book have been laid out on the assumption that you will read the chapters and sections through in sequence (perhaps skipping some sections in ways suggested below), rather than dipping into it in the manner of a reference book. At the same time, I have provided a certain amount of cross-referencing in later chapters, so that, if necessary, you can refresh your memory about basic concepts introduced earlier.

Chapters 2 to 6 are concerned principally with theory, and the remaining chapters with application, but the two cannot be kept entirely in separate compartments. In order to appreciate the pros and cons of various methods of application, it is necessary to be familiar with the description in the earlier chapters of modes of reasoning, testing hypotheses, and so on.

Chapters 2 and 3 cover two topics that are fundamental to further understanding, namely deduction and induction. Deliberately, both are introduced by means of non-economic illustrations; the aim is to establish the ideas firmly in the first place, to lay a sound foundation on which to work through subsequent discussions of their economic significance. Judging from my experience of the taught course, some readers may wonder 'where the argument is going' during these early stages. I would ask you to take on trust their direct relevance to economic questions, and not only to theory but to applied economics as well. For example, the scheme of reasoning called the *syllogism*, introduced in Chapter 2, will turn out to be basic to later discussion of economic prediction and the testing of economic theory, as well as to the appraisal of econometric method. Likewise in Chapter 4, which discusses the widely accepted formulation of scientific procedure known as the *hypothetico-deductive account*, the discussion is deliberately carried on mainly in terms of 'science generally', and the economic illustrations used are only incidental. This again is done with a purpose: an important task of subsequent chapters will be to discuss ways in which economic method may differ from the method of 'science generally', and this can only be done with clarity if we first establish firmly what in fact this method of 'science generally' is. To centre the discussion on economic examples at too early a stage would merely have muddied the waters.

If, on the way through Chapters 2, 3, and 4, you do feel the need to reinforce your understanding by reference to economic instances, you can do so by working through the sets of discussion points which follow each chapter. These discussion topics are also given after Chapters 5 and 6, with the same objective of allowing you, if you wish, to check your understanding of the subject matter as you go along. (Where the book is being used as a text on a taught course, I hope these discussion questions will also be useful as essay topics or for class discussion.)

The presentation of the subject matter is self-contained in the sense that, if you wish, you can read it without referring to any other methodological literature whatever. But if you would like to broaden your knowledge of logic or the philosophy of science, or read at first hand some of the methodological controversies between economists, then the end-of-chapter reading guides will enable you to do so. In the case of Chapters 7 to 10, the reading guides lead you to sources of detailed information on the practice of applied economics. In compiling the reading guides, I have kept the lists of sources as short as possible, selecting them simply as being the most useful and interesting that I have come across.

Especially if you are a student reading this book without the direction of a teacher, I would pass on to you the good advice Professor Joad gave about how to read any philosophical book: at any one time, only keep on reading for as long as you are *understanding* what you read. Sooner or later, at any one reading session, there will come a moment when you realize that the words are passing before your eyes without conveying any message: as soon as this happens, put the book away for the day.

I have tried to make the argument accelerate as one progresses through the chapters, up to the end of Chapter 6. You will find that while the basic ideas of Chapters 2 and 3 are set out in a fairly leisurely way, the presentation becomes more condensed through Chapter 4, and is more so still in Chapters 5 and 6. In certain sections of Chapters 5 and 6, the argument goes at the kind of rate you would expect to find in journal literature. Since Chapters 7 to 10 deal with the application of concepts developed in the earlier chapters, you should find them relatively easy going by comparison with Chapters 5 and 6.

How much of the book you can skip depends on how interested you are in the philosophical side of things. If you want to carry your interest on into the journal literature of economic methodology, then you will have to plough through every section up to the end of Chapter 6, as well as casting an eye over the remaining four chapters. However, *at a first reading*, you might wish to pass over Sections 5.1.8, 6.3.5, and 6.3.6, coming back to them at leisure later, perhaps after you have had a go at some of the journal reading indicated in the reading guides.

If you are interested in the main ideas of economic methodology but do not intend to read beyond the present book, you can if you like omit altogether the three sections just listed. On the other hand, if you are totally uninterested in controversies over the nature and testing of *theory* in economics, you can skip the whole of Chapter 6, as well as the section of Chapter 5 just mentioned, and go straight to the chapters on applied economics; you will then find the occasional obscure reference to something in Chapter 6, but this will not disable your reading of these later chapters.

You may, of course, have another reason for skipping, namely that you are already familiar with some of the subject matter; you may already know, say, what a syllogism is, or be well acquainted with the elements of econometric analysis. I leave the choice of such skips to your own good sense. If you do skip in this way, you may find it useful to consult the Glossary in order to confirm that your own usage of technical terms corresponds to that in the text.

Reading guide: Chapter 1

A classic of economic methodology is the work by Lord Robbins, *Essay on the Nature and Significance of Economic Science*.[70] Read his Chapter 1 along with my first chapter. We shall see later that Robbins's *Essay* is a statement of one particular view of economic method. As it happens, I (and many other people) think that it is a correct view in all substantial detail, but you should follow the argument through to my Chapter 6 before forming your own opinion. Try also Chapter 1 of Kenneth Boulding, *Economics as a Science*;[7] perhaps slightly more difficult going than Robbins for the first-time reader, this book is a collection of essays by another distinguished economist and methodologist.

For further reading on the general philosophy of science, there is an excellent text by Peter Caws, *The Philosophy of Science*.[10] A great strength of this book is that, very unusually among texts in its field, it explains jargon terms as it goes. Chapters 1 and 13 are directly relevant to my first chapter; look also at his Preface, and skim if you like through the other chapters of his Part I, though this contains more philosophical detail than is strictly necessary for our present purpose. As regards the philosophy of social science, there is a comprehensive text by Abraham Kaplan, *The Conduct of Inquiry*.[36] Kaplan writes in a more academic and discursive style than any of the other three writers cited here; read through his Chapters 1 to 4, skipping intelligently, and not worrying overmuch if there are allusions which you do not understand at this stage.

All these four sources will be cited frequently as the present book goes on. They, and all other sources mentioned in the end-of-chapter reading guides, are listed in the References (page 231).

Look at your texts on general economics and see if they contain sections on methodology. If you find such sections in more than one text, compare different writers' accounts to see if they agree or disagree, and how they differ in emphasis.

Finally, our first journal reading is by Fritz Machlup, 'Are the social sciences really inferior?'.[50] This anticipates to some extent what we will be discussing in Chapter 5 about the distinctive features of economic data, but is so eminently readable that I am citing it now as a preview.

Discussion topics: Chapter 1

Obviously, at this early stage, any discussion topics must anticipate what is to come in later chapters. But by way of preview, you may like to think around the following few points.

1. Consider these five scientists: nuclear physicist; astronomer; biochemist; economist; criminologist. For each one, jot down a few problems he might be called upon to investigate; the data he might collect in doing so; and the kind of instrumentation (recall page 4) which you might expect him to use.

Now compare the economist with each of the other four scientists in turn. For each comparison, consider what problems over collecting and interpreting 'facts' have to be faced by each scientist. For instance: how might error arise in observation? How likely is it that the results of one observation will be repeated on other occasions of observing the same phenomenon? How easy is it for each scientist to predict the future behaviour of the things (or people) he is observing? Is it easy or difficult for him to convey to other scientists, and to non-scientists, the exact content of his observations and the meaning of his interpretation of these observations?

In fact, the five scientists were listed above in what would probably be accepted as declining order of the 'hardness' of their respective disciplines. From the points you have just considered, see if you can arrive at any definition of this notion of 'hardness'. (Then if you like, check out your view against the article by Fritz Machlup given in the reading guide to this chapter.)

2. If an economist and a fortune-teller gave you conflicting advice on an economic policy decision, whose advice would you prefer to follow—and *why*? (Note: the question is not as facetious—nor as easy—as it seems.) Suppose that in the event, the fortune-teller's advice turned out to be right and the economist's to be wrong: whose advice would you take on future policy decisions—and, again, *why*?

11

3. In your everyday reading of the newpapers, look out for uses of the word 'scientific' ('A scientific study has shown that . . .', 'This product has been scientifically tested', etc.). Try to establish what meaning of 'scientific' is implied in each context. Does it indicate that instrumentation has been used? If so, what might have been an 'unscientific' way of doing the same investigation? What, if anything, do the 'scientific' results tell us which the 'unscientific' findings would not?

2

Deduction

The style of argument called *deduction* is central to economic reasoning, as indeed it is to the reasoning of all sciences and of everyday life. Whenever we do any theoretical economic thinking—whether it be working through the familiar textbook 'models', or hammering out new theoretical ideas —then we do so by means of deduction. And, as later chapters explain, deduction also plays an essential part in the testing of theory against reality, as well as being indispensable whenever we try to predict the economic future. In this chapter, we acquire a basic knowledge of what makes up a deductive argument.

2.1 The nature of deduction

The word 'deduction' comes from Latin *deducere*, 'lead away from'. In deductive reasoning, we start with certain given statements and work *from* them—according to certain rules—to derive a conclusion. In other words, we *deduce* that conclusion.

The 'rules' to which we have to work are simply rules of correct reasoning. You might say these are no more than the rules of common sense, and so they are in a way. But the problem is that except in the very simplest of situations, it is by no means always immediately obvious what constitutes common sense and what constitutes error.

These 'rules of correct reasoning' are also familiarly known as the 'rules of logic'. And indeed, the ancient discipline of *logic* can be defined as the study of reasoning—or, some say, the study of correct reasoning. The job of the logician, in his traditional field of study, is to consider the ways in which reasoning can be right or wrong, and to draw up his findings in sets of rules which will make it easier for the rest of us to judge the correctness or otherwise of our own reasoning, and, more important perhaps, the correctness of other people's reasoning.

While we are dealing with definitions, it is worth mentioning a study closely related to logic, namely *epistemology*: 'the study of knowledge'. The distinction between studying *knowledge* and studying *reasoning* may at first sight seem both obscure and unnecessary; and indeed, in practice, the two disciplines overlap to a large degree. A clue to the difference between them can be given in this way: it is possible to engage in *reasoning* without necessarily saying anything at all about the real world, i.e., without concerning oneself with *knowledge*. If, at this stage, that proposition seems pretty much of a conundrum, I would ask you merely to file it away until the notion is looked at more closely in Section 2.4 below.

2.2 The syllogism

A traditional mainstay of deductive reasoning is the *syllogism*. This is an argument consisting of two statements which, taken together, lead to a conclusion. For instance:

1. All politicians are corrupt;
2. Bloggs is a politician;
3. therefore Bloggs is corrupt.

Or:

1. All businessmen are profit-maximizers;
2. farmers are businessmen;
3. therefore farmers are profit-maximizers.

We can show the general form of this kind of reasoning by using an approach similar to that of algebra, and putting symbols in place of politicians, businessmen, and so on:

1. All A's are B;
2. C is an A;
3. therefore C is B.

The items designated A, B, and C in this generalized example—corresponding to *politicians, corrupt,* and *Bloggs* in the first example—are called the *terms* of the syllogism.

The statements on which the conclusion is based—the ones labelled 1 and 2 in the examples above—are called the *premises* of the syllogism. (The singular of the word is *premise*; less often nowadays, you may also find the spellings *premisses* and *premiss*.) To distinguish the two premises from one another, we use another two technical terms: the premise that says 'All A's are B' is called the *major premise*; and the one that says 'C is an A' is called the *minor premise*.

Needless to say, in real-life argument, premises and conclusion need not always be arranged in this neat 1–2–3 order. The arguer might, for instance, boldly state his conclusion first, then go on to give the statements which led to that conclusion; or he might state the minor premise before the major premise.

In this introduction to the syllogism, I have given only the barest bones of a description; just enough to enable us to go on to discuss the place of deductive reasoning in economic work. In fact there are very many variants of syllogistic reasoning, both correct and incorrect: if you are interested in learning more about these, any introductory textbook on logic (such as those cited at the end of this chapter) will help you to do so.

Needless to say, everyday discussions are not carried on in terms of carefully constructed syllogisms. Nor, for that matter, is most scientific reasoning. People may very often, for instance, leave a premise unsaid —implicit—instead of stating it explicitly. Returning to our friend Bloggs, we might argue: 'Bloggs is a politician, therefore he is corrupt.' This turns out to be our first example all over again, except that the premise 'All politicians are corrupt' has been left unsaid.

It may occur to you that this practice of leaving out one of the premises (which, by the way, logicians call *enthymeme*) may lend itself to the construction of misleading arguments, either accidentally or deliberately. In this you would be correct, and we shall come back to the point when we look at deductive fallacies (Section 2.5).

To complicate matters still further, even where the stages of an argument are all stated explicitly, there are few occasions when real-life reasoning will be in the straightforward 'textbook' form of the syllogism. You find people stringing several premises together before reaching an eventual conclusion, or using the conclusion of one argument as a premise in the next one. Arguments may be phrased negatively instead of positively. (Try this: 'No opportunist is an honest man, and dishonest men are willing to take bribes. There is not a politician who is not an opportunist. Bloggs, being a politician, is willing to take bribes.' Well, is he?).

Logicians since the Ancient Greeks have delighted in putting together complex strings of argument in this way—with or without deliberate mistakes—and once again I would refer you to texts on logic if this kind of puzzle takes your fancy.

All the examples of syllogisms given in this section have been of the type called *categorical syllogisms*. They are so called because all the statements in them assert simply 'something-or-other is the case' (e.g., 'Bloggs is a politician', 'all farmers are businessmen', '*C* is *B*'). Statements like this are called *categorical statements* (or sometimes just *categoricals*), hence the name given to this form of syllogism.

Quite often, we can leave out the word 'categorical', since, if we refer to a 'syllogism' without further qualification, the term will usually be taken to mean a categorical syllogism. However, we do have to put in the word 'categorical' if we are comparing this kind of syllogism with another kind—which, in the next section, we go on to do.

2.3 The hypothetical syllogism

A *hypothetical syllogism* is one in which the major premise has the form: 'if . . . then . . .'. The generalized form of this kind of syllogism, in its most straightforward version, is:

15

1. If *A* is true, then *B* is true;
2. *A* is true;
3. therefore *B* is true.

For instance, we might say:

1. If Bloggs is a politician, then he is corrupt;
2. Bloggs is a politician;
3. therefore Bloggs is corrupt.

In an economic context, we could argue:

1. If farmers are businessmen, then they are profit-maximizers;
2. farmers are businessmen;
3. therefore farmers are profit-maximizers.

Or:

1. If the demand schedule for good *X* rises, its price will rise;
2. the demand schedule for good *X* is rising;
3. therefore its price will rise.

As later chapters will show, the hypothetical syllogism is a style of reasoning that plays a crucial role in scientific method; it is therefore especially important to be familiar with the construction of this kind of syllogism and to know the technical names given to its various parts.

As we saw, the hypothetical syllogism is defined by the fact that its major premise is an 'if . . . then . . .' statement. This kind of statement is usually called a *hypothetical statement* (or just a *hypothetical*)—hence the name given to this kind of syllogism.*

In some books, an 'if . . . then . . .' statement is called a *conditional (statement)*, and a syllogism starting from this kind of statement is correspondingly called a *conditional syllogism*. Here, I will stick to the term 'hypothetical', and I mention the alternative simply to save confusion if you come across it in other texts. Come to that, some authors, with admirable simplicity, simply use the term 'if–then statement' and leave it at that, though I have never seen anyone referring to an 'if–then syllogism'.

It is important that we now 'home in' on the hypothetical statement itself

---

* Some texts follow a different nomenclature, and reserve the term 'hypothetical syllogism' for a syllogism in which *both* premises are hypotheticals (and, of course, the conclusion is also a hypothetical). Still other books use the term 'pure hypothetical syllogism' to indicate a syllogism with two hypotheticals in the premises, and apply the contrasting term 'mixed hypothetical syllogism' to a syllogism that has one hypothetical and one categorical as its premises, i.e., to what I am here simply calling a 'hypothetical syllogism'.

and take it down into its constituent parts. Indeed, it is rather obvious that in an 'if . . . then . . .' statement there are two parts: the 'if . . .' part and the 'then . . .' part. However, these are not normally referred to in these simple words, but have their own technical names: the 'if . . .' part is called the *antecedent*, and the 'then' part is called the *consequent*.

In order to remember which is which, you may find it useful to keep in mind the Latin derivations of these two words: 'antecedent' means 'that which goes before' and 'consequent' means 'that which follows'. It need, perhaps, hardly be added that this is not necessarily a matter of the order in which the two parts of the statement appear; if we said:

Bloggs is corrupt if he is a politician;

the 'if . . .' clause would still be the antecedent. When we talk about 'going before' and 'following', we mean in terms of what causes what, not the order in which they appear on the page. Here again, we have looked at the hypothetical syllogism only in the barest detail, and texts on logic will introduce you to several variants of it. We shall ourselves be meeting it again very shortly. For now, only one more point about it needs to be made: we can, if we like, make the 'if . . .' clause of the hypothetical refer not just to one condition, but to two or several. For instance, we might say:

If Bloggs is a politician (and if the times are hard for politicians, and the anti-corruption laws are not strict), then Bloggs will be corrupt;

in which the antecedent contains not one but three conditions.

If we take this kind of hypothetical, with more than one condition, and use it as the major premise of a syllogism, we see that in order to reason correctly to the conclusion, we must be able to assert *all* the conditions as true in the minor premise. Suppose, for instance, that our major premise is the hypothetical just given: it is now no longer enough to say 'Bloggs is a politician; therefore Bloggs is corrupt'—what if the times were *not* hard for politicians, or if the anti-corruption laws *were* indeed strictly enforced?

Thus the generalized correct form of this kind of syllogism runs as follows:

1. If A_1 (and A_2, A_3, . . . , A_n) are true, then B is true;
2. A_1 (and A_2, A_3, . . ., A_n) are true;
3. therefore B is true.

It is not enough in the minor premise to say just 'A_1 is true'—at least, not if we want to be able to reason rigorously to the truth of B. Instead, we must also be able to say that *all* the A's in 'A_2, . . . , A_n' are true; if any of these A's were not true, then B might also not be true.

By this stage, you may already have realized why the hypothetical syllogism is so important in scientific procedure. We shall be discussing the point in detail later, but before leaving this section we may have a brief preview. Consider this hypothetical:

If hydrogen and oxygen are mixed, then water will be the result.

Now, of course, you need to do more than just mix these two elements to get water; they need to be mixed under specific conditions. Not being a chemist, I am not sure of all the conditions necessary, but can think of the most obvious one and add a few rows of dots to symbolize the others. We can add these to the antecedent of the conditional:

If hydrogen and oxygen are mixed (and if they are brought to a certain temperature, and if . . . , and if . . .), then water will be the result.

This of course is a hypothetical corresponding to the one in the generalized example, i.e., 'If A_1 (and A_2, . . . , A_n) are true, then B is true.'

In fact, it is in this form that a physical scientist will usually phrase experimental results—either the established result of an experiment which has already been carried out, or the expected result of one which he is about to carry out.

Now recall the economic instance of the hypothetical syllogism given on page 16; it began with the hypothetical:

If the demand schedule for good X rises, its price will rise.

When you saw that example, you may perhaps have protested: 'That is not a good example—because in economics we would never be able to suggest that a rise in demand *need* bring a price rise, unless we knew also what was happening on the supply side.' And of course, this is correct. In order to make the hypothetical into a more acceptable economic proposition, we would need to say something like:

If the demand schedule for good X rises (and if there are no offsetting movements in the supply schedule, and if the supply curve is neither perfectly elastic nor perverse), then the price of good X will rise.

If we wanted to be totally punctilious, we would need to put in quite a few more conditions in order to exclude all situations in which demand for the good might rise without this bringing about a rise in its price.

So, once again, we have a hypothetical with several conditions in the antecedent. Your knowledge of economics already has brought it home to you how much of the everyday reasoning of the subject is expressed in this way.

When a hypothetical is used in a scientific context, its antecedent is very often given an alternative name: the *assumption* or *assumptions*; and the consequent is renamed the *prediction*. In later chapters, we shall consider the appropriateness (or otherwise) of these alternative terms.

At this point, we can temporarily take our leave of the hpyothetical syllogism. Although we have seen how certain statements in scientific procedure can readily be cast into the form of hypotheticals, we have not gone on to look at the way in which the hypothetical syllogism itself is used in scientific reasoning. That important issue will be taken up shortly.

2.4 Logical 'truth' v. material truth

Consider this syllogism:

1. All politicians have two heads;
2. Bloggs is a politician;
3. therefore Bloggs has two heads.

Ludicrous as it may seem at first sight, this is a flawless piece of deductive reasoning. The syllogism is correctly constructed, as may be seen if you substitute 'are corrupt' for 'have two heads' in the major premise, and make the corresponding amendment in the conclusion.

The general point to be noted is this: the correctness of deductive reasoning does *not* depend on the factual truth of the premises. Correct deduction can proceed from factually false premises (as in the example just given, assuming that we can agree that in reality politicians do not have two heads). Contrariwise, we may find incorrect reasoning applied to factually correct premises; and to complete the permutations, we have the possibilities of 'factually correct premises, correct reasoning', and 'factually false premises, incorrect reasoning'. Additionally, we may start our deductive reasoning from premises whose factual truth is regarded as unknown. You may like to pause and compose a few examples of each type. (Deliberately, for the present, we shall not be looking at the question of *how* one goes about establishing whether a statement is or is not to be regarded as 'factually true', since this issue will be explored in later chapters. For the purpose of making up your examples, you can simply use statements that seem to you to be factually 'obviously' true, false, or unknown.)

So far in this section, I have used the phrase 'factually true' to describe statements that are true of the real world. However, in methodological writing it is more usual to use a technical term which means the same thing, and to refer to such statements as *materially true.*

Contrasted with these are the statements which we 'take as given' purely for the purpose of a deductive argument; in the jargon, we are taking these statements as *logically true*. In this second technical phrase, the word 'true' is perhaps rather a confusing one, since it is difficult to conceive of a statement like 'All politicians have two heads' as being 'true' in any normal sense of the word. However, we had better go along with established technical usage, perhaps adding mental quotation marks round the word 'true' when we mean 'logically true'.

This distinction between material and logical truth may seem strange if you are coming to the idea for the first time, and so may the proposition that the correctness of deductive reasoning is independent of the material truth of the premises. Perhaps, though, a training in economics helps to make the general notion of the distinction familiar, even if economists do not usually use the philosophers' jargon terms; you cannot get far into any textbook of economics before you meet some mention of what happens in the 'real world' as compared to what happens 'in theory'. This mental device is of course commonplace in economic teaching and economic reasoning. Scientists in other fields are, generally speaking, much less accustomed to making this *explicit* distinction between the 'real world' and the 'world of theory' as part of their everyday reasoning, though, as we shall see, it is a fundamentally important idea in scientific methodology.

2.5 Deductive fallacies important in economics

2.5.1 The nature of a fallacy

In everyday conversation, when we use the word 'fallacy', we usually just mean something like 'mistake' or 'common error'. But logicians give 'fallacy' a stricter sense: they apply the term to any argument in which the premises do not lead *necessarily* to the stated conclusion. In other words, when a logician calls an argument fallacious, he is not saying 'this reasoning is necessarily wrong', but rather 'this reasoning is not necessarily right'. By the way, we see from the discussion in the previous section that the words 'right' and 'wrong', in this context, need not mean the same as 'materially true' or 'materially false'. A perfectly correct argument, in logical terms, will lead you to materially false conclusions *if* you start from materially false premises—but such an argument will not be fallacious, as far as the logician is concerned. On the other hand, you may possibly use a fallacious argument and 'just happen' to come up with a materially true conclusion.

Traditionally, three main types of fallacy can be distinguished. *Logical fallacies* (sometimes called *formal fallacies*) involve breaches of the rules of correct inference—that is, they arise because of faults in the structure of the syllogism. *Verbal fallacies* (their alternative name is *semilogical fallacies*) are those in which the correct rules of inference appear to be followed, but on closer inspection are seen not to be. The third class, *material fallacies*, is rather a ragbag category, and includes several kinds of misleading argument; as the name implies, some material fallacies take us to the borderline between questions of correct reasoning and questions of material truth or falsity.

In this section, I am most certainly not trying to list all the very many individual possible fallacies that logicians can pick out—once again, a textbook of logic will do this for you if you want to follow the matter up. Here, my intention is simply to highlight the fallacies which seem to have most relevance to economic work; I am not suggesting, of course, that these are the *only* fallacies which can arise in economics.

Of the fallacies listed below, the fallacy of affirming the consequent is a formal fallacy; the fallacy of composition is a verbal fallacy; and all the rest are material fallacies.

2.5.2 Affirming the consequent

Think back to the hypothetical syllogism (Section 2.3). Recall that in its generalized form, it went:

1. If A is true, then B is true;
2. A is true;
3. therefore B is true.

Remember also that the hypothetical statement in the major premise can be split up into the antecedent ('if A is true') and the consequent ('then B is true').

Now in order to get to the conclusion, 'B is true', we must be able to say in the minor premise that A is, indeed, true. In other words, we state the truth of the antecedent of the hypothetical statement; in technical terms, we *affirm the antecedent*. Once we have done so, we see that the conclusion *must* necessarily follow. (Or, at any rate, its logical truth must follow; we are talking now only of deductive argument, and paying no heed to whether the premises or the conclusion are materially true.)

Consider what happens, though, if we try a different form of argument, like this:

1. If A is true, then B is true;
2. B is true;
3. therefore A is true.

This time, as you can see, we have the hypothetical statement in the major premise, as before. But instead of affirming the antecedent, we have *affirmed the consequent*: we say 'B is true' as the minor premise, and try to argue from this to the truth of A. Is this correct reasoning? The answer is no, as an example will illustrate:

1. If Bloggs is a politician, then Bloggs is corrupt;
2. Bloggs is corrupt;
3. therefore Bloggs is a politician.

Clearly, it is no longer the case that the conclusion *must* follow from the premises. Suppose a lot of other people, apart from politicians, were corrupt—businessmen, policemen, economists even? Then Bloggs might quite well be a businessman, policeman, economist, instead of a politician. In other words, the conclusion no longer follows *necessarily* from the premises—and in the logician's terms, that means that this form of argument is formally fallacious.

If we make the same transformation on another of the examples of the hypothetical syllogism we have already met (page 16), we get this fallacious argument:

1. If the demand schedule for good X rises, its price will rise;
2. the price of good X has risen;
3. therefore the demand schedule for good X has risen.

You should have no difficulty in making out a catalogue of various other things, apart from a rise in demand, that might well have caused the rise in the price of good X.

In fact, the fallacy of affirming the consequent crops up not only in economic science, but in a far more general scientific context. As we shall see, it is a fundamental feature of the testing of scientific theories, and in later chapters we shall be looking in detail at how this occurs.

2.5.3 The fallacy of composition

Suppose a crowd are waiting to see a procession. The first carriages appear round the corner. One man stands on tiptoe, and is pleased to find that this gives him a better view of the procession. But then everybody around him notices what he has done, and they all stand on tiptoe as well. What happens? With everybody on tiptoe, nobody gets a better view.

This example (for which I am indebted to Professor Samuelson) gives a good illustration of the way in which the fallacy of composition can arise in everyday human action. Expressed in more general terms, the fallacy of composition arises when you assume that *something which is true of the part must also be true of the whole*. In the example above, the fallacious argument would run: 'One man is seeing better by standing on tiptoe—therefore the crowd will see better if they all do the same.'

It is not difficult to see how the fallacy of composition may play a part in economic problems. For instance, there is the paradoxical situation that faces policy-makers and advisers in agriculture. The individual farmer faces a horizontal demand curve for his produce—in other words, he can increase his own output by any amount he likes without affecting the price he is able to get for that produce on the market. So, for an individual farmer, it may often be perfectly sensible business policy to adopt some innovation—a new machine, say—that has the effect of increasing output, and hence, he expects, increasing revenue. So far so good. But what happens if not just one farmer, but many farmers, all have the same idea? The *total* market demand for most agricultural goods, far from being totally elastic, is markedly inelastic. So if a lot of farmers do adopt the innovation and thereby increase their output, the arrival of the extra produce on the market is likely to push prices down considerably. The end result can be—and in practice, often is—that individual farmers finish up getting *less* revenue from that product than they did before the innovation was adopted. It is the 'standing-on-tiptoe' principle all over again.

Another example is the famous 'paradox of thrift'. Suppose people decide to increase their savings. This they begin to do, and on the 'Keynesian diagram' the 'savings' schedule rises. The level of national income sinks to its new, and lower, equilibrium point. If we have drawn the 'investment' schedule sloping upwards from left to right (that is, if we portray investment as a positive function of national income), the savings and investment schedules must now intersect at a lower level of saving than they did before. In other words, people's attempt to save more has actually resulted in a *fall* in total saving.

There is one interesting feature that is common to all three of these examples (and which comes up also in other economic problems of a similar kind). That is, in every case, the decisions taken by the individuals concerned are perfectly sensible for them *as individuals*. And this is so even if the people taking the decisions know that other people are likely to follow their example and produce an unwanted effect at mass level. For instance, the farmer in our second example was quite right in thinking that his most obvious way to increase revenue was to increase his output. The fact that in the end he did not succeed in doing so was not the fault of any action taken by him as an individual; it was simply the result of a lot of other people all taking similar decisions at the same time. And even supposing that he was aware that this self-defeating effect was likely to happen, it might still be that he would go ahead and increase output anyway, since, as he might argue: 'I can see lots of people increasing their output of this product—so you can bet the price is going to go down. But I cannot stop this happening. So I may as well do the same, and increase output myself, because then at least I will get the lower price on a bigger amount of product, and avoid my revenue going down any more than it has to.'

You can easily work out the similar reasoning that applies in the 'paradox of thrift' example. In both these cases, and in other instances where the fallacy of composition may arise in economics, the basic situation is the same: a certain action is sensible when one individual does it; but when many people do it, the total outcome is undesirable.

Awareness of the fallacy of composition helps the economist to alert policy-makers to this kind of difficulty. Admittedly, policy can not usually give a solution that will be satisfactory from everyone's point of view, since there may often be a genuine conflict of interest—the interest of the individual versus the mass interest or 'public interest'. The economist will have performed a useful function, though, if he is able to warn in advance of the existence of the conflict.

The fallacy of composition can also arise in forms that are easier to spot and to deal with, and which result simply from ignorance of economic theory. An instance of this is the old-time politicians' argument: 'The wise household balances its budget—income just equal to outgoings. Therefore, the country, to stay stable and prosperous, should likewise aim for a balanced budget.' Nowadays, thanks to the acceptance of Keynesian ideas, we know better. Or, at least, most of us do. It is still worth while, though, to look out for instances of the 'ignorant' fallacy of composition coming up in political speeches and the like.

2.5.4 Post hoc ergo propter hoc

The witch-doctor is worried because Spring is here and the crops still have not started coming up. But he knows what to try: he casts the appropriate spells—and, very soon afterwards, the crops start to sprout. The witch-doctor breathes a sigh of relief: he has proved his ability, at least till this time next year.

The politician is worried because the balance of payments is running in deficit. But he knows what to try: he applies deflationary measures at home—and, very soon afterwards, the deficit turns into a small surplus. The politician breathes a sigh of relief: he has proved his ability, at least until the next deficit comes along.

Witch-doctor or politician—both the characters in these examples have fallen foul of the fallacy called *post hoc ergo propter hoc*. This resounding Latin mouthful means simply 'after this, therefore because of this', and that phrase accurately describes the nature of the fallacy. It lies in *assuming that because event B happens after event A, then event B is necessarily caused by event A*.

This fallacy comes into the picture very often when people are appraising the results of economic policy measures. Think back to our witch-doctor casting his spells, and our politician applying his deflationary measures. Neither of them could ever be *certain* that it was his own action, and not some other factor altogether, that brought about the result he observed. The reason for this is simple: neither the witch-doctor nor the politician has any way of knowing what would have happened if he had *not* taken the action he did take. For all he knows, the aimed-for result might have happened if he had done something entirely different.

If this logical realization were accepted as the only guide for real-life action, the sensible thing to do would be never to try to influence the future course of events in any way—a view of the world that few people would accept as a workable one. The fact is, of course, that in reality we take it for granted that we can exercise judgement about whether a certain action *did* produce a particular result or not. For instance, most educated people would fairly certainly agree that the witch-doctor was mistaken in thinking he needed to cast his spells in order to make the crops come up. And most economists would probably agree—though the certainty is much lower this time—that deflation at home helps to some extent to correct a balance-of-payments deficit.

But if our politician were to assert flatly: 'My deflationary policy cured the balance-of-payments deficit', he would be laying himself open to the fallacy of *post hoc ergo propter hoc* just as much as did the witch-doctor with his spells. And, of course, as a glance at the papers will show, people do talk in this way all the time. For politicians, this kind of oversimplification may be permissible. But for the economist appraising policy, it is not. He can never afford to forget that a policy measure and the observed events that follow it may or may not be linked causally—and that even if there is a causal link, it may be a close link or a remote one.

The problem of the 'witch-doctor's fallacy' is made more pressing by two features which are typical of economic policy-making. First: individual policy measures are very seldom applied on their own—more often a 'blunderbuss' approach is used. For example, to deal with a balance-of-payments deficit, governments would seldom stop at applying internal deflation. They would, say, apply currency restrictions and import controls, to name but two of the possible measures that come to mind. The result of this is that it becomes very difficult to tell what contribution each of these individual measures makes to the eventual outcome, or whether it makes any contribution at all.

Second (and this is a more elusive point): suppose a government is faced with some economic problem, takes what it judges to be the right policy measures, and that the problem in question does *not* disappear after these measures have been taken. It is very tempting to conclude from this that the policy measures taken were 'not the right ones', or that they 'had no effect'. But a conclusion like this is merely a negative form of the 'witch-doctor's fallacy'. This is so because, once again, we have no way of knowing what would have happened if the policy measures concerned had not been taken; for all we know, but for these measures the problem might have finished up much worse than it in fact did. A real-life example of this was the 'barley explosion' in the UK—the big increase in the production of this crop that started in the early 1960s and went on for the next five or six years. The government, alarmed at the support payments they were having to make because of the downward pressure on barley prices, cut the guaranteed price for the crop for several years in succession. But farmers just kept on growing more. The naïve conclusion is that 'the level of guaranteed price did not affect farmers' readiness to grow barley'. But in reality, we cannot say anything of the kind—since we can never tell for sure how the production of barley *would* have gone if these cuts in the guaranteed price had not been made. In this case, as in all questions of policy application, all we can do is use our economic judgement to try to work out how far the policy measure and the events which followed it were connected by cause and effect.

You may justifiably ask 'But what *is* this thing called "judgement"? Given that we cannot say event *B* is caused by event *A* just because event *B* comes later in time, how *can* we go about checking the causal link between them?' This question takes us away from the topic of deductive fallacy, and will be taken up when we come to consider the nature of explanation in Chapter 4.

2.5.5 *Argument by analogy*

In generalized form, an *argument by analogy* is one that says: '*A* is similar to *B*; therefore whatever is true of *A* is also true of *B*.' Put in this bald manner, the statement is easily seen to be unsound. But there are various contexts in which it can seem at first sight to be a valid argument.

First of all, this fallacy comes up importantly in discussions of scientific methodology; it arises particularly when we consider the use of 'models'. Once again, this is a topic that will be taken up later on (Chapters 6 and 10).

In everyday economic reasoning, argument by analogy can turn up in the form of comparisons between countries, economic sectors, groups of workers, and so on. A real-life instance, only too familiar to economic policy-makers, is that of arguments over wage differentials. Surface workers in the coal industry, for example, might argue: 'Face-workers have just been awarded a certain percentage wage increase; therefore, since we are miners too, we should get the same percentage rise.' The problem with this style of reasoning, of course, is that while there are similarities between the wage-bargaining position of face-workers and surface workers, there are also dissimilarities; and it is a matter of debate whether the similarities or the dissimilarities are more important. The point to note here is simply that argument by analogy is not a conclusive argument in itself, but depends on whether the analogy is a good one—that is, whether *relevant* similarities exist or not.

Argument by analogy, in cruder but more pictorial form, is a favourite with politicians (and therefore is outside the area of economic science—but nevertheless needs to be recognized by the economist when he is appraising policy statements). The 'ship of state'—which is usually running on to the rocks or going down without trace—is one hoary old example, out of favour now because it has become a cliché. But in fact, the 'ship of state' still seems to be around by implication; we are fairly often told that the only way to 'keep our heads above water' is to adopt some economic policy or other. Or we are urged to decide whether we 'sink or swim'. Since in reality the country is unlikely to sink with all hands—no matter how bad the economic situation may become—it follows that this particular analogy provides no support at all for whatever policy is being urged on us. As another example of the same kind of thing, which also turns up frequently in political utterances, we are assured that the country will 'go bankrupt' if *x*, *y*, *z* are not done. But 'bankruptcy' is a financial state of affairs, very well defined in legal terms, in which businesses and individuals may find themselves: there is no such well-defined notion that can be applied to a country's finances. So once again we are left asking what, if anything, the argument really means: since the country is not in fact going to 'go bankrupt', what *is* going to happen if x, y, z are not done?

These examples, and any others like them which you may like to collect, admittedly seem laughable. But the trouble with such arguments is that they may obscure the real nature of any problem that exists, or may even make it seem that there *is* a problem when in fact there is none.

As a final example, argument by analogy often turns up in the teaching of economics (as in the teaching of many other subjects), and can both help and hinder understanding. For instance, it is very common for textbooks to illustrate Keynes's 'circular flow of income' by analogy with water flowing through a pipe—investment corresponding to water pumped into the system, and savings to a leakage of water out of the system. This is a good illustration in so far as it gives a striking mental picture of the nature of the 'circular flow' and the roles played by investment and saving. But the economy is not in fact a water-pipe; and if we are asked, say, '*Why* does national income fall when savings rise over investment?', there is not much practical value in replying: 'Because savings leak out like water from a pipe.'

The only safe rule for dealing with argument by analogy is to recognize it when it appears, and once again to use our judgement in deciding how appropriate is the analogy and hence how valid is the conclusion reached.

2.5.6 *Appeal to authority*

This is the argument that runs: '*A* is true because **** says so.' For the row of asterisks, insert the name of some deity, some political (or economic) figurehead, or even, in recent times, the name of some ideology. In Communist countries, at the time of writing, a particular choice of economic policy would be considered justified by many simply because it 'conformed to the principles of Marxism-Leninism'.

A lightly disguised version of the appeal to authority is to be found in an argument which I take the liberty of calling the 'fallacy of government infallibility'. It comes up in statements like this: 'In such-and-such a year, the government applied internal deflation, import controls, and currency restrictions. From this we can conclude that the problem of balance-of-payments deficit was the main one facing the economy.' To argue thus is to imply that the government's interpretation of economic situations is always correct—or more simply, that the government is infallible.

2.5.7 Argumentum ad hominem

Here also, personalities come into the picture, but for the opposite reason. The Latin phrase means 'argument directed at the man', and *argumentum ad hominem* consists in trying to demolish someone's argument by making unfavourable comments about him or her. This is another favourite with politicians, usually being based on reference to the political party that the person under attack belongs to. Alternative approaches are to cast aspersions on his or her honesty, personal habits, racial origin, or state of mental health.

2.5.8 Begging the question

In everyday conversation, the phrase 'begging the question' is often used in a variety of incorrect or vague senses. But it in fact has a precise meaning: it's the fallacy which arises when we base our argument on a proposition which has not been proved (or has not been agreed) to be true. The Latin name for this, often used in textbooks, is *petitio principii*.

This fallacy can arise when we are using a syllogism in which one of the premises is implied rather than stated—a very common state of affairs, as mentioned in Section 2.2. For instance: 'Progressive taxation redistributes income; therefore progressive taxation is good.' In this example, of course, it is the major premise that has not been stated, and it would have to run: 'Anything that redistributes income is good.' If, in argument, you stated this premise instead of leaving it out, then an opponent of income redistribution could only accuse you of having mistaken views on the matter. But if you did leave the premise unstated, he could accuse you not only of being mistaken in your views, but also of trying to mislead him by begging the question.

2.5.9 Circular reasoning

'Redistribution of income is a good thing.'
'What make you think so?'
'Because all the best economists say so.'
'But what makes you class these economists as the best economists?'
'Because they're the ones who support the redistribution of income.'

This is circular reasoning—the mistake that arises when we take as given in our argument the very point that we originally set out to prove. Usually, as in the example given here, circular reasoning is quite easy to spot, and it probably comes up more often in arguments over opinions rather than arguments about facts. (By the way, it may occur to you—correctly—that circular reasoning is a special case of begging the question.)

It is worth mentioning that, quite often in economic argument, we come across what seems to be circular reasoning but in reality is not. To quote the most obvious example:

'Why are prices rising?'
'Because wages are rising.'
'And why are wages rising?'
'Because prices are rising.'

This is perfectly correct reasoning, since the argument is that there really is a circular process of cause and effect going on. In other instances, though, apparent circular reasoning can arise from vagueness in stating theory:

'In the Keynesian model, a rise in consumption brings about a rise in national income.'
'And what happens to consumption when national income rises?'
'The rise in national income brings about a rise in consumption'.

This kind of proposition tends to leave people asking themselves: 'Well, what is it that brings about what?' The problem here is not circular reasoning in the precise sense; both the statements are true as they stand. But they fail to make clear the causation involved. The point is, of course, that the phrase 'rise in consumption' is being used to mean two different things: the first time it appears, it means 'an autonomous rise in the consumption schedule', and the second time 'a movement along the consumption schedule'.

Reading guide: Chapter 2

Caws, *The Philosophy of Science*,[10] Chapters 14 and 15.
    For further detail on syllogisms and formal logic generally, there are many textbooks you can consult; use of their indexes and contents lists will lead you to the topics discussed in this chapter. One well-established text is by Irving M. Copi, *An Introduction to Logic*,[20] Read his Chapters 1, 3, 6, and 7.

Discussion topics: Chapter 2

1. (a) Sketch out the usual textbook picture of the demand curve (and, if you like, write out its algebraic equation). Now express it in words, in the form of a *hypothetical*.
(b) Add (arbitrary) numerical scales to the axes of your diagram, and reword your hypothetical to include this new detail.
(c) Recall that the antecedent of a hypothetical often includes not just one condition, but many (Section 2.3). List as many as you can of the extra conditions you might wish to add to the hypothetical expressing the demand curve, in order to specify that it keeps its simple 'textbook' form. (Hint: many of these will be statements about things that do *not* happen: can you think of the phrase which 'packages' all the statements of this kind?)
(d) Of all the statements you now have in the antecedent of your hypothetical, which would you say have material truth, and which have only logical 'truth'? (Make this judgement purely on commonsense grounds for now; in later chapters, we shall explore the detail of *how* the material truth of statements can be investigated.)
    If you like, repeat all these steps for the 'textbook' pictures of the Keynesian consumption function and the consumer's indifference curve.

2. Given that some of the starting statements you have listed do have only logical 'truth', *why* do you think economists use statements like this in their reasoning? (Keep a note of your answer, and compare it later with the discussion in Chapter 6.)

3. In the following statements, see if you can identify examples (apparent or real) of the deductive fallacies listed in Section 2.5:

(a) 'Keynesian measures taken in the early 1970s failed to slow down the rate of inflation.'

(b) 'This appraisal of Soviet economic policy is misguided: it has been made by bourgeois economists.'

(c) 'Commuter rail services into large cities should be cut, because the average commuter finds it more convenient to travel by car.'

(d) 'The government should cut direct taxation, because this increases the incentive to work and hence promotes economic activity and encourages growth.'

(e) 'The price of corn is high because the rent of corn-land is high.'

(f) 'Profit margins in meat retailing are higher than those in the retail sector generally; this shows that meat retailers are inefficient.'

4. In the imaginary example on page 26 about the wage-bargaining position of face-workers and surface workers, we saw that the mere argument by analogy, 'we are all miners', was not a sufficient argument for wage-bargaining parity. What other arguments (first economic, then if you like political) might be brought in to support or deny the surface-workers' claim, i.e., the appropriateness or otherwise of the analogy?

3

Induction

When, as an economist, you are observing and interpreting your real-world data, there are two procedures which you will find yourself using time and again. One is to study a sample (of consumers, of firms, and so on) and to use your sample data to arrive at a general result. The other is to look at how a particular economic variable has changed over a number of past time-periods, working out from this an idea of its time trend. In both these cases, you are using the style of reasoning called *induction*.

In the introduction to the topic given in this chapter, I use non-economic instances exclusively. Here, as elsewhere, the aim of this is partly to establish the basic nature of the reasoning as vividly as possible. But importantly also, as later chapters will explain, there are controversies as to whether we can use inductive reasoning in economics in quite the same way as we use it in physical science. To avoid begging this important question, then, we start with some instances of induction taken not from any scientific field, but from everyday experience.

3.1 The nature of induction

What makes you think the sun will rise tomorrow morning?

In fact, of course, we take it so much for granted that the sun *will* rise each morning that, in the normal way of things, it would never occur to us to think about the matter. For all intents and purposes, we are 'sure' that it will be so; and you might think therefore that it would be obvious to us *how* this certainty comes about. But, unless you have already met the idea of induction, it proves not to be at all an easy matter to explain. Before reading any further, you may like to pause and work out your own explanation.

If we were to put the explanation into words, it would have to run something like this: I have made observations of very many mornings in the past, and on all these occasions the sun has risen; therefore I conclude that it will continue to do so in future.

This is an example of inductive reasoning at work—though, of course, the reasoning in this particular example takes place at an unconscious level in the normal way of things. If it were not for such unconscious induction, everyday learning would be impossible. For instance, we take it for granted that if we drop a solid object, it will fall towards the ground rather than staying in mid-air or moving sideways. We are aware that if we do not eat, we will get hungry, and that if we do eat, this is likely to relieve the hunger. Other possible examples are numberless. The one about the 'sun rising in the morning' is an old favourite in philosophical textbooks; and to quote another classically hackneyed instance, it is also by inductive reasoning that we are able to say crows are black, rather than white or grey.

Not all inductive reasoning, of course, is carried on at this unconscious level. As we shall see in the coming chapters, a lot of scientific investigation is based on a purposeful use of induction. But the pattern of inductive reasoning, whether simple or sophisticated, is always essentially the same: we look at a number of *individual* cases, and on the basis of this evidence we reach a *general* conclusion.

This process is reflected in the derivation of the word 'induction'. It comes from Latin roots implying 'to lead into': our several individual observations lead us into the general conclusion. (Recall the contrasting meaning of 'deduction', page 13.)

Very often in induction, the various individual cases come at successive points in time, and the general conclusion is then really a statement about the future, e.g., 'Whenever I have observed it in the past, the sun has risen in the morning; therefore I believe that in the future it will continue to do so.' But this time-spread is not strictly necessary for induction—we could, for instance, observe a few dozen crows sitting in a tree, note their colouring, and draw the general conclusion 'Crows are black'.

The description thus far outlines only the barest bones of inductive reasoning. Thick books have been written about the niceties of induction, and there is still disagreement among philosophers over the detail of what is entailed in inductive reasoning and how it can be used in science. We shall ourselves be looking at a few more basic aspects of induction in this chapter; and, as the book goes on, we shall be coming across it again many times. We shall see, for instance, that statistical techniques, in economics or any other field of study, are inductive in nature.

3.2 Proof and disproof

In talking about the end-product of induction, I have so far deliberately used the vague phrase 'general conclusion'. But what kind of a beast is this? And, particularly important from the point of view of the scientist, is it the kind of statement that he can take as conclusive *proof* of a proposition?

The answer is: 'No, induction cannot prove for certain that a statement is true.' When you think about the matter, it is not difficult to see intuitively that this is so. For instance, thinking again about the sun rising, I am forced to admit that I have no reason to say certainly that it will do so tomorrow, or on any other morning. All I can say, strictly speaking, is: in the past the sun has risen each morning, and so I have developed a very strong belief that it will continue to do so in the future. But I cannot see *for certain* into the future, any more than anyone else can. My past observations of the sun refer to the past, and no more; and it will always remain just possible that, one morning, the sun might *not* rise.

Then again, reconsider our flock of crows sitting in their tree. From observing these, we come to the general conclusion 'Crows are black'. But, lurking somewhere in the world, there might just conceivably be a white crow. For this reason, once again, we are unable to say that our general conclusion is one which will hold as *proof* in all conceivable circumstances.

This view of induction—that it can never prove a statement—is where texts often let the matter rest. But it is worth raising a minor query which does have relevance to economic work. Suppose, continuing with our previous example, that we *did* look at all the crows in the world—that we carried out what the survey researcher calls a *100 per cent enumeration* of crows. Suppose—and it is a pretty unrealistic supposition, but just possible nevertheless—that we had some way of being sure that we had indeed looked at all the crows in the world; and suppose we had confirmed that each and every one of these was black. Do we not then have conclusive proof, by induction, for our statement 'crows are black'?

It should be obvious, first of all, that in real-life investigations there are few situations where this kind of proof can be afforded, mainly because it would be very difficult to be sure that our '100 per cent enumeration' really has covered all the individuals we want to consider. Nevertheless, as we shall note in later chapters, there are certain investigational circumstances in economics where we can take it as established for all practical purposes that we really have managed to carry out a 100 per cent enumeration.

There is a much more fundamental difficulty to face, however, in any investigation where your 'individual cases' are at different points in time, and where your inductive conclusion therefore takes the form of a prediction. Obviously, here a genuine '100 per cent enumeration' would require us to look at all possible *future* cases of whatever we are investigating, as well as all past cases. If we had the crystal ball that would enable us to do this, we would not need to take the trouble of making inductive predictions in the first place.

Because of this second difficulty in particular, it seems inappropriate to talk of the 100 per cent enumeration as 'providing proof by induction' —though some philosophers have done just this, referring to the process as 'perfect induction' or 'complete induction'. Other philosophers, though, have got round the problem in an ingenious way, by suggesting that 100 per cent enumeration is not induction at all—since, they point out, it does not entail generalizing from known cases to unknown cases. From now on in this book, I shall follow this second usage. So we can say about the 100 per cent enumeration: *if* we can be sure for practical purposes that our coverage really is 100 per cent, then we do end up with conclusive proof on whatever it is we are studying—but this 'proof' is best not regarded as inductive, and applies only to the past. And yet another important qualification has to be made: when we say 'you have conclusive proof', we should really add '. . . *if* nobody chooses to argue with you over the ways in which you have observed or interpreted your data.' This last point anticipates a much later part of our discussion (Section 4.4.3), so you need only note it and file it away for now.

We come back, then, to our general conclusion that induction can't provide proof. But there is something else which, in given circumstances, it certainly can do, and that is to provide *disproof*. If, at this moment, I looked out of the window and saw a white crow flying past, my previous conclusion that 'crows are black' would most certainly be disproved.

But a complication arises here. When we say, for instance, 'Crows are black', are we talking about *all* crows? Or are we only referring to 'crows generally'—that is, to 'most crows' or 'some crows'?

If indeed we do mean 'all crows', then the position is exactly as I have just described it: we only need to see one white crow, and our statement is disproved. But if, instead, we are really talking about 'crows generally', we could still find a white crow—or even a few of them—without necessarily feeling that our general statement about crows had been shown up as untrue.

What *would* it take, then, to disprove such a statement about 'crows generally'? Before reading on, you may care to make out your own answer to the question.

Disproof would only come, in fact, if we saw *so many* white crows as to make us admit that our original statement—even though it was not meant to apply universally—had now been so badly discredited that it could no longer be taken as 'true'.

'If we saw *so many* white crows . . .'—but *how* many would we need to see before we had to admit that our original idea had been wrong? In everyday life we can leave the number unspecified, and just say 'When I have seen enough to convince me!' In scientific investigation it is seldom thought good enough to rely on undefined standards of this kind. Instead, the investigator will set certain *limits* as regards the number of contrary observations he allows himself to record before he must admit that his original statement has been disproved. For instance, he might start by saying, not just that 'crows generally are black', but 'not fewer than 99 per cent of crows are black'. He then makes his observations. If they give him reason to believe that fewer than his declared 99 per cent of crows are black, he will admit that his contention is disproved.

However—and this is a crucial point—even when he uses limits of this kind, he can still never *prove* his original statement by means of induction. If he *does not disprove* the statement, all he can say is just that and no more, i.e., that the statement has not been disproved by the observations he has made so far. No matter how many observations he makes, he can strictly speaking still not claim proof, since it must always remain remotely possible that further observations will take him past the limits he has set as the borders for disproof.

Admittedly, what the scientist can do 'strictly speaking' does not always correspond very closely with what he actually does in his everyday work. There are innumerable inductive conclusions, both in scientific work and in everyday life, which for all practical purposes are taken as certain; even the most punctilious philosopher would be mightily surprised if the sun did *not* rise tomorrow! And, as we shall see in Chapter 4, the weight of direct inductive evidence is seldom the only factor which is to be taken into account in judging the material truth of a statement.

3.3 The deductive basis of induction

Let us think again about the sun, still reliably rising each morning despite all philosophical quibbles. You will recall that, if I were pressed to say why I thought it would continue doing so, I would be forced to reply: 'In all the times I have observed it in the past, the sun has risen in the morning; therefore it will continue to do so in the future.'

But why 'therefore'? As we have also noted, I can never observe the future. So by what reasoning can I judge what the future behaviour of the sun is going to be, merely by observing its past behaviour? Before going on, you may like to pause once again and try to work out your own answer.

As a first clue, look back again at this piece of reasoning about the sun rising. There is obviously a conclusion there, the part which starts 'therefore . . .'. And there is one premise. We realize, therefore, that this type of argument is none other than our old friend the syllogism—a syllogism with one of the premises implied rather than stated. Now here again you may take a moment's pause (if you have not already jumped ahead of my reasoning) and work out, first: is it the major premise or the minor premise that is missing? And second: what would have to be the wording of the missing premise?

It is of course the major premise that has been missed out, and if we had to construct the full syllogism it would run something like this (putting the minor premise down first):

1. In all the times I have observed it in the past, the sun has risen in the morning;
2. what the sun has done in the past it will continue to do in the future;
3. therefore in the future, the sun will continue to rise in the morning.

This example illustrates an important feature which is common to all inductive arguments: *to reach a general conclusion by induction from the observation of individual cases, we must use syllogistic reasoning.*

When we are using induction predictively, the major premise of our syllogism must always have the sense 'what has happened in the past will continue to happen in the future'.

When we use induction in a non-predictive sense, the major premise still conveys a similar idea, saying something like 'what is true of observed cases is true also of non-observed cases'. Check this out on the reasoning which enables us to say that 'crows are black'.

We might decide to work out an all-purpose form of words for the major premise, which we could use in all instances of inductive generalization. The one just mentioned, 'what is true of observed cases is true also of non-observed cases' would do quite well, since of course it includes as a particular case the situation where our 'non-observed cases' are in the future and our 'observed cases' are in the past. Or, more picturesquely, we might say 'Nature is uniform'. Some philosophers, in fact, have called this premise a 'proposition of regularity' or 'proposition of uniformity'.

As far as anyone has ever been able to tell, the use of this proposition of regularity is absolutely indispensable whenever we reason to a general conclusion by means of induction. Admittedly, the proposition of regularity is almost always implied rather than being stated, but nevertheless it must always be there.

3.4 The logical problem of induction

This brings us to the final point about induction in this chapter, and a surprising point it is too. We can work to it by asking: from where do we get the evidence for the proposition of regularity?

The thoughtless answer might be something like: 'Well, you have looked at a lot of cases of whatever it is you are examining, and formed a general conclusion about these observed cases—and *that* is the evidence that your unobserved cases are likely to be subject to the same conclusion.' For instance, this naïve explanation might go on: 'You have seen the sun rise every day in the past—now that is a great many days, and on each and every one of these days the sun has risen. So what more evidence do you need in order to say the same will be true in the future?'

Attractive as this kind of answer is, we know from what has already been said in this chapter that it is wrong. To confirm this, we can spell out the syllogism by which we reason that 'the sun will rise tomorrow', adding the points just mentioned in the naïve argument:

1. I have observed that, every day in the past, the sun has risen (and, certainly, that is a lot of days, and a very uniform pattern);
2. what the sun has done in the past it will continue to do in the future;

3. therefore I conclude that the sun will rise tomorrow.

The qualifications about numbers of past observations and the uniformity of these observations come into the *minor* premise, not the major premise. It is obvious why they must do so: the qualifications themselves relate to the past. They are *not* part of the major premise, i.e., not part of the proposition of regularity.

Furthermore, they do not give us any grounds for reasoning *to* the proposition of regularity. In the syllogism we are reasoning, as always, from both premises to the conclusion. There is no way in which we can reason from the minor to the major premise.

This feature of inductive reasoning is quite general, and it brings us to this important realization: when we are generalizing inductively from a number of individual observations, *these individual observations themselves can never act as evidence for the proposition of regularity*. This is still so, even if we have revealed a very uniform pattern.

But having now discovered where we *do not* get the proposition of regularity from, we are right back at our initial question: where do we get it from?

Philosophers have had various ingenious stabs at answering this question, but none of the answers has ever been accepted generally as being the correct one; in fact, none of them seems very satisfactory. It seems that the proposition of regularity—this universal ingredient of inductive reasoning both in everyday life and in science—just floats in from nowhere, as a sort of assumption for which there can never be any conclusive evidence. Needless to say, philosophers of science have often been rather unhappy with the idea that scientific induction could be founded on anything as vague as this—hence the effort that has gone into trying to put the proposition of regularity on a firmer basis (or alternatively, to set up an account of scientific reasoning in which the investigator's findings did not depend on a proposition of regularity).

We shall shortly be considering how these features of inductive reasoning affect economic work, and in particular how they come into the reasoning of statistical prediction.

Reading guide: Chapter 3

Caws, *The Philosophy of Science*,[10] Chapters 26 and 35.
Copi, *An Introduction to Logic*,[20] Chapter 12.

Discussion topics: Chapter 3

1. What data would economists collect as inductive evidence of the real-world shape of (a) the supply curve for a particular product, and (b) the consumption function in a country's economy?

2. For both (a) and (b) above, work out the wording of the *assumption of regularity* which has to be introduced in order to reach the inductive conclusion. (Keep a note of your answer and compare it later with the discussion in Section 5.1.)

3. For both (a) and (b) above, try as hard as you can to find some evidence among the data you have collected about your *observed* cases (the firms you have checked on, the years in which you have noted consumption and income) which gives you any grounds for applying the assumption of regularity to your unobserved cases (the firms you have not checked, future years' relations between consumption and income). The objective here is that you confirm for yourself—I hope—that you can never get any such evidence.

4

Hypothetico-deductive method

In Chapter 1, we saw that though there is no widely accepted definition of 'science', there are nevertheless two features of 'scientific' procedure that are common to pretty well all suggested definitions. First: a science is based on certain patterns of thinking, which serve to define the subject matter of the science in question and which, taken together, are called the 'theory' of that science. Second: science is empirically based—that is, the scientist must always be prepared to confront his reasoning with factual observation. We now begin consideration of the ways in which the scientist goes about bringing his theory into contact with empirical reality.

Just as there is no one universally accepted definition of 'science', so there is no universally accepted description of 'scientific method'. However, there is one particular account of scientific procedure which, in one version or another, would be accepted by most methodologists as being somewhere near the truth. According to this account, scientists proceed by means of what is called the *hypothetico-deductive method*, and discussion of this method will occupy the present chapter.

Before we go on to look at the nature of hypothetico-deductive method, it is important to take note of two cautions. First: just because scientists are seen to proceed according to a certain method, it is not necessarily the case that they are consciously following that method; as far as they themselves are concerned, they may just be 'doing what comes naturally'.

Second, and more important from the point of view of this book: the 'hypothetico-deductive' account was originally put together to describe the procedure (or idealized procedure, anyway) of *physical* science. Among economic methodologists, there have been wide differences of opinion about the transferability of hypothetico-deductive procedure to economic science. Some writers have taken the view that it should be transferred lock, stock, and barrel—that economics, by trying to approach as closely as possible to the procedure of the physical sciences, could make progress towards attaining the empirical 'hardness' of these sciences. Other economic methodologists have put forward various modifications in hypothetico-deductive method as being more suitable for the particular characteristics of economic investigation: while still others have insisted that hypothetico-deductive method, in the sense in which it is pictured by the philosopher of physical science, is totally inappropriate for economic science, and that economics needs to construct its own account of scientific procedure. These differing views will be explored in Chapter 6. But to prepare the ground for that discussion, we need first to make sure of some basic features of hypothetico-deductive method, and examine (in Chapter 5) some of the special characteristics of investigation in economic science.

4.1 The stages of hypothetico-deductive method

In using the hypothetico-deductive approach, the investigator does not begin simply by making a set of random observations and rely on chance to decide what the nature of his conclusion may be. Instead, he starts by formulating a statement which takes the form of a *guess* at the likely outcome of his investigation. When I use the word 'guess', I do not mean that scientists normally employ a process of blind trial and error; their guesses are, most often, very well-informed guesses. Nevertheless, informed or not, the mental process used at this initial stage is essentially one of guesswork. The initial statement, though, is not called a 'guess': it is called a *hypothesis*.

Once he has formulated his hypothesis, the investigator's next task is that of *testing*. This is just what its name implies: making observations and seeing whether or not they are consistent with the hypothesis.

Often, though, it is not possible to go on to this second stage directly from the original hypothesis, since this hypothesis will often refer to things that are not themselves directly observable. When this is so, the investigator needs to *deduce consequences* of his original hypothesis which *are* directly observable, and carry out his testing on those. (You will now realize, by the way, how the name 'hypothetico-deductive' is derived.) In the textbook account of hypothetico-deductive method—coined, as I have said, mainly to describe the procedure of physical science—it is usual to give examples in which the original hypothesis refers to something very far from the world of everyday observation, and for which it is thus necessary to work out complex chains of deduction in order to arrive at consequences that *are* observable. It should be clear, incidentally, that in this kind of situation the 'chain of deduction of consequences' includes the design of an appropriate experimental set-up, and that this can sometimes be as difficult as any of the more abstract reasoning involved. One thinks, for instance, of the various ingenious ways physicists have evolved for tracking the paths of subatomic particles; or of the development of the electron microscope, which has made visible the 'genes' within the living cell, originally hypothesized in the theory of heredity.

It is not difficult to see why such formidable achievements of physical science have caught the imagination of methodological writers. But it needs to be pointed out that in the world of everyday scientific investigation, hypotheses are very often relatively near to direct observability, and the necessary chain of deduction of consequences is correspondingly short, often being no more than translation into the terms of investigational procedures which themselves are drawn up on well-accepted lines (such-and-such a solution turns litmus paper blue; such-and-such a percentage of mice die after being given such-and-such a dose of substance X).

It is obvious that in social science, and in economics particularly, hypotheses are likely to be relatively close to direct observability. In economic science, we are not confronted with problems like trying to view electrons or work out what is going on inside the living cell. Come to that, we are not faced with the need to test hypotheses about such unobservables as the subconscious mind or group morale, instances of the sort of thing which our colleagues in the other social sciences may well have to investigate. Economics may or may not be a 'miserable science', but it certainly is a matter-of-fact science.

At the same time, even in economics it is rather seldom that a hypothesis will be phrased in directly observable terms. Some 'deduction of consequences' is almost always necessary, even if this only takes the form of specifying the series of figures which the investigator is going to use as data. For instance (anticipating an example which we shall look at again in Section 4.2), suppose we formulate a hypothesis about how wage inflation is affected by the level of employment. Here, our observables are the published series of figures for money wages and for unemployment percentages. So, starting from our hypothesis that inflation is affected by the level of employment, we have no difficulty in moving to the deduced consequence: 'Then the series of figures for wage-rate changes will be related in some systematic way to the series of figures for employment percentage'; and it is this latter proposition that we would test directly.

Suppose next that the investigator has completed his testing. He can, strictly speaking, never *accept* his hypothesis as being true. The most he can do, if his observations were indeed in accordance with his hypothesis (or with its deduced consequences), is to register that the hypothesis has not been disproved. Instead of *acceptance*, he should speak of *non-rejection*.

In our discussion of induction in Section 3.2, we saw why this should be so: we noted that our observations could never be regarded as giving us *proof* of a statement, no matter how consistent the pattern of these observations might be, since it would always remain possible that future observations would throw up enough contrary instances to take us over the limits we had set for disproof. (Nearly all scientific observation is inductive, in fact. In some disciplines it has occasionally been possible to test a hypothesis by just one do-or-die observation; but, for reasons that will be brought out in Section 4.4.3, not even this kind of once-off test can be said to afford proof positive.)

Often, hypothetico-deductive procedure includes yet further investigation. The scientist may go on to deduce further consequences of his non-rejected hypothesis, and to test these in turn. Very often, where inductive testing has been used, these 'further consequences' will take the form of happenings which the investigator predicts but which have not yet been observed. If these deduced consequences then turn out to be true of the real world, even more support is given to the possibility that the original hypothesis is a correct statement of the facts.

It is worth noting, however, that not even this last stage can establish the truth of a proposition once and for all—because it will always remain possible that some day, someone might make observations that contradicted the deduced consequences, just as they might contradict the original hypothesis.

4.2 An economic illustration

By way of real-life illustration, we shall look at a famous example of hypothetico-deductive method from economics: the investigation which led to the formulation of the 'Phillips curve'. Here, the *hypothesis* was: '. . . the rate of change of money wage rates in the United Kingdom can be explained by the level of unemployment and the rate of change of unemployment . . .'.

As we see, this hypothesis relates to things which are very much part of the everyday world—it is relatively close to direct observability. All we need to do by way of 'deducing testable consequences', in fact, is to translate the idea of 'unemployment explaining wage-rate changes' to the observable consequence of a systematic relationship between the figures for unemployment and the figures for wage-rate changes.

At the stage of *testing*, these sets of figures were compared with one another, and the relationship between them turned out to fit in very well with the hypothesis. So the result was *non-rejection*.

Phillips then went on to the next stage, that of deducing and testing further consequences of his non-rejected hypothesis. We saw that in this kind of inductive enquiry, such 'further consequences' will usually take the form of predictions. Now in 1958, at the time of writing his paper, Phillips could obviously not subject his hypothesis to tests against what would happen in the future, for the obvious reason that the data he would have needed were not yet available. However, instead of this, he used a device that is frequent practice among researchers in this field: he 'predicted the past'. This meant that at the intitial stage of testing his hypothesis, instead of using figures for all the past years at his disposal, he left out those for a run of the most recent years; then at the stage of 'testing further consequences', he worked out what his non-rejected hypothesis *would have predicted* for these recent years, and compared these 'predictions' with the actual results for these same years. Once again, the comparisons were pretty close, lending yet more support to Phillips's hypothesis.

In subsequent years, many investigators did carry out further checks on the hypothesis, by testing the genuine predictions of the 'Phillips curve' against the observed figures of unemployment and wage rates in the years following 1958. For several years it turned out that these predictions also were notably accurate.

It is worth mentioning, though, that this particular example also illustrates the danger of regarding any hypothesis as having been 'proved' by means of the hypothetico-deductive method. There is always the danger, as we have said, that future observations will contradict our hypothesis, and this is exactly what happened in the case of the Phillips curve. After a number of years of good prediction, the Phillips relationship broke down. Just exactly why it broke down is a question that is still being discussed; all we know is that circumstances have changed in such a way that the relationships underlying the 'curve' no longer seem to hold.

4.3 Hypotheses

4.3.1 The nature of a hypothesis

A hypothesis, we said, is in the nature of a guess—some people would prefer to call it a suggestion—as to the outcome of a scientific enquiry. In this section, we look briefly at one or two features of hypotheses.

First, a point of terminology: there are some differences among philosophers over the exact meaning of 'hypothesis'. One meaning of the word has just been given in Section 4.2, and this is almost always the sense in which 'hypothesis' turns up in the everyday language of economics. Methodological writers, though, sometimes use the word in a broader sense, implying 'any general statement forming part of a scientific theory'; indeed, some people go even further in this direction, and reserve the term 'hypothesis' for a theoretical statement which is remote from direct observability. (These notions will be fully explained in Section 4.6.)

In this book, I shall continue to use 'hypothesis' in the everyday sense in which the word usually occurs in economics, except where I specifically state otherwise.

Traditionally, hypotheses are phrased as statements rather than as questions. For instance, you would hypothesize 'Consumption varies with income', rather than putting the question 'Does consumption vary with income?'. This is purely a matter of convention. Indeed, in many ways it might be better if hypotheses were phrased as questions; the process of testing certainly amounts to 'questioning' the hypothesis. However, the habit of putting hypotheses in the form of statements is so well established by now that we had better go along with it.

4.3.2 Derivation and functions of hypotheses

Exactly how do we arrive at hypotheses in the first place? And are there any rules we can learn that will help us to turn up hypotheses that are useful and which are supported by observation? Since the hypothetico-deductive method is such a cornerstone of the exact sciences, you would think at first sight that rules of this kind would have been drawn up long ago. But in fact, philosophers and methodologists have drawn an almost complete blank on this question. Far from having any systematic set of rules for hypothesis-making, we are still almost completely ignorant of the mental process by which hypotheses are produced. There is general agreement on the obvious proposition that hypothesis-making depends to some extent on the investigator's previous knowledge of the subject under study. For instance, before we can hypothesize 'consumption varies with income', we need to know what is meant by the two concepts 'consumption' and 'income'. Just as important, we need to appreciate the nature of the problems which national income theory has to deal with—since it is this appreciation which leads us in the first place to think that the relationship between consumption and income might be worth looking into.

This much having been said, though, most writers simply admit that we know nothing more about how hypotheses are derived. If a book of 'rules for successful hypothesizing' ever comes to be written, I suspect that its author will be a psychologist, not a philosopher.

In some books on the philosophy of science, you find the statement that for every problem there is an 'infinite number of hypotheses' that can be suggested as possible answers. In the world of abstract philosophical discussion, this is strictly true. For instance, there is nothing to stop me hypothesizing that national income varies with the phases of the moon, with changes in the population of rabbits, and so on for any number of items that I like. In any practical investigation, of course, it is ridiculous to suggest that you start from an infinite number of hypotheses; what you do is to start from one or from relatively few hypotheses, which you have selected as good ones to start from because they seem to be sensible possibilities. Your judgement of whether they *are* sensible possibilities comes, as we have seen, from your previous knowledge of the field and appreciation of its problems, and probably also from your interests, common sense, skill as a hypothesizer, and likes and dislikes as regards investigational method. The question of whether these 'sensible guesses' are or are not supported by the facts is one that can only be checked by empirical testing.

By discussing how hypotheses are arrived at, we also come to see what are the benefits—and what are the drawbacks—of using hypotheses at all, rather than just investigating around in all directions. One point of starting from a hypothesis, of course, is to direct investigation along a closely defined path right from the beginning. This should, one might expect, mean that investigational resources are used with maximum effect on the specific problem under study, instead of being diffused over a wider area. More fundamental from the philosophical point of view is this: by declaring his hypothesis *before* starting to work, the scientist voluntarily binds himself to abide by whatever the facts may show. If the real world disappoints him by not conforming to what he had expected to find, he cannot slip out of the situation by saying: 'Well, that is not really what I meant in the first place.'

Clearly, the first of these advantages of using hypotheses can also be a disadvantage, if the hypothesis happens not to be the right one. In that case, resources are certainly directed along a well-defined path, but the path leads to a dead-end. At the same time, perhaps this problem should not be emphasized a great deal, since 'rejection of hypothesis' is by no means always the same thing as 'failure of investigation'. As many methodologists have pointed out, science progresses just as much by the failure of investigations as by their success. (Unfortunately for the practical researcher, this view does not always seem to be shared by the bodies who give out grant money for research work.)

A much more significant possible disadvantage of using hypotheses is that by their very function of directing the scientist's attention in one direction, they may distract him from looking in other directions which in the end may prove to be more informative. And in the same way, they may reduce the chance of that 'happy accident' which can sometimes start scientific investigation off on new and fruitful paths (classic instances, of course, being the discoveries of X-rays and of penicillin). Again, the balance of pros and cons probably is determined by how good the individual scientist is at hypothesizing; as we have seen, a hypothesis comes into being often as much by inspiration as by intellect, and it may be that in the end there is no sharp distinction between 'good hypothesis' and 'happy accident'.

4.3.3 Deterministic v. statistical hypotheses

A *deterministic hypotheses* is one that suggests something about *all* the members of the group of objects under study. For instance, going back to our example from the previous chapter, the suggestion 'All crows are black' is in the form of a deterministic hypothesis. It can be disproved by the sight of even one non-black crow.

The statement 'some crows are black', on the other hand, has the nature of a *statistical hypothesis*, since it is suggested as applying to only *some* of the group under study; and we cannot take it as disproved until we have seen quite a few non-black crows.

The name 'statistical hypothesis', strictly speaking, does not necessarily mean that we use statistical testing in conjunction with this kind of hypothesis—but, in practice, we usually do. You will remember that in Section 3.2 we talked about 'setting limits for contrary observations': if the investigator got more contrary observations than the limits he had set himself, we said, he reckoned that his original statement had been disproved. Now, for 'original statement' we can read 'hypothesis'; and the 'limits' in question are those set by various statistical tests of significance and correlation.

In fact, deterministic hypotheses have relatively little importance in scientific work—and in economics, it is fairly safe to say, they have no importance at all. Very often a hypothesis may be phrased *as if* it were a deterministic hypothesis, while in fact it is intended as a statistical hypothesis and is taken as such by investigators and by anyone reading their results. Indeed, where an investigator uses statistical testing, it is obvious that his hypothesis must have been intended as a statistical hypothesis—if it were not so, then there would be no need to go in for the complications of statistical testing, since just one contrary observation would knock his hypothesis out of court.

For instance, suppose we hypothesize: Aggregate consumption varies with total disposable income, other things being equal.' Now, is this a deterministic or a statistical hypothesis? At first sight, it might look like the former, since we are after all only talking about *one* national income—not about *some* national incomes. Nevertheless, people can and do use statistical testing to investigate this proposition. And of course, on reflection, we see that it is indeed a statistical hypothesis. What we are really hypothesizing is that a *group* of measurements of consumption, made at specified time-periods, shows a correlation with a group of measurements of national income made at these same time-periods. Even if some of the measurements in the two groups do not fit into the general pattern, we do not take the hypothesis as having been disproved, unless and until such contrary observations exceed the statistical limits we have set ourselves.

4.3.4 Testability and non-testability

We have seen that an essential part of hypothetico-deductive procedure is the testing of hypotheses—that is, the comparison of hypotheses with what is observed in the real world. It follows from this that a hypothesis, if it is to be of any use to the investigator using hypothetico-deductive method, must be in such a form as to be *testable* against reality. In this section, we look at the features which determine whether a hypothesis is or is not testable.

Once again, before beginning, it is necessary to say that in methodological literature there is considerable difference of opinion over what exactly is meant by 'testable'. Here, I shall try to cut as many corners as possible, and simply draw up a brief all-purpose summary of the factors which seem to me to be most relevant to the question of testability in economic investigation. Even more briefly, I shall sketch out some of the main problems of interpretation attaching to each factor in the list.

We may start from the very obvious proposition that, in order to be testable, a hypothesis must say something that can be compared with factual observation. This allows us to pick out three kinds of statement which (most writers would agree) are *not* testable; they are given under headings (a), (b), and (c) below.

(a) Definitional statements   Very often, economic reasoning includes propositions which simply consist in defining something in terms of something else. An obvious example comes from national income theory, in which national income is defined as being the sum of consumption and investment

(with various possible frills, depending on how simple or complicated your textbook happens to make it). You may be aware that this relationship is correctly shown in symbols by using the 'identity' sign ($Y \equiv C + I$) and not the 'equals' sign. There is clearly no sense in trying to test this definition: for the purposes of our reasoning, it is so simply because we have defined it as being so.

(b) Vaguely phrased statements   Suppose an economist were briefed to check the statement: 'Margins in retailing are high'. As it stands, this is not a testable proposition, because its exact meaning has not been well enough specified. What do we mean by 'high'? Whose margins, and at what times and places? What exactly do we mean by 'retailing'? It is obvious that this kind of non-testable statement can be made testable by giving precise answers to these questions of specification. At the same time, this carries the danger that the statement you eventually test may not really mean what the original ill-specified statement was intended to mean by whoever made it.

(c) Normative statements   In Section 5.2.1, we shall be looking in some detail at the nature of a normative statement; for now, we may define it as 'a statement that is purely an expression of the speaker's personal tastes'. For instance, the proposition 'Progressive taxation is a good thing' is not a testable hypothesis. It is hardly necessary to say why this kind of statement is non-testable: it simply sets forth the speaker's own preference, rather than describing the facts of a situation; and so no facts can ever be brought forward to show whether the statement is objectively 'right' or 'wrong'.

4.3.5 Tautologies

As I have indicated, there is little dispute about the non-testability of statements of the three kinds just described, i.e., definitions, vague statements, and normative statements. However, there is quite a bit of controversy over the testability of some other kinds of statement in economics, and we go on to look at these debatable areas in this section and the one following.

A *tautology* (or *tautologous statement* or *tautological statement*) is a statement that says the same thing twice over in different words. In a scientific context, we might add that it could say the same thing in symbols as had already been said in words, or vice versa, or even say the same thing twice over in different symbols. To put the same idea in another way: suppose we have a statement 'X is Y'. Then that statement is tautologous if, on inspection, it turns out that the Y merely consists of a restatement of what has already been said in X.

Obviously, then, any definition is a tautology (in other words, you can if you like regard a definition as a particular kind of tautologous statement; come to that, you can take things from the other end, and view any tautology as an extended kind of definition). We have already noted that the Keynesian '$Y \equiv C + I$' is a definition, or, in algebraic jargon, 'identity'; now we see that it can also be called a tautology.

We also get a tautology, more complex in nature, when we reason deductively to any conclusion within an abstract system of logic or mathematics. For instance, the proposition:

$$(a + b)^2 = a^2 + 2ab + b^2$$

is tautologous; the expression on the right-hand side is merely another way of saying what is on the left-hand side. (Just to be awkward, this kind of proposition in algebra is almost always expressed with the two-line 'equals' sign, rather than the more correct three-line 'identity' sign.) Likewise, the theorems of Euclid's geometry, or of any alternative geometry, are usually considered to be tautologous, since once again they can be viewed as a restatement of the few postulates on which the geometrical system is founded.

In so far as a tautology can be viewed simply as a kind of definition, then, like any definition, it must be untestable. It must have logical 'truth', at least for the purposes of the system of reasoning we happen to be following, just because we have defined it as such. And it retains its logical 'truth' irrespective of anything that may happen in the real world.

When we speak, in contrast, of a statement which is *not* tautologous—that is, a statement to which material truth or falsity can be attached on the basis of real-world observation—we call this a *contingent statement*.

Sometimes philosophers use alternative phrases to express the two contrasting ideas just described: when they are referring to a proposition arrived at by wholly deductive reasoning within some abstract system, they may describe this as an 'analytical statement'. The contrasting term is 'synthetic statement'—that is, a statement which has been reasoned out from premises, some at least of which are contingent.

At the beginning of this subsection, I mentioned that we were entering an area of controversy. In fact, the controversy is not over the suggestion 'tautologies are non-testable'—since everyone agrees that tautologies are, indeed, non-testable, for the reasons just discussed. The real cause for argument is this: in scientific investigation, it is not always possible to establish to everyone's satisfaction just what statements *are* tautologies and what others are contingent. It is easy enough to agree that simple definitions like '$Y \equiv C + I$' are tautologous; the same is true of algebraic manipulations like the identity given above. But when we get a bit more complex in our reasoning and move even a slight distance from purely abstract deductive systems, it gets much more difficult to recognize whether a statement is tautologous or not. For instance, though geometry is quite often cited in texts as a tautologous system, some philosophers have argued that it really is nothing of the kind: you can, they point out, go and measure a right-angled triangle to test Euclid's suggestion about the square on the hypotenuse. Come to that, you can do the same with arithmetic—instead of just taking it on trust that two and two make four, you can put two bricks together with another two bricks and count the result.

If there is this potential difficulty in distinguishing tautologous from contingent statements in relatively abstract systems like geometry and arithmetic, it goes without saying that this difficulty is much greater in the physical and social sciences. The economic implications of this will be taken up in Chapter 6.

4.3.6 Testability in practice and in principle

Consider the proposition: 'In 1987, the consumer price index in the UK (to base 1970 = 100) will be between 400 and 450.' Is this testable or not?

The fact is, of course, that in its form and phrasing, the statement *is* testable; the only problem is that we do not have the data—at the moment at least—by which it can be tested. The simplest way round this is to class such statements as *testable in principle*. These can be contrasted with statements which are *testable in practice*, i.e., those which can be tested against currently available data.

Needless to say, this distinction between testability 'in principle' and 'in practice' is another fruitful source of methodological argument, in science generally and economics in particular. For a start, there is always room for differences of opinion about the dividing line between 'principle' and 'practice' in any instance where testing is called for. Obviously, this line is always shifting, partly because we move forward in time (so that predictions can eventually be tested against what turns out in reality), and partly because new techniques of testing come to be developed: in one rather old textbook, the statement 'the moon is made of green cheese' is cited as being testable in principle only, whereas nowadays it is testable in practice, and indeed actually has been tested.

In economics, most of the problems in this area arise because, as we have seen, very many of the hypotheses in which we are most interested are not themselves *directly* testable, but must instead be translated into terms of relations between observable data. The scope for argument lies in the appropriateness or otherwise of the figures used in the translation. The size of the problem varies as between different economic concepts. For instance, there is not much controversy about what figures an investigator should use in translating hypotheses about 'national income' or 'balance of payments' into directly testable terms. With rather vaguer concepts like 'economic activity' or 'pressure of demand', the room for differences of opinion is greater. And when it comes to notions like 'welfare', 'consumer satisfaction', 'amenity', and so on, many economists simply throw up their hands and say that, as far as they can see, there is no way in which these ideas can be translated into terms of observable data. Hence, they argue, propositions about them must be regarded as non-testable—certainly as non-testable in practice, and perhaps even non-testable in principle. At the same time, other economists are ingeniously trying to find convincing ways of translating these same concepts into observable terms; and still other economists are arguing about their success in doing so.

4.4 Testing

4.4.1 The logical problem of testing

We now go on to look more closely at the reasoning behind hypothetico-deductive testing. In doing so, we renew acquaintance with some ideas that were first introduced in Chapter 2, in the discussion of deductive reasoning.

Think back to what we have learned about the process of testing a hypothesis. Usually, we saw, our hypotheses are not phrased in terms which are directly testable; they have therefore to be translated into other terms which are open to direct testing—even if, as often in economics, this translation just entails choosing which sets of figures best express the notions about which we are hypothesizing.

Now, what is the pattern of the reasoning underlying this translation of 'not directly testable' to 'directly testable', and of the testing process that goes with it?

Let us work this out by going back to the economic example that we used in Section 4.2, the 'Phillips curve'. As we saw, Phillips's hypothesis spoke of 'wage inflation being explained by the level of unemployment . . .'. In choosing the sets of statistical observations for testing, and in deciding on his criterion for non-rejection, what reasoning did Phillips have to employ?

In fact, he necessarily had to reason in this way: 'If I am correct in hypothesizing that wage inflation is explained by the level of unemployment, *then* it will be the case that the figures for wage inflation show a statistical relationship with the figures for unemployment.' (For brevity here, I am of course simplifying both Phillips's hypothesis and the specification of what is entailed in a 'statistical relationship'.) I am not suggesting that Phillips *consciously* engaged in this sequence of reasoning—perhaps he did, more probably he did not. The fact is, though, that this is the form of reasoning which *must* underlie the translation of any hypothesis that is not directly testable into directly testable terms.

When Phillips went on to test this formulation, he was able to look at the results and say: 'Yes, there *is* a statistical relationship between these two sets of figures.' From this, as we said, he was able to assert that his hypothesis stood as non-rejected.

Having mentioned that we were going to meet some old acquaintances from Chapter 2, I perhaps need not bother to say what form of reasoning is in the picture here: you will probably already have recognized it as a hypothetical syllogism. Let us draw it out in formal style:

1. If inflation is explained by unemployment, then the figures for inflation and for unemployment will show a statistical relationship;
2. these figures do show a statistical relationship;
3. therefore inflation is explained by unemployment.

So far, so good. Or rather, so far, so bad—because you will probably have spotted something else about this syllogism: it is formally fallacious.

If you are in any doubt about this, check it by putting the syllogism in generalized form:

1. If *A* is true, then *B* is true;
2. *B* is true;
3. therefore *A* is true.

This is, of course, none other than the fallacy of affirming the consequent.

I am not suggesting for a moment that Phillips somehow 'made a mistake' in his reasoning. The fact is, that in setting up his hypothesis for direct testing, there is no other kind of reasoning he could have used. You may like to think of some other instances, from economics and other sciences, where the results of observation are used to check a hypothesis that is not directly testable, and confirm that in every case the reasoning used must commit the formal fallacy of affirming the consequent.

Now, as you may guess, all the innumerable scientists who have used hypothetico-deductive testing cannot all have been guilty of false reasoning. (Or, to be more exact, they conceivably may have been, but it seems very unlikely; for a start, most scientific findings *work* when they are applied to the real world.) The fact is, that although the reasoning we are speaking of is formally fallacious, this is not to say that it leads to 'wrong' conclusions or that it tells us nothing. What we need to establish is: what kind of conclusions *does* it lead to, and how are they reached?

As a first step in working out the answer, we look again at the generalized *incorrect* form of the hypothetical syllogism:

1. If *A* is true, then *B* is true;
2. *B* is true;
3. therefore *A* is true.

As we have already said, the syllogism is incorrect because we cannot assert the *necessary* truth of the conclusion on the evidence of the premises. But if we cannot necessarily say '*A* is true' on this evidence, what *can* we say about *A*? Before reading on, you may care to work out your own answer.

We can, in fact, say something like this:

1. If *A* is true, then *B* is true;

2. *B* is true;
3. therefore *A* is perhaps true.

You may feel like retorting: 'Fair enough—it is obvious that you can say "*A* is perhaps true" on the basis of these premises. But couldn't you have said "*A* is perhaps true" on the basis of no evidence at all? In other words, does your reasoning tell you anything you could not have guessed already?'

The answer is that it does tell us something new. In order to see why it does, let us do something we have not done up to now, and put the hypothetical syllogism in its *negative* form, as follows:

1. If *A* is true, then *B* is true;
2. *B* is not true;
3. therefore *A* is *not* true.

In the technical terms we learned in Section 2.5.2, we are here *denying the consequent*. And as you can see, this *is* correct reasoning: once we have said '*B* is *not* true', it follows necessarily that *A* also is *not* true. If you are at all in doubt about this, it may be useful to spend a few minutes thinking over this syllogism—if you like, replacing *A* and *B* with some of the concrete instances from the examples in Chapter 2.

The correct negative form of the syllogism, then—in which we deny the consequent, saying '*B* is *not* true'—allows us to reach the conclusion: '*A* is necessarily untrue.' Now, look back once again at the incorrect positive form, in which the consequent is affirmed, and see if you can establish what the reasoning of that syllogism has allowed us to say about *A* which we could *not* have said without the evidence of the premises.

We see, in fact, that the formally incorrect positive form of our reasoning does convey some useful information, as follows:

1. If *A* is true, then *B* is true;
2. *B* is true (that is, *B* is not not-true);
3. therefore *A* is perhaps true and is *not necessarily-not-true*.

I have added the hyphens to 'necessarily-not-true' in an effort to make clear the meaning of what is being conveyed. To repeat the same idea in more straightforward English: by being able to assert that '*B* is true', we have not managed to show for certain that *A* is true; but we *have* managed to *exclude the possibility that* A *is not true*.

Now, so far in talking about these cases of deductive reasoning, I have been using 'true' in the sense of 'logically true', without necessary reference to material truth or falsity. And correspondingly, of course, words like 'necessarily', 'possibly', 'for certain', and so on, have all been intended to relate to logical 'truth' and not necessarily material truth. But, since after all we are discussing the problems of empirical investigation, we should now work out what these logical findings imply for the process of hypothetico-deductive testing.

First of all: we see one reason why some present-day philosophers of science lay stress on the idea that testing is a process of attempted *falsification* rather than attempted *verification*. Strictly speaking, the scientist is never in a position to say that he has verified a hypothesis by reference to observed data—because, as we have seen, in order to try to reason to the truth of his hypothesis, he must commit the fallacy of affirming the consequent. But if, on the other hand, we think of testing as a process of setting a hypothesis up for possible falsification, then this logical problem is avoided. (By the way, I say 'avoided' rather than 'solved', for reasons that we shall come to shortly.) If, when the scientist checks his real-world data, he finds for certain that they do not show the relationships that his hypothesis had predicted, then he can use correct logic to conclude that his hypothesis is indeed false.

And what if, on the other hand, the real-world data do *not* run counter to the hypothesis? In that case the hypothesis has 'stood up to an assault by the facts', and hence the possibility of its truth can be regarded as better substantiated than before the experiment. The more violent the 'assault' which the real-world investigation arranged to provide, then so much the greater is the strength revealed in the hypothesis which has stood up to that assault.

Moreover, to continue the same figure of speech: the strength of a hypothesis can be gauged also by the number of assaults it has stood up to, and the range of different kinds of assault it has withstood. In other words, if a hypothesis has stood as non-rejected against a relatively high number of different attempts to falsify it, and if these attempts have been based on relatively varied kinds of factual observation, then the strength of that hypothesis—that is, the degree of confidence placed in it—is correspondingly heightened.

You may feel, in following this reasoning through, that all the parts of the picture have fallen into place like the neat pieces of a jigsaw (I certainly did when I first came across this account). We have now arrived at a satisfying picture of a 'logic of disproof', not only elegant in itself but able to help us to understand some features of what is involved in real-life testing. In one sense, this pleasing picture is also an accurate one—accurate, that is, so long as we are talking only about an idealized notion of what can be achieved in testing. Unfortunately for our mental comfort, we now must abandon this idealized scene, and look at the kind of testing that is possible in real life.

4.4.2 *Falsification v. verification*

Perhaps you have already spotted the real-life problem. It lies in a 'deliberate mistake' that came into a sentence a few paragraphs back: 'If, when the scientist checks his real-world data, he finds for certain that they do not show the relationships that his hypothesis had predicted, then he can use correct logic to conclude that his hypothesis is indeed false.' The trouble is that in real-life scientific investigation, the scientist is almost never able to show *'for certain'* that a predicted relationship does *not* hold, any more than he can show 'for certain' that a predicted relationship does hold.

In Section 3.2 we saw why this lack of certainty arises in instances where the observation used is inductive in nature (and you will remember, observation *is* inductive in the great majority of scientific investigations). We said that, in the usual methodological view, induction 'could provide disproof'. But we then went on to note that this 'disproof' depended essentially on the fact that the investigator had started out by setting certain 'limits for contrary observations': in other words, if his testing revealed more observations contrary to his hypothesis than he had allowed himself in these pre-set limits, then he regarded his hypothesis as having fallen. The point to emphasize now is this: nowhere in the rules of logic is there any indication of *what* these 'limits for contrary observations' should be. In fact, the choice of these limits is up to the investigator; and they will depend on the nature of the investigation, as well as being dictated largely by what the investigator, and his readers, think is 'sensible'. So in the event, inductive enquiry cannot give a certainty of disproof: it can only give a *probability of disproof*.

We saw that there was only one possible exception to this general finding, namely, where the hypothesis being tested was deterministic rather than statistical. For such a hypothesis, certainty of disproof would come from the sight of just one contrary instance. But, as we said, deterministic hypotheses are of exceedingly little importance in science. Indeed, it is not difficult to see now why they are unimportant: by simple common sense, scientists realize that the real world is not a world of certainties, but of probabilities and possibilities. For sure, you *could* decide to be very hard on your hypotheses, and take them as disproved if even one contrary observation were noted. But for most practical purposes, this is just too tough a test; its consequence would be that almost every hypothesis would fall before real-world observation—not a very constructive result as far as scientific progress is concerned.

In technical jargon, we often say that the findings of inductive observation are *probabilistic*—that is, that they must be expressed in terms of probabilities rather than certainties. (If you want to use a technical word to contrast with 'probabilistic', the usual one is 'deterministic'.)

Now, what does all this imply for the reasoning of hypothetico-deductive testing? Let us go back to the logically correct negative form of the hypothetical syllogism that we last saw on page 52. It said:

1. If A is true, then B is true;
2. B is not true;
3. therefore A is not true.

As before, let B stand for the relationship that the scientist predicts in his real-world data; and let A stand for the hypothesis on the basis of which he makes this prediction—that is, the hypothesis which is being checked against the real-world observations. Are we to interpret the minor premise as meaning 'B is (certainly) not true'? If so, we are taking a pretty impractical view, since, as we have said, real-life observation can virtually never provide this certainty of disproof.

Suppose now we rephrase the minor premise to conform with the kind of result that we *can* get in real life: it is clear that we would also have to reword the conclusion correspondingly. Before reading on, you may like to think out your own reworded syllogism.

In fact, it would go something like this:

1. If A is true, then B is true;
2. B is perhaps not true;
3. therefore A is perhaps not true.

In your own reworded version, you may quite well have said 'probably' or 'possibly' rather than 'perhaps', and any of these words will do in this all-purpose context (though, as we shall see in Section 4.4.4, it is not entirely clear that 'probably' means the same thing as the other two words).

Thus, we see that in the non-ideal world of real-life observation, we no longer have a logic of disproof—rather, we have a logic of probable or possible disproof. Notice, by the way, that *this* 'perhaps' is not a result of any formal fallacy in the syllogism: as we said, this negative form—in which the consequent is denied—is logically sound. The 'perhaps' here arises instead from the inconclusive nature of real-world observation.

Just as a final flourish to this section: what happens if we apply this same wording to the formally fallacious positive form of the syllogism, in which the consequent is affirmed? Looking back to Section 4.4.1, we see that before we brought probabilistic reasoning into the picture, this form went:

1. If A is true, then B is true;
2. B is true;
3. therefore A is perhaps true.

If we now reword it in order to allow for the inconclusiveness of observations, it needs to go:

1. If A is true, then B is true;
2. B is perhaps true;
3. therefore A is perhaps perhaps true.

Compare the wording of the probabilistic versions of the logically correct syllogism (in which the consequent is denied) and the formally fallacious one (in which the consequent is affirmed). In particular, compare the two conclusions. The logically correct syllogism leads us to conclude 'A is perhaps not true'; and the formally fallacious syllogism gives the conclusion 'A is perhaps perhaps true'.

The distinction between these two statements is subtle, to say the least. From the logician's point of view, the first of them is obviously the more satisfactory, since it has only one 'perhaps', instead of two (that is, the conclusion is affected only by the probabilistic nature of real-life observation, instead of being affected both by this and by formally fallacious reasoning as well). However, if you get the feeling that as far as the working scientist is concerned, the difference does not really matter much, you would (in my opinion) be right.

The fact is, that whether you choose to talk about a 'logic of possible disproof' or a 'logic of possible proof', what you end up actually doing in real-life investigation is pretty much the same. Probably, nevertheless, it is more acceptable in methodological circles to talk in terms of 'falsification' rather than 'verification', for the logical reasons sketched out here; and this view is reflected not only in the methodological statements to be found in some economics textbooks, but also in some of the conventions of statistical procedure (as you will probably already be aware, in statistical testing we usually set out to falsify a 'null hypothesis').

Some methodological writers have quite sensibly opted out of controversy over whether we should talk about 'falsification' or 'verification' of hypotheses. Instead, they use the all-purpose term *validation*, to convey the idea of assessing hypotheses against the probabilistic results of observation. Currently, too, some philosophers are working on the development of a view whereby hypotheses, instead of having to be 'falsified' or 'verified', have varying 'degrees of confirmation' attached to them. Certainly, this notion seems well in line with our intuitive feelings about the 'strength' of a hypothesis—that is, the amount of confidence we can place in it.

4.4.3 The epistemological problem of testing

Having taken a look at the logic of hypothetico-deductive testing, we shall go on to consider another question, which, for convenience in labelling, we may call the epistemological problem of testing.

It can be introduced by means of a well-worn old parable. Philosopher X rushes up to philosopher Y, bursting with good news: all his life he has been trying to observe a white crow, and now at last he has managed to spot one.

'Ah', replies philosopher Y discouragingly, 'but how can you tell that the white thing you saw was actually a crow?'

The general point illustrated is this: no matter how carefully we set up our investigations, there will always be some room for argument over the interpretation of our results. It is always possible, or at least always possible to argue, that what we think we observed may not actually have been what we did observe; or that what we were observing may not have been what we really should have been observing in order to check our hypothesis; or that the conditions under which we made our observations were not what we thought they were, or were not fully enough specified.

It is important to realize that this source of inconclusiveness in observation is *not* the same thing as the inconclusiveness which results from using induction; the two sources of inconclusiveness are quite distinct, and, in investigations which do use induction, the one source is additional to the other.

To reinforce this idea, we can register that an experiment which did not use induction, but depended instead on a once-off observation, would nevertheless still give results that were subject to doubt. For an illustration of this kind of thing, we need to go outside economics and into the physical sciences, where some experiments of this kind have become famous (and are much quoted in methodological texts). To give a legendary example: when Galileo wanted to test the proposition that solid bodies all fall at the same rate, regardless of their weight, he did so by climbing up the Leaning Tower of Pisa carrying two cannonballs, one large, the other small; he dropped both cannonballs from the top of the Tower, letting them go at exactly the same time, and checked whether they struck the ground together. (As it happens, historians now believe that the whole story is a myth, and that Galileo never did anything of the kind; but this need not stand in the way of a good illustration.) This is quite often quoted in texts as a 'crucial experiment', on the reasoning that if the two cannonballs had *not* hit the ground simultaneously, then just this once-off observation would have provided certain disproof of Galileo's hypothesis.

And yet, when Galileo dropped those mythical cannonballs, was it perhaps just possible that he did not let them go at exactly the same time? Or that one ball did strike a little earlier than the other, but that Galileo's assistant failed to notice this? Could it be that the atmospheric conditions around the Leaning Tower of Pisa were very unusual, or that cannonballs fall in a very special way which is not really typical of solid bodies in general? By any chance, did Galileo's boldness in making this test annoy the Deity, so that He sent a couple of invisible angels to interfere with the rate of fall of the balls, thus fooling Galileo and everyone else? It is clear that such questions are numberless.

Considering the image of the scientist as someone above all concerned with the pursuit of objective truth, it is 'strange but true' that, in the last analysis, the resolution of questions like these is a matter of opinion—of agreement or disagreement among scientists—and not something that can be got from any epistemological rule-book. Clearly, the scope for disagreement will vary from one investigational situation to another. If we note 'Solution Z turns red litmus paper blue', we need not expect a great deal of methodological argument over the inference to be drawn about the nature of solution Z. But we are in quite a different situation if we are called on to draw conclusions from, say, the ways in which different people interpret a set of ink-blots, or the way in which figures for income and consumption relate to each other.

We see, then, that not even the most rigorous scientific investigation can strictly claim to be 100 per cent *objective*. This is *not* to suggest that scientists need let their personal prejudices, political views, and so on, interfere with their scientific detachment. The point is, rather, that even the most detached scientist may find intellectual reason to disagree about the interpretation which other scientists place on investigational findings.

To express the idea of 'agreement among scientists' over the interpretation of observational results, we can use the term *intersubjectivity*.

We can go on to formalize these notions a little more, starting from what we already know about the reasoning underlying empirical testing. We said that very frequently, a hypothesis was not directly testable; and that what the investigator then needed to do was to deduce directly testable consequences (often called 'predictions') from this hypothesis.

Now, of course, this prescription misses something out. We have spoken about 'deducing consequences' from a hypothesis. But to deduce something, you need premises. And from just one premise, you can deduce nothing; you need at least one other premise in order to be able to reach a conclusion. This leads us to the important realization: *from one hypothesis standing alone, no consequences can be deduced*.

In fact, the scientist needs to introduce other premises than the hypothesis in which he is primarily interested. These other premises will be in the nature of statements about investigational conditions, the procedures by which observation is carried out, and the ways in which these are to be interpreted.

As a case-study of this, we could perfectly well use Galileo's cannonball experiment, but let us return to economic instances and look again at the 'Phillips curve' investigation, already familiar from Section 4.2. As we know, Phillips was interested in the main hypothesis that wage changes in the UK were explained by the unemployment rate. He was going to take this hypothesis as non-rejected if the sets of figures for wage change and for unemployment showed a close relationship one with the other. What were his premises? In other words, what additional hypotheses did he need to introduce in order that he could reason from his main hypothesis to its prediction?

First of all, and importantly, he needed to say: 'In all cases where two sets of events are causally connected, the sets of figures providing appropriate measures of these events will be closely related one to the other.' As you will realize, this hypothesis is not controversial; it is so widely accepted that scientists do not usually bother to state it explicitly. (By the way, that is not to say that one would expect it *always* to hold; what we mean is that this hypothesis is *intersubjectively* very well accepted as being materially true in most circumstances, or often enough to form a working basis for observation.)

Putting this together with his main hypothesis, Phillips was then able to reason: 'Figures providing appropriate measures of price change and unemployment in the UK will be closely related one to the other.' But he was still not at the end of his necessary chain of deduction. To get to the specific prediction he was making, he needed to say two more things. First: 'The sets of figures I have *are* appropriate measures of price change and of unemployment in the UK'; and second: 'The statistical procedures I am using *are* able to demonstrate whether or not two sets of figures are closely related.'

Once again, these were not hypotheses which Phillips was actually setting out to check in his investigation; they are matters for intersubjective judgement. If we wanted, we could spell out the detailed points of intersubjective agreement which are necessary for the acceptance of each of these hypotheses (for instance, the amount of observational error which is judged to attach to the figures of price change and unemployment; the interpretation of the tests of correlation between the sets of figures; and so on). Each of these more detailed points would appear in the reasoning as a separate hypothesis put forward for intersubjective judgement.

We have confirmed, then, that in order to get to his specific prediction about what he would observe, Phillips had to bring in several hypotheses additional to the one in which he was mainly interested. This requirement is universal in hypothetico-deductive reasoning. If you like, you might try making a list of all the additional hypotheses which Galileo had to bring into his reasoning when he was carrying out his legendary observation on the cannonballs.

In technical language, these statements which I have so far called 'additional hypotheses' are usually known as *auxiliary hypotheses*. Very often, as in the example about the Phillips curve, the material truth of auxiliary hypotheses is so widely accepted intersubjectively that scientists do not feel the need to test them specifically (and very often, also as in the example, they are not even explicitly stated).

We could, if we liked, spell out a separate syllogism for every auxiliary hypothesis, working through one syllogism after another, chainwise, till we eventually arrived at our specific prediction. However, it is much more convenient to package all the auxiliary hypotheses together into a single hypothetical statement, where the main hypothesis and all the auxiliary hypotheses come into the antecedent, and the 'deduced consequence' is the consequent.

In our example of the Phillips curve, we recall from page 50 that his hypothetical, in simple form, could be phrased '*If* I am correct in hypothesiz-ing that wage inflation is explained by the level of unemployment, *then* it will be the case that the figures for wage inflation show a statistical relation-ship with the figures for unemployment.' Now that we have registered the various auxiliary hypotheses which were necessary in order to reason out the prediction, we can expand the hypothetical to take account of them:

> If wage inflation is explained by the level of unemployment;
> . . . *and if*, in all cases where two sets of events are causally connected, the sets of figures providing appropriate measures of these events are closely related one to the other;
> . . . *and if* the sets of figures I have are appropriate measures of price change and of unemployment in the UK;
> . . . *and if* the statistical procedures I am using are able to demonstrate whether or not two sets of figures are closely related;
> . . . *then* these sets of figures will show a close relationship, according to my statistical procedures.

Because this kind of reasoning is so central to hypothetico-deductive method, we can generalize it by using a few symbols. We can label the original hypothesis—the one we are really interested in testing—with the symbol H. We can call the auxiliary hypotheses, like those spelled out above, $A_1, A_2, A_3, \ldots, A_n$ (the A_n showing that the number of auxiliary hypo-theses is not determinate, but is decided by intersubjective agreement). Finally, we can use the label P for the deduced consequence or 'predic-tion'.

So the complete hypothetical comes out in this form:

> If (H and $A_1, A_2, A_3, \ldots A_n$) are true, then P is true.

This kind of statement—a hypothetical with several conditions in the antecedent—is not new to us; we met it briefly when we first looked at the hypothetical syllogism in Section 2.3. We noted then that in order to argue to the truth of the consequent in a statement like this, we need to be able to assert the truth of *all* the conditions in the antecedent.

Now, what is the situation in the context of empirical testing, where we are trying to reason in the other direction—that is, *from* consequent *to* antecedent?

Suppose that when Phillips did his statistical tests, his two sets of figures had *not* shown a close relationship—in other words, suppose that his 'deduced consequence', labelled P by us, had proved materially false. Would this necessarily have falsified H, his original hypothesis? Strictly speaking, it would not. Instead of H, it may have been any of the A's that was false.

And we are in no better case if we try to use the formally fallacious reasoning of verification, rather than that of falsification. We know that Phillips's two sets of figures did show a close relationship. Does this lend support to the original hypothesis? Again, not necessarily. If we choose to believe that any of the A's was really false, then it follows that the whole antecedent also becomes false, irrespective of anything we may observe about P.

We have already noted that from one hypothesis standing alone, no consequences can be deduced. Now we can complete this picture. In order to deduce testable consequences from a hypothesis that is not directly testable, we must bring in additional premises (at least one, and more usually, several). Thus when we carry out our test, it must inevitably be not just a test of our original hypothesis, but rather of the *original hypothesis together with all the auxiliary hypotheses*.

Some philosophers have argued that, strictly speaking, we can never be sure that we have specified all of the auxiliary hypotheses which may be relevant to any investigational situation—and hence that we can never be sure whether our 'test' is really a test or not. This argument is convincing in itself, but like several other 'strictly speaking' arguments, it does not stop scientists from doing their best to test hypotheses against real-world observations. As we have seen, an important practical device is to put all or most of one's auxiliary hypotheses up for *intersubjective* acceptance—very often by implication only.

At the same time, it is desirable that the investigator should be aware that auxiliary hypotheses do enter into his reasoning. The greatest danger arises, as some methodologists have pointed out, when an important auxiliary hypothesis is brought into the reasoning un-noticed—that is, when the scientist takes this proposition so much for granted that he is not even aware of it. To take a classic example from physical science: until Einstein, nobody thought of questioning the proposition that two different events could be unambiguously observed to happen 'at the same time'. At a fair guess, the reason why this belief had not been questioned was that most people were unaware of even holding it. But Einstein did question it, and this insight was one of the foundations of his theory of relativity.

Though the economist, unlike the physical scientist, is not called on to design complicated experimental set-ups and interpret their results, nevertheless, he is not immune to the necessity of bringing auxiliary hypotheses into his reasoning. Nor is he proof against the possible danger of unknowingly taking for granted the truth of an important auxiliary hypothesis which may in reality be false, or at least doubtful.

4.4.4 Certainty, uncertainty, and ignorance

From the discussion of the last few sections, one feature to emerge is this: in the context of empirical investigation, we are never entitled to say that anything can be known 'for certain'. In scientific discourse, the word 'certain' can only be used of one type of finding—and that is a finding that is arrived at purely by sound deduction from 'given' premises. (Recall that we can speak of this as being an 'analytical', as opposed to a 'synthetic', finding.) The trouble is that this word 'certainty', as used of deductive conclusions, means something distinctly different from the notion of 'certainty' which we might associate with empirical observation.

The clue to this distinction in meaning is to be found in the distinction between logical 'truth' and material truth. When we talk of analytical findings as being 'certain', we are referring to 'certainty' in terms of logical 'truth'—and all we really mean is that our conclusion has been reached by means of logically correct reasoning from premises which we have chosen to call 'logically true' for the purposes of our argument. Really, it would be a great deal better if some other word than 'certainty' were used to convey this meaning; but, here as elsewhere, this ambiguous usage seems to be firmly established in philosophical writing, and so we had better conform to it—registering mentally, though, the difference between these two meanings of 'certainty'.

By the way, just as real-world observation can never show anything to be certain, neither can it show anything to be impossible. The reasoning behind this is easily seen if we translate 'impossible' into 'certainly not-true'. Here again, the only context in which impossibility (i.e., certain non-truth) can be justifiably spoken of is the context of wholly deductive reasoning—and the 'impossibility' we speak of in that context is in terms also of logical 'truth', not material truth.

Now, given that empirical findings can never be either certainly true nor certainly untrue, what *can* they be? In trying to sort this question out, by the way, we enter an area that has not been all that well explored by philosophers of science, whether in the field of economics or outside it.

The tempting answer is that if empirical findings are neither certain nor impossible, then we must be able to express them in terms of probabilities. But in fact, this is only part of the correct picture. The non-certainty of empirical observation, as we shall now see, comes about because of two classes of causes, only one of which has its effect in terms of probabilities.

To look first at the issue of probability: here, I do not intend to dive into the murky philosophical controversy over what probability actually *is*: on this point, philosophers have various notions, to which the references at the end of this chapter will lead you if you want to pursue the matter. I will simply take it that we know intuitively what is meant by saying that something is 'more probable' or 'less probable' than something else. To be a bit more explicit, you can visualize a scale on which something absolutely certain is graded at '1' and something absolutely impossible is put at '0'; relatively probable things are put relatively near to '1', while relatively improbable things are nearer to '0'. This gives us a conventional scale on which to express measurements of probability.

There are various ideas, too, about how you go about allotting a 'high' or a 'low' probability to different events. You can work the whole thing out in terms of purely abstract mathematical reasoning (you may well have come across typical examples in which imaginary black and white balls are drawn out of imaginary urns); by the way, as we now know, it is only in such abstract examples that you will ever get to the limiting values 'certainty' or 'impossibility' (i.e., probability values of 1 and 0 respectively). Other accounts lay stress on the subjective aspects of probability—that is, the ideas of the probability of various outcomes which the observer had in his own head before beginning his investigation. Still others look upon probability as being something that you establish on the basis of empirical observation—that is, if you want to get an idea of how probable a certain event is, then you observe the world and count up how many times that event happens out of the total number of times it possibly could have happened. It is obviously this last view which will most often be in mind when people speak of the 'probability' of events in the context of empirical observation in science.

I repeat: these theories of probability have been sketched here only very briefly, and you should go to the appropriate texts in order to get a fuller account. My only aim here is to depict in the simplest terms what is meant by probability, so that we are able to distinguish it from the other component that helps to account for the inconclusiveness of empirical findings.

This 'other component', as I have mentioned, is very much less well recognized than is the idea of probability. Many texts on statistics or econometrics make no specific mention of it whatever. It does not even have a generally accepted name; yet it is an inevitable feature of all empirical observations.

It is possible to put together a sensible terminology to describe this 'other component'. We can first of all distinguish the idea of the *probability* of a given outcome, in the terms just described; and we can say that we are correspondingly faced with *uncertainty* about that outcome. But turning now to the 'other component', we can speak of *possibility*; and we can say that in instances where we are dealing with possibility rather than probability, we correspondingly face not uncertainty, but *ignorance*. While these terms were not coined by me (in fact, they have been collated from suggestions made by other methodological writers), I must stress that this is *not* generally accepted terminology. A great many texts either make no mention of 'possibility' and 'ignorance', or use the terms interchangeably with 'probability' and 'uncertainty'.

Let us, though, take up the terms just suggested. What is ignorance, and how does it differ from uncertainty?

In fact, we already have the knowledge on which to work out the answer to this question. First: in Section 3.2, we noted that we could never regard an inductive generalization as 'certain', because there always remained the possibility that further observations would take us over the statistical limits which we had set for contrary instances. Second: in Section 4.4.3 we saw that in any task of empirical observation, no matter how carefully the scientist might set up his investigation, there would always be some scope for argument over the interpretation of the results. On the terminology just suggested, the first of these features is the source of uncertainty; and the second is the source of ignorance.

In other words: if we *could* set up the 'perfect investigation'—if we could make sure to everyone's satisfaction that all the conditions of our observational set-up were perfectly specified, and that the data we were observing were indeed exactly those data that we needed to observe in order to check our hypothesis—then there would still be uncertainty attaching to the results, for all the reasons that we discussed in Chapter 3; but there would be no element of ignorance about these results. As it is, of course, in real-life investigations we are never able to achieve this perfect investigational set-up, and in so far as we are not, our results will be affected both by an element of uncertainty and by an element of ignorance.

There are two other and rather more obvious ways in which ignorance can enter the investigational picture. If we extend our idea of 'empirical observation' to mean not just the results of one specific investigational exercise, but rather the overall knowledge we have of one area of subject matter, we may often face ignorance simply because certain features of that subject matter have not been investigated fully, or indeed have not been investigated at all. It may even have to be admitted that in that area, we are not at all sure what it is we should try to investigate (in other words: we do not know what it is we do not know). To quote an instance given originally by B. J. Loasby, a writer who has stressed the importance of this concept of 'ignorance': in economics, what we call the 'theory of the firm' depends to an important degree on assumptions about businessmen's actions and motives; but, in fact, the empirical evidence we have to support these assumptions is very sketchy indeed, because relatively little convincing work has been done in investigating many of these actions and motives. Thus, correspondingly, we face a considerable element of ignorance about businessmen's real-world behaviour—as well as the uncertainty attaching to the results of those investigations that *have* been carried out.

Lastly: it can be argued that any prediction about future events must carry an element of ignorance as well as an element of uncertainty. This 'problem of prediction' will be discussed in some detail in Chapter 5. Here, we can merely note this: if we believe that the occurrence of future events can be predicted in terms of probability, then that corresponds to saying that our predictions face only uncertainty. But if, instead, we believe that it is not sensible to try to predict future events only in terms of a probability value, then we are saying that our predictions are affected by ignorance as well as uncertainty.

4.5 Explanation v. prediction

In the description of hypothetico-deductive method which has occupied us in this chapter, the procedure of science has perhaps been made to seem a pretty mechanical affair. All the scientist does, seemingly, is to start off from a hypothesis, churn it through the hypothetico-deductive machinery, see whether the answer he gets is 'maybe yes' or 'maybe no', then go on to the next hypothesis that happens to come into his head. You may well suspect that there's more to scientific endeavour than this—and indeed, nearly all present-day philosophers of science would agree with you. It is now pretty well recognized that scientific enquiry, instead of just setting out to say 'what happens', or even 'what will happen', needs to tackle the much more difficult question 'Why does it happen?'. In other words, science should set out to *explain* phenomena, not just describe or predict them.

Not so long ago, there was a powerful school of philosophers who dissented from this view. They felt that true scientific practice should indeed confine itself to just describing, and perhaps also trying to predict, the course of real-world events. Any attempt to speak of 'causes' operating behind this description or prediction, in the view of this school, was scientifically taboo.

At first sight, this may seem an extraordinary attitude to adopt, for a scientist or anyone else. But let us pause for a moment or two to discuss why this view, though extreme, had its own rationale.

In fact, we have already come across the reasoning which underlies this philosophical position. In talking about the fallacy of *post hoc ergo propter hoc* (Section 2.5.4), we saw that just because event B follows event A, you cannot say for certain that event B is caused by event A. When we came to look at the related topic of the logical problem of testing (Section 4.4.1), we again noted that you could never tie up cause and effect conclusively.

Now, if you extend this reasoning just a little, you realize that it amounts to saying that a cause can never be observed. You can observe that every time (or most times) an event of type A arises, it is very soon followed by another event of type B—but that is all that is open to observation. If we then introduce the notion of 'cause', it can only be because we have done so out of our own heads. And this is where we come back to the philosophical viewpoint we are now considering: these philosophers felt that it must be unscientific to bring in notions which were just a matter of the investigator's imagination, and that he should keep to statements about what he could observe happening in the real world; QED, the scientist should make no reference to causes.

It is fairly safe to say that this extreme viewpoint would nowadays hardly find any supporters among philosophers of science (though, as we shall see in Chapter 6, its tattered remnants still turn up from time to time in some of the methodological pronouncements of economists). It is by now recognized that 'ideas brought in out of the scientist's own head', far from being foreign to science, are fundamental to it—the idea of cause among them. Further, if science wants to say anything *useful* about the real world, it must deal in answers to the question 'why?'

Given that science deals in explanations, it still proves not to be too easy to describe what we mean by an 'explanation'. Before reading on, perhaps you would like to pause and consider: what *do* you mean by saying you have 'explained' something?

As this section goes on, you can keep in mind your own suggested definition of 'explanation', and see how it corresponds to the various ideas that are bandied around by philosophers of science.

Some ingenious souls, first of all, have managed to take up a position that largely preserves the spirit of the old 'no explanation' school we have just discussed, while actually departing from the letter. In order to do this, they stretch the meaning of the word 'explanation', and say that prediction and explanation *are one and the same thing*—in other words, that if you can predict outcomes in a given investigational situation, then you have 'explained' that situation. (By the way, this is another notion that will turn up in the review of ideas in Chapter 6 on the testing of economic theories.)

In reality, there is literally no argument with this point of view—since, if a philosopher chooses to define 'explanation' as meaning 'prediction', or vice versa, then that is purely up to him. However, without being too unfair, one can say that in current methodological thinking, this particular approach has been consigned to the same rubbish-bin as the older and more extreme viewpoint from which it was derived. Our common sense tells us, in fact, that you can easily come across situations in which people can make successful predictions, without providing anything that could be called an 'explanation' in any normal sense of the word. To borrow an example from Abraham Kaplan:[36] the astronomers of the ancient world were able to make predictions of the movements of heavenly bodies that compete in accuracy with any that can be made nowadays; yet their 'explanations', in so far as they existed at all, were totally out of line with reality. Then again, remember the witch-doctor whom we met in Section 2.5.4. He might be very successful in predicting the appearance of the crops at a given time of year; but, for him, the explanation of this event would be that he had put on his green robe and cast some good spells.

You may have noticed that in the two examples in the paragraph above, I begged the question by suggesting that the explanations provided by the ancient astronomers and the witch-doctor were not really explanations at all. But how do we judge if an explanation *is* an explanation? We have just noted that it is not just a matter of good prediction. Of what, then, is it a matter?

It is generally accepted, first of all, that a 'cause' is indeed something that can never be directly observed, since it exists only in the mind of the observer.

Its existence can only be inferred indirectly, on the basis of events observed to happen in the real world.

Next, it is also well accepted that an observed correlation between events, though it can never tell the whole story about causal connections, is nevertheless evidence for their existence. Again, this is just a matter of simple common sense. Whether in science or in everyday life, if we note that events of type A are always, or very often, followed by events of type B, then we can sensibly take it that there is likely to be a causal link running from the former to the latter. In recognizing this ground for explanation, we are also admitting that the philosophers who said 'prediction was what mattered' were partly right; the point is that when we predict anything on the basis of real-world observation, then this can only be because of some correlation we have noted in past observation. (In Chapter 5 we will be looking at this notion in some detail, so you may wish to take it on trust for now.) The present-day view, though, just says that prediction (i.e., correlation) tells *some* of the story about explanation—not that it tells all of the story.

From this point on, current lines of thought divide into two main streams, though these are complementary rather than contradictory to one another.

According to one of these accounts, we have 'explained' an event when we have succeeded in fitting it into the pattern of what we already know about the subject matter in question. Or, to put the same idea in different words: we explain an observation, or a hypothesis, by showing how it is consistent with other propositions in the theory we are using.

For instance, going back to our contrasting examples of the witch-doctor and the politician: why do we take the witch-doctor's explanation as false? After all, it may be that the inductive evidence in favour of it is pretty strong; since, the witch-doctor might protest, every year he *had* cast his spells, and every year without fail this had been followed by the sprouting of the crops. But nevertheless, the witch-doctor's 'explanation' is out of line with very many well-supported generalizations of biology: for instance, that the sprouting of crops is brought about by temperature, time of year, changing day-length, and so on. It is also out of agreement with some broader facts of empirical observation—for instance that, as far as is known, the casting of magic spells does not exercise any effect on physical or biological phenomena.

When by contrast, the politician explains his shrinking balance-of-payments deficit in terms of the policy measures he has just taken, we accept that his explanation may well be a reasonable one (whether or not we agree with it entirely). Note that the inductive evidence in favour of the politician's explanation may well be *less* convincing than that for the witch-doctor's—there are many and many occasions when a government may impose import controls and currency restrictions, institute deflationary measures at home, and so on, without any perceptible benefit to the balance of payments. Yet the politician's explanation does fit in with some generalizations of economic theory which—though a great deal less well supported than the ones from biology that we have just met—nevertheless get some credence from most economists.

From these two examples, you will note an important feature of this account of 'explanation'. It is that when we 'explain' a given event in terms of a given theory, then our confidence in the explanation must depend on the confidence we place in that theory. The witch-doctor might develop a reasonably consistent 'theory' to account for the sprouting of the crops after he had cast his spells (in fact, complicated 'systems of magic' do exist); but scientists prefer the biological explanation because it fits into a theory that is well supported by empirical observation.

It follows in turn that when a theory falls under the assault of factual evidence, then explanations in terms of that theory have to be discarded. To use a much-quoted illustration from the history of physical science: not so long ago, there existed a well-developed body of theory about 'phlogiston', the 'principle of combustion' which was supposed to be released by burning substances. This theory gave perfectly sensible 'explanations' for a wide range of phenomena connected with combustion, oxidation, and so on. But when eventually the entire phlogiston theory was abandoned in favour of present-day ideas, then even the serviceable explanations provided by it had to be replaced; there was no longer any pattern into which these old explanations could be fitted.

Furthermore, if two competing theories exist in a given field of study —that is, if there is still argument about which theory *is* better supported by observation—then they will generate competing explanations. There was a long period, for instance, when the phlogiston theory was still in competition with theories of chemical combination, and so the events concerned could be explained in either way, according to the scientist's own choice of theory. Much nearer home, you will have no difficulty in recognizing the 'monetarist v. neo-Keynesian' wrangle as an example of the same kind of thing, with economists in each school setting out to explain inflation in terms of their preferred theory.

Going on to the second of the two main streams of thought regarding the nature of scientific explanation: we can say we have 'explained' a situation when our 'explanation' enables us to influence that situation in the way we desire. If we interpret astronomical observations in terms of the movements of sun, stars, planets, and so on, in a three-dimensional space, then it turns out that we are able to send vehicles off on an accurate rendezvous with Mars; in these terms, we have made a good explanation of our observations. We could, if we liked, choose to believe that what we observe as the sun, stars, and planets were in fact powerful lanterns, situated a few miles above the earth's surface and propelled through the sky by invisible angels. But if we sent a balloon up with the idea of bringing one of these back to earth as a cheap source of light, we would discover that our interpretation of events was unserviceable as an explanation.

It is easy to see how this second notion of 'explanation' is closely related to the first. If we talk about fitting an observation or hypothesis into the pattern of a theory, we mean that we are working out how this observation or hypothesis is causally connected with other observations or hypotheses relevant to the theory; and to work out the nature of these causal connections is much the same thing as working out how to influence the situation concerned.

However, the second of the two views of explanation is rather wider than the first (we can say that it defines explanation less stringently). This is because it is sometimes possible to influence the course of events even though we have no theory into which we can satisfactorily fit these events. This is often the case in medicine, for instance; we know that we can use certain chemicals as stimulants or depressants, but doctors have hardly the beginnings of a theory which will say *why* the presence of the chemical produces the observed mental changes.

Just as you can predict without fitting your predictions into a theory, so you can predict without being able to influence what you are predicting: both Keynesian and monetarist economists, at the time of writing, can very readily predict inflation in developed economies!

There is one final point to make about the relationship between explanation and prediction: just as prediction is part of the story of explanation, so explanation is a partial aid to prediction. In looking at the mechanics of inductive reasoning in Chapter 3, we concentrated on the way in which the evidence for empirical prediction came from inductive observation, aided, as you will recall, by a 'proposition of regularity'. However, there were hints that the inductive evidence in itself was not all we would consider when making a prediction. For instance, we noted that philosophers would be very surprised if the sun failed to rise of a morning, despite the fact that the inductive evidence could never make that event certain. Why would they be very surprised? Not just because of their past observations of the sun, though of course these provide a large part of the evidence; but also because if the sun failed to rise, it would be contradicting most of the statements of the theory of celestial mechanics, to say nothing of half a dozen other theories.

In other words, we can make a prediction more confidently on the basis of inductive evidence plus theoretical reasoning than we can on inductive evidence alone. At the same time, it is very difficult to quantify the importance of this theoretical back-up. Statistical analysis tries quite explicitly to put a measure on the confidence that we can place in a prediction on the basis of the *inductive* evidence—that is, according to the number of observations we have made and the configuration of the results. (Note that, advisedly, I said 'tries to', not 'does', for reasons we shall consider in the next chapter.) But no one has got far in trying to apply the same kind of analysis to the element of confidence that comes from having some theoretical support for our prediction—largely because, very often, the assessment of this theoretical support is as much a matter of hunch as of systematic reasoning.

4.6 Some formal notions

This section introduces no new ideas. Instead, it formalizes what we have already learned in this chapter about the structure and validation of scientific theories, briefly introducing some of the technical concepts and terms used by philosophers of science in discussing this subject.*

There are several reasons why this is worth doing. It will help to consolidate understanding of the material that has been worked through in the earlier sections of the chapter. It will assist you in further reading on the general philosophy of science, if you choose to pursue this topic. Most important, it will provide some powerful aids to understanding in our coming discussion of the nature and validation of economic theory.

We can start from a notion that we have already used several times in this book, and which we noted as being a familiar idea to economists: the two-way division between the 'real world' and the 'world of theory'. Philosophers of science have various technical usages to describe this distinction, and here I shall follow one of the most usual. They speak not of two 'worlds', but of two *domains*. The 'real world' is rechristened the *domain of protocols*, or *p-domain* for short; and the 'world of theory' is correspondingly called the *domain of constructs*, or *c-domain*.

The word *protocol*, here, has nothing to do with diplomatic good manners; in philosophers' jargon, it means (roughly speaking) 'something that is observed happening', whether the 'observation' in question is done by the scientist's own unaided senses or with the help of observational instruments.

A *construct* is so called because it is an idea put together in the scientist's own mind—'constructed', that is, by his imagination.

There are several important contrasts which we can draw between the contents of the c-domain and those of the p-domain. First of these is the one we have just noted as defining the difference between the two domains: namely that constructs proceed from the scientist's own imagination (in the first instance anyway), while protocols are matters of observation. As we shall see, the other comparisons follow from this first one.

Next: the c-domain is systematically organized; its contents are coherent, and the various propositions it contains are logically connected, even though the logical connections may have breaks in them here and there. In terms of everyday reasoning, these features simply add up to the fact that any sane person—scientist or otherwise—has, inside his head, a picture of the world that 'makes sense'. By contrast, the p-domain has no organization of its own; it must have organization *imposed on it* by the observer. Every waking hour, we are assailed by 'observations' of all kinds; and, whether in scientific studies or just in the business of everyday living, we need to select some of these data and ignore others. When, for instance, a market-research

---

*For the expositional approach of this section, I acknowledge a debt to the essay by Professor Margenau, 'What is a theory?'.[54]

interviewer is at work, he confines himself to taking in what is being said by the interviewee; he does not attempt to note down the news broadcast coming from a nearby radio set, nor to add comments on the fact that his feet happen to be hurting—to name just a couple of the many impressions that may be impinging on him at that moment. You can appreciate that our choice of which sense-data to select and which to leave out will be determined by what we are trying to do at any one time: when our interviewer completes his interview, he may 'tune in' to the news broadcast, or make off to buy a new pair of shoes. So it is also in scientific reasoning: our selection of data from the p-domain is determined by the content of the theory we happen to be examining. We shall shortly register how the contents of the scientist's c-domain—his theories—are organized, and how he goes about selecting his data from the p-domain.

Going on to the next contrast between the two domains: a construct need not be something that is directly observable (though it can sometimes be). A protocol, on the other hand, must by definition be directly observable. This ties up with a notion we came across in Section 4.1, namely, that a hypothesis, while it sometimes could be directly tested against observation, very often could not be; and if not, then the scientist had to deduce directly testable consequences. Now we can register that in a 'directly testable consequence', *all* the constructs we are speaking of must be identifiable with protocols; whereas a hypothesis that is not directly testable will be so because it contains at least some constructs which are not directly identifiable with protocols. For instance, Phillips's hypothesis about 'wage change being explained by unemployment' could not be directly tested against observation, because none of the three constructs it contains is identifiable with a protocol (the three constructs are 'wage change', 'unemployment', and 'being explained by'). By contrast, in Phillips's directly testable prediction, all the constructs mentioned are indeed directly identifiable with protocols, i.e., with specific things that can be observed; 'This set of figures for wage change is correlated with that set of figures for unemployment.'

Lastly: a construct can be exact—or, we can say, propositions in the c-domain can be envisaged as being 'certain'. The contents of the p-domain, by contrast, are inexact, vague, uncertain, partly unknown. Once again, this is no new idea to us. In Section 4.4.4, we spoke of the 'certainty' which could attach to analytical statements—though that 'certainty' was to be interpreted in terms of logical 'truth', not material truth. Statements about the real world could never be put forward as certain: they would always be subject to uncertainty and ignorance.

Having drawn these four contrasts between the c-domain and the p-domain, we next need to 'home in' on each domain in turn, or at least on that part of each domain whose content is relevant to the practice of science.

Looking first at the c-domain: we said that it was systematically organized. More precisely, this means that the propositions in the part of the c-domain relevant to a given field of science—that is, the propositions making up the theory of that scientific field—should be linked by valid deductive reasoning. Ideally, every one of the deductive links in a theory might be spelt out. In practice, this still has not been achieved in any field of science, not even in theoretical physics. Recognizing this, philosophers of science have made a variety of less ambitious suggestions about what criteria we should apply in order to judge whether a set of statements is or is not to be regarded as a 'theory'. Of these, probably the two most obvious and most important are: that no two of these statements should be mutually contradictory; and that the statements should all be relevant to one another. In recognizing these criteria as sensible in principle, it need hardly be added that sometimes there are great problems in judging whether two statements *are* mutually contradictory or mutually irrelevant.

We can say that some statements in a theory are more *general* than others. Formally, this notion can be expressed as follows: let A be a statement in a theory. Then, if there is a set of statements $B_1, B_2, \ldots, B_n$ in the same theory, such that the truth of A entails the truth of $B_1, B_2, \ldots, B_n$, then the statement A is more general than any of the statements in the class $B_1, B_2, \ldots, B_n$. I choose this rather starchy way of describing the idea because, if one tries to describe it in plainer English, one runs into problems of mixing up the generality of statements with some other, related but distinct, ideas.

Illustrations make the notion clearer. For instance, take these two statements:

'Mrs Bloggs will buy less bread if its price rises'; and
'Mrs Smith will buy less tea if its price rises'.

The truth of both these statements is entailed in the truth of the more general statement: 'Consumers buy less of a commodity if its price rises.' In turn, this latter statement is entailed in even more general statements about the way consumers maximize satisfaction. Or, progressing the other way, i.e., from higher to lower generality: if we start from the statement 'businessmen maximize profits', then this implies that 'businessmen will produce where marginal cost equals marginal revenue'; and this in turn implies 'businessman Bloggs (and Smith, Jones, . . .) will produce where marginal cost equals marginal revenue.' You will realize once again that we have already come across these ideas expressed in different words. 'Reasoning downwards in generality' means deducing consequences—making predictions—from hypotheses; while 'reasoning upwards' corresponds to the hypothetico-deductive 'testing' process, where a hypothesis that is not directly testable is checked by reference to a directly testable consequence (or where a more general hypothesis is assessed by reference to one that is less general).

We have already noted that philosophers love to coin jargon terms, and when it comes to a choice of terms to describe this idea of 'higher and lower degrees of generality', the jargonsmiths have had a field-day. Here, I shall use the simplest wording of all, and one that has now been widely adopted.

Instead of the 'degree of generality' of a statement, we speak of its *level*. Thus, to go back to the description I originally gave, we can say that statement A is of a higher level than statements $B_1, B_2, \ldots, B_n$. If we want to speak of the most general statements of all in a given theory—those from which all other statements in the theory can be deduced—we can call them the highest-level statements. The lowest-level statements in the theory will be those that are the least general of all—and that means statements that are to be compared directly with observation, i.e., with protocols.

It would take pages to spell out all the variations in terminology that different texts have used to express these ideas, and even more pages to clear up the confusions of interpretation as between different jargon sets. However, as some guide to further reading, I had better mention the most common of these alternative terms. The highest-level statements of a theory are sometimes called *axioms* or *postulates*. The statements at the next level down in generality are often called *hypotheses*—though this term can be also used to describe the idea which I have just designated by 'axioms'. The word 'hypotheses', as we noted earlier, is used by some philosophers to mean not just highest-level statements, but any statement in a theory; others use it to mean a fairly high-level statement, employing other words for lower-level statements. Sometimes we find the alternative term *theorems* used to imply high-level statements which are not themselves axioms.

At the lower end of the scale of generality, we find people talking simply about *predictions*; or about *experimental statements* or *protocol statements*. Slightly higher than these are *empirical generalizations*. To increase confusion still further, some writers use these last three terms in relation to the contents of the p-domain, not the c-domain at all; while still others use them about both domains.

With that, we can thankfully abandon this look at terminology, and note a practical point about the idea of designating statements as high- or low-level: just as in real-life science it can be difficult to say whether two statements are mutually contradictory or mutually irrelevant, so it can often be difficult to say whether one statement really is of higher or lower level than another.

Before leaving the c-domain, it is worth mentioning two of its occupants, which you may not always find described as such in the textbooks. They are, first, the notion of *cause* (Section 4.5); and the 'proposition of regularity' (Section 3.3). Both of these are constructs, and they enter into the reasoning of every scientific theory, as also, indeed, into the reasoning of everyday life.

Going on now to the p-domain: for our immediate purpose, it is not necessary to say nearly as much about it as about the c-domain. As we have seen, the p-domain consists of a churning mass of data, from which we have to abstract and organize what we need for the purposes of our scientific work. Philosophers of general science have had a lot to say about what is really entailed in observation and its interpretation—which is not surprising, given the emphasis there has traditionally been on the methodology of physics, where investigational apparatus is often complex. There are also many subtle problems in the observation of economic events, which have received rather less attention from methodologists; Chapter 5 looks at the most important of these.

We have, then, our two domains, one consisting of constructs and the other of protocols. The c-domain is the domain of theory; and the scientist is free to fill it with whatever constructs he likes. He can construct a theory about unicorns and little green men, in a theoretical world where two and two make five one day and three the next. If he is ingenious enough, he may even be able to build up this theory in such a way that it contains no mutually contradictory nor mutually irrelevant statements. In its own internal terms, this would be a satisfactory theory. But it is not a scientifically sound theory, for reasons that are obvious to us: when it is compared with the p-domain, it will be seen not to correspond with anything observed there. In more straightforward terms, it does not fit the facts. And as we noted right at the beginning of our discussion, the mark of scientific endeavour is that the facts are always given precedence; if the scientist's ideas do not correspond with them, then the ideas must go, not the facts.

In the framework of the philosophical ideas we are now discussing, this idea of 'confronting ideas with facts' corresponds to setting up comparisons between the c-domain and the p-domain. Traditional accounts of scientific method have often suggested that only the very lowest-level statements of a theory can be compared with protocols. Nowadays, it is widely accepted that this is too formal an idea, and that it may well be possible to compare not just lowest-level statements, but also those of rather higher level, directly with real-world observation. This obviously is likely to depend on the subject matter of the theory in question; as we shall see in Chapter 6, the point has relevance to the testing of economic theory.

In comparing his two domains, the investigator has to choose which low-level statements to compare with which protocols; and he has to devise some convincing means of making the comparisons. This, again, is an idea we have already met: in Section 4.4.3, we saw that in the process of testing, the scientist had to specify an investigational set-up as an integral part of the 'deduction of consequences' from his original hypothesis. We noted that it was a matter of intersubjective agreement whether a given investigational set-up was or was not appropriate for the checking of a given hypothesis.

In any one field of science, at a particular time, notions on how to carry out investigations are usually pretty well agreed among scientists. Indeed, you could conceive of drawing up a set of 'rules' specifying what data should be chosen, how these should be collected and analysed, and what interpretation should be put on them. In the terminology just introduced, we speak of these as *rules of correspondence*.* It is worth repeating that they are only 'rules'

*This terminology follows Margenau.[54] Other writers (e.g., Caws)[10] use 'rules of correspondence' to mean something quite different, viz., the rules by which a calculus is related to its interpretation in the form of a specific theory.

in the sense of being intersubjectively agreed procedures. They are not imposed from somewhere outside science. They can and do change as time goes on; and in some fields of science, two or more sets of competing rules may exist at the same time, or there may be only vague ideas of what the rules of correspondence should be.

We are now able to translate the whole sequence of hypothetico-deductive enquiry into the technical terms introduced in this section. Professor Margenau describes it effectively, as a 'circuit from p-domain into c-domain and back again'. The scientist starts by making an observation, or a set of observations, of events in the p-domain. Using rules of correspondence, he interprets these in terms of low-level statements in the c-domain. From these, he reasons upwards to higher-level statements. If his observations seem to be inconsistent with any of these higher-level statements, he may tentatively revise the statements concerned. Next, he reasons downwards again from these statements (revised or not) until he arrives at some further low-level statements that can in turn be directly compared with the p-domain via rules of correspondence. From there, the whole process can start again (and, of course, the scientist can also begin completely new 'circuits' starting from different sets of data). At each circuit, the higher-level statements of the theory are either regarded as better substantiated than before—if they stand up to the assault from the facts—or are revised as necessary. If, over a period of time, evidence builds up contrary to a number of the theory's high-level statements, then there may come a point at which the whole theory has to be regarded as untenable. If this happens, the theory must be wiped out of the scientific c-domain, and replaced by one that can be compared more convincingly with the p-domain.

Having reviewed this neat formal picture, it is worth calling to mind the caution that was sounded right at the beginning of the chapter. Real-life scientific procedure can not often be related very closely to this idealized account; and even when it can, it is by no means safe to assume that scientists are *consciously* following any 'method' whatever. In recent years, some philosophers of science have suggested that over the longer term, progress in science comes not from revisions of theories in hypothetico-deductive style, but from other processes altogether—and that these other processes are as much sociological as intellectual. Interesting as these suggestions are, I am not going to examine them here, since their subject matter shades out of methodology and into the history of science and the history of economics. The references at the end of this chapter will introduce these alternative accounts of change in science.

4.7 Postview

We are now at the end of this introduction to the hypothetico-deductive account of scientific method. Before going on, I shall pause briefly to re-emphasize just what it is we have been looking at, and from what angle we have been viewing it.

Deliberately, not much use has been made of economic examples so far. The hypothetico-deductive account has been discussed simply as a method of investigation for 'science generally'. Where economic examples have been used, no questions have been asked about how well such examples represented what is actually done, or should be done, in economic science. The objective has been to establish a firm mental picture of what is entailed in hypothetico-deductive method—simply because, until we have acquired this mental picture, we are not in a good position to go on and examine how far this standard version of the hypothetico-deductive account can be considered appropriate to economic investigation.

From now on, this emphasis will be reversed: we shall be looking first and foremost at economic method, and where examples from physical science are given, these will only be for purposes of comparison with economic practice. Indeed, the hypothetico-deductive account itself (coined originally, as we saw, as a means of codifying the practice of physical science) will be used as a yardstick with which to compare various accounts of economic method.

Reading guide: Chapter 4

Caws, *The Philosophy of Science*,[10] Chapters 24–35; Copi, *An Introduction to Logic*,[20] Chapters 13, 14; Kaplan, *The Conduct of Inquiry*,[36] Chapters 5–7, 11, 15, 25, 26, 34–36.

There is a very useful volume of essays on economic methodology edited by S. R. Krupp, *The Structure of Economic Science*.[42] Read the essay in it by Henry Margenau, 'What is a theory'. (I think his very last paragraph gives a slightly over-optimistic view of what economic science has achieved to date.) This collection of essays will come into the reading for many of the coming chapters.

If you would like to go to 'the horse's mouth' for the detail of the Phillips curve, read the original article by A. W. Phillips, 'The Relationship between Unemployment and the Rate of Change of Money Wage Rates in the United Kingdom, 1861–1957'.[65] For a non-technical indication of the way the curve relationship broke down, see the chapter by M. C. Kennedy[37] in A. R. Prest and D. J. Coppock (eds), *The UK Economy*.

The principal name associated with the 'falsificationist' view of scientific method is that of Karl Popper. However, some methodological writers—economists among them—have recounted a naïve version of 'falsificationism' which is a vast oversimplification of what Popper actually said. To check on what he actually did say, read his masterly book, *The Logic of Scientific Discovery*.[67] From it you will find, for instance, that Popper is very well aware that empirical observation can never provide conclusive *falsification* any more than it can provide conclusive verification—a point on which he has been consistently misunderstood by these 'naïve falsification-ists' (see his p. 50).

For two writers' views on the nature and implications of *ignorance* in economics, see B. J. Loasby, *Choice, Complexity and Ignorance,*[48] and T. W. Hutchison, *Knowledge and Ignorance in Economics.*[32]

Of the writers who have portrayed scientific advance as a sociological process, T. S. Kuhn has attracted a great deal of attention with his book, *The Structure of Scientific Revolutions.*[43] Another methodologist, Imre Lakatos, has offered an alternative account in his 'methodology of scientific research programmes'. He states it not in any single book, but in various essays and journal articles. Kuhn and Lakatos (like Popper) are authors who are probably cited more often than they are read, by economists at least. If your interest is in the philosophy of economic science rather than of science generally, you may find that your scarce reading time is better used by finding out how Kuhn's and Lakatos's ideas have been applied to economics, in the relevant sources cited in the reading guide to Chapter 6.

Discussion topics: Chapter 4

1. (a) Sketch the usual textbook version of the Keynesian saving function. Suppose you are going to test it empirically: what would be the wording of your *hypothesis*?
(b) What series of figures would you set against one another in order to test this hypothesis?
(c) List as many as possible of the *auxiliary hypotheses* on which you would need intersubjective agreement in carrying out your testing.
(d) Suppose your hypothesis stood at first as non-rejected: can you think of any possible changes in economic circumstances which might lead to its later rejection?

If you like, carry out all these steps also on the textbook version of the supply curve.

2. (a) List half a dozen economic constructs which are totally *unobservable* (that is, which are not directly identifiable with any protocol).
(b) Then list another half dozen which *are* directly identifiable with protocols. (Hint: make sure that you make this latter list *specific* enough. For instance, the construct 'price', familiar as it is to us as an everyday idea, is certainly *not* identifiable with any protocol, unless you specify the price of *what, when, where.* Check back on this point after you have read Fritz Machlup's article 'Operationalism . . .'.[51])

3. Are the following statements tautologous or contingent?
(a) 'National income equals total expenditure'.
(b) 'If the marginal propensity to consume is 3/4, then the multiplier is 4.'
(c) 'Consumers maximize their satisfaction'.

4. Sketch out the textbook supply-and-demand diagram, showing the familiar proposition 'equilibrium comes where supply equals demand'. Now try writing down each of the individual hypotheses which have to be used in order to reason out this familiar conclusion. (Take it that we are working purely in the c-domain, so that you can forget about all the auxiliary hypotheses we would need to add if the proposition were being put up for empirical checking. Even so, your task is not nearly as easy as you might think. As just one hint, remember that you will need to specify hypotheses not only to describe the two schedules, but also to say what equilibrium *is*, and *why* it comes where it does.)

Once you have what seems to be a complete list of these hypotheses, look at each one and see if you can think of a *higher-level hypothesis* which entails the truth of the hypothesis in question. Try to continue this process until you cannot get any higher in level—that is, until you have the set of axioms from which supply-and-demand equilibrium can be deduced. By the way: if you succeed in doing this beyond all reasonable argument, you will have achieved what the most eminent theoreticians in economics have so far failed to do.

5

Distinctive features of economic data

The economist and the physical scientist are both concerned with facts; and each faces his own particular problems in establishing and interpreting these facts. But while the detail of the physical scientist's task has been well explored by methodologists of general science, much less attention has been given to the special problems of observing and interpreting economic data. This chapter will examine some of these distinctive problems of economic science. In particular, the question will be asked: how far *are* the procedures of physical science appropriate for use in economics, given the difference in the kinds of data which scientists in the two fields have to handle? This discussion will help to set the scene for the treatment in Chapter 6 of the relationship between economic theory and reality, as well as for several of the questions of economic application which are covered in later chapters.

5.1 The problem of prediction

5.1.1. The meanings of 'prediction'

To what extent are economic events predictable? This question, long the subject of controversy, has not yet been conclusively answered. It is hardly necessary to spell out why the issue is significant both from the point of view of the academic economist and from that of the policy adviser. In this part of the chapter, we take a detailed look at this important data problem.

Our first step, as always, must be to sort out confusion over terms. In economic literature, the word 'prediction' seems to be used in at least three separate senses—and just to confuse matters even further, these three different meanings are not entirely independent of each other: to some extent, they overlap.

First: as was said in Section 2.3, in methodological writing the term 'prediction' is sometimes used as an alternative to 'consequent', when one is talking about the hypothetical syllogism. I have indeed used it in that sense in parts of the discussion of hypothetico-deductive method (e.g., on pages 50, 73). According to this terminology, we usually rechristen the antecedent as well, referring to it as the 'assumption' or 'assumptions'. This meaning will come up again in Chapter 6, when we come to look at another con-troversial question: is economic theory to be 'tested by assumptions' or tested by predictions'?

Second: often when we talk about the 'predictions of economic theory', what we are implying is merely that theory gives us some reason to predict the *direction* in which a certain variable will move—rather than predict *how far* it will move. A moment's thought will reveal this kind of interpretation in every department of economic theory. 'If the demand schedule for good X rises, then (other things being unchanged, and given a normally sloping supply curve) its price will rise.' 'If planned investment falls while planned saving stays the same, then (other things being unchanged) the equilibrium level of national income will fall.' To confirm how frequently this kind of reasoning appears in economic theorems, you may like to work out a few instances from other areas of theory—remembering that 'no movement at all' is one 'direction of movement'. This meaning of 'prediction' is sometimes specified by calling it *qualitative prediction*.

Sometimes, as you may realize in thinking of other cases, this kind of 'prediction' does entail some hints about the amount of movement (as well as its direction), but these hints are themselves phrased in relative and general terms, implying just that one variable moves proportionately more than, or less than, another.

In some instances, you may come across 'predictions' which are worked out in numerical terms, but which arrive at their numerical results purely because of the arbitrary choice of numbers at the start of the reasoning. For instance: 'If the marginal propensity to consume is $2/3$, then an increase in government spending of £1 million will produce a final multiplied increase in national income of £3 million.' Here, the numbers are purely illustrative—we might as well have said $3/4$, £10 million, and £40 million respectively; or, come to that, c, X, and $\Delta Y = X/(1-c)$.

Third: our last sense of 'prediction' is the most obvious one in terms of everyday conversation, and simply indicates a statement of future outcome in quantitative terms. 'In the spring of the coming year, unemployment in Great Britain is expected to be such-and-such a figure'. 'The X Research Institute have forecast that the rate of price inflation in the UK over the coming six months will be so-and-so many per cent.' And so on; each day's news reports bring a crop of examples.

However, it is worth mentioning a point which will come up again in later discussion: quantitative prediction need not always contain a specific reference to the future. As often as not, the predictive element is implied in the phrasing. To anticipate a famous example: if we say 'the elasticity of demand for herring is 1.3', and do not qualify our remark any further, then we are clearly implying not only that the figure has been 1.3 in the past, but that it will *continue to be* 1.3—or thereabouts—in the future.

In beginning this section, I mentioned that these three senses of 'prediction' overlapped. Without trespassing too much on the discussion of later sections and chapters, it is worth while here briefly reviewing these overlaps of meaning. First: when we talk about 'predictions of economic theory'— when, that is, we talk of the consequent clauses of hypotheticals occurring as statements of economic theory—we may either mean qualitative or quantitative 'predictions'. In fact, writers often have not made it clear which they mean, and the potential confusion of interpretation is relevant to the question of how economic theory is to be tested, a point which we shall look at again in Chapter 6.

Second: it is rather obvious that you can make qualitative predictions without at the same time making quantitative predictions, but not vice versa. There would not be much point in predicting, say, a change of 500,000 in the total of unemployed by next spring, if at the same time you failed to say whether the change was expected to be upwards or downwards. In fact, there is no sharp dividing line between 'qualitative' and 'quantitative': as I have already said, some qualitative predictions can be considered quantitative in a rudimentary way, simply because some numerical values happen to be injected into the reasoning for illustrative purposes. But if we extend this process so that the numbers we inject are not just arbitrary, but are intended as sensible estimates of real-world values; and if we also take care to specify the conditions in which our variables interact, again trying to get as close as we can to a real-world situation—then the prediction we reason out will correspondingly be intended as a quantitative suggestion of the real-world outcome.

Third: it is possible to speak of the 'predictions of theory' without implying that we are necessarily talking about the real-life future. We *may* indeed intend to set our theoretical predictions against something that is to be observed in the future. But we may quite well talk about events that theory did or did not succeed in predicting in the past. Or, very often, our theoretical reasoning deals with a generalized economic situation which is not placed in any specific time, and the 'prediction' is then also correspondingly timeless; it is simply a deductive implication following from whatever premises we have chosen to start from in our theorizing.

All these points of interpretation will, as I have said, come into our discussion again in later chapters. But in the examination of the 'problem of prediction' as a special feature of economic data, in the sections immediately following, we shall be using 'prediction' in its most straightforward sense: that is, as indicating a statement in quantitative terms of the future value of some economic measure.

5.1.2 *The controversy*

When I speak of a 'controversy' over the question of economic prediction, I do not intend to convey that it is a matter of non-stop argument among economists or even economic methodologists; simply that two viewpoints can be distinguished, more or less opposed to one another, and that the disagreement between these two schools has not been resolved to the general satisfaction of everyone. Let us call these two camps, purely for descriptive convenience, the 'predictionists' and the 'non-predictionists'—though, as perhaps I need hardly add by now, there is no clear-cut dividing line between the two, and we will find some methodologists who 'sit on the fence'. By way of a lead-in, we may look at quotations from two well-known writers, one from each camp. Here first is the predictionist view, put by Professor Lipsey in *An Introduction to Positive Economics:*

> Whether human behaviour does or does not show sufficiently stable responses to factors influencing it as to be predictable within an acceptable margin of error is a positive question that can only be answered by an appeal to evidence and not by *a priori* speculation.
>
> In fact it is a matter of simple observation that when we consider a group of individuals they do not behave in a totally capricious way but do display stable responses to various stimuli. The warmer the weather, for example, the higher the number of people visiting the beaches and the higher the sales of ice-cream. It may be hard to say when or why one individual will buy an ice-cream, but we can observe a stable response pattern from a large group of individuals: the higher the temperature the greater the sales of ice-cream.
>
> Many other examples will come to mind where, because we can say what the individual will probably do—without being certain of what he will do—we can say with quite remarkable accuracy what a large group of individuals will do.

And here, by contrast, is a famous passage from Lord Robbins's *Essay on the Nature and Significance of Economic Science.* He is talking about a mythical economist called Blank, who had been doing research into the elasticity of demand for herring:

> Let us assume that in 1907–08 Blank had succeeded in ascertaining that with a given price change in that year, the elasticity of demand was 1.3. . . . what reason is there to suppose that he was unearthing a constant law? . . . The demand for herrings . . . is a function of a great many apparently independent variables. . . . (*As examples of these, Robbins cites fashion, promotional campaigns, transport changes, discoveries in the art of cooking, even theological views, among other influences.*) Is it possible reasonably to suppose that coefficients derived from the observation of a particular herring market at a particular time and place have any permanent significance—save as Economic History? . . . Rough ideas relating to the elasticity of demand in particular markets are indeed essential if we are to make full use of the more refined tools of economic analysis. But they have no claim to be regarded as immutable laws. However accurately they describe the past, there is no presumption that they must continue to describe the future. . . . If we wanted to be helpful about herrings we should never dream of relying on the researches of the wretched Blank who was working in 1907–08. We should work the whole thing out afresh on the basis of more recent data.

Our job as methodologists is to try to evaluate the soundness of each point of view. As with many other similar tasks, the first and perhaps the most important question to resolve is simply: what is it that each side *is* arguing, anyhow? Some wordy methodological wrangles could have been dispensed with if their writers had paid more attention to this starting question.

We begin by noting two points which neither side would dispute. First: no one, not even the most committed predictionist, would suggest that we have any useful way of predicting the economic actions of *individuals*. The predictionist position is, instead, that when we can view the economic actions of people in reasonably large groups, then the *mass* outcome will be predictable. We shall shortly be examining the reasoning behind this view.

Second: not even the most enthusiastic non-predictionist would argue that mass economic behaviour is *never* predictable. The non-predictionists say rather that mass economic behaviour is in some ways less easily predictable—or, perhaps, less often predictable—than the predictionists think.

Even with these two nonarguments out of the way, the position of each side is still pretty vaguely defined—too vaguely to allow sensible discussion of the case. (Which has not prevented a lot of controversy over just these two ill-defined positions.)

We can get nearer to a sensible starting-point for discussion if we get very slightly more technical over the nature of 'mass outcomes'. The point is, of course, that when you observe any phenomena in groups, then you can use statistical techniques to analyse the results. So, in these terms, what the predictionists are suggesting is that mass economic behaviour can be predicted with the aid of statistical techniques; and the non-predictionists are disagreeing with this view, though the strength of the disagreement varies from writer to writer. If we 'strike an average' of non-predictionist positions, then we come out with something very like what Robbins argues in his 'herring' example: not that mass economic action is *totally* unpredictable in a statistical sense, but rather that the predicted relationships are likely to hold for only a relatively short time after the prediction has been made—often too short a time, suggests Robbins, to be of any use in real-life policy decisions.

In the passages quoted from Lipsey and Robbins, each writer supports his own viewpoint by referring to the predictability—or otherwise—of purchases of one particular good, rather than by advancing arguments about economic behaviour generally. (Though Professor Lipsey's remarks about the predictability of ice-cream sales are sensible in themselves, they do not make up the wide-ranging 'appeal to evidence' which he himself calls for.) Both writers, of course, do argue their cases more generally in other passages. And we have to do the same: when we are assessing the predictability of economic behaviour, we must try to come up with an answer that applies to economic behaviour generally, and not just to selected cases.

Furthermore, since we are looking at scientific procedure, we need to take up Professor Lipsey's challenge and base our assessment on 'an appeal to evidence', not on '*a priori* speculation'. Let us begin in true scientific style, then, and try to work out what *hypothesis* about predictability is being asserted or denied by each side, instead of just talking in vague terms of an 'argument'.

We can phrase our hypothesis in positive rather than negative terms, i.e., we can word it so as to express the predictionist viewpoint. On the basis of the discussion so far, it would run something like this: 'By using statistical techniques, mass economic behaviour can be predicted; and the stability of the predicted relationships is great enough to make these predictions serviceable in the testing of economic theory and the formulation of policy decisions.'

Predictionists, in putting this hypothesis forward, would very probably want to be more specific about the conditions in which its truth could be expected to hold. The two most important of these conditions would probably be: that the necessary data should be available; and that the investigator should use a procedure appropriate to the statistical characteristics of these data.

Admittedly, this is only one possible way of wording the predictionists' hypothesis. Perhaps some less ambitious predictionists would want to drop the reference to the 'testing of economic theory'; and others, less ambitious still, might even simply want to assert that 'by using statistical techniques, mass economic behaviour can be predicted more accurately than by mere random guessing'. (Though unless it can be asserted that the predictions thus made are good enough to be *useful* for something, economic prediction is relegated to the status of a mere intellectual puzzle—which, many non-predictionists would say, is exactly what it is.) However, for the moment, let us accept the more optimistic wording, already given above, as being near enough to what the predictionists are asserting and the non-predictionists denying.

How about the testability of this hypothesis? As far as can be seen, it is testable in principle: all we need to do is to look at the observed results of economic prediction, taking a sufficient number of instances to allow us to make a sensible generalization, and making sure that our observations cover instances of prediction from all the different areas of economic subject matter (since our hypothesis is about economic prediction generally, and not just prediction in certain branches of the subject).

And, of course, in practice we can do none of these things. Or, at least, we cannot do them nearly well enough to convince either side in the controversy. There is no body of empirical data against which the predictionist hypothesis can be directly tested in any remotely convincing way. Admittedly, a great many economic predictions have been made by a great many people over the years, on many different subjects and using many different techniques. But the most that can be agreed about their results is: some have been very close to the mark, some have been ridiculously wide of it, with the rest falling somewhere in between—hardly a firm basis on which to judge the soundness of a hypothesis about economic prediction generally.

There is another explanation of the fact that the predictionist hypothesis is not testable in practice: both the predictionist and the non-predictionist positions really assert something about what economic prediction is potentially *capable of*, and not just what it actually *has* done to date. Predictionists have often implied that where current techniques fail to produce good predictions in a given case, the fault lies in the current techniques, rather than in any feature of the economic situation itself; future improvements in technique, they feel, will bring the looked-for success in prediction. Contrariwise, non-predictionists have brought forward the notion of some inherent unpredictability in economic action, such that no improvements in statistical technique could ever bring about a useful degree of accuracy in prediction. It is clear that neither the predictionist nor the non-predictionist interpretation here is open to testing against any existing real-world data.

So, given that the predictionist hypothesis cannot be convincingly tested simply by looking at the results of past exercises in economic prediction, must we therefore leave the matter there, and accept that an inconclusive answer is the only one we are able to get in the present state of knowledge? In the coming sections, I shall suggest that the position is not quite so bad as this. Though indeed we cannot test the baldly phrased hypothesis 'economic prediction works', we can nevertheless learn something useful by looking further into the reasoning behind prediction in general and economic prediction in particular.

Let us look first at two arguments which, though often used, turn out on examination not to tell the whole story about the practicability of prediction in economics. They should be viewed as inadequate arguments, not 'wrong' arguments: as we shall see, some of the points made are very relevant to the problem of prediction, even if they do not quite succeed in making out a watertight case.

5.1.3 The role of free will

Non-predictionists sometimes argue along these lines: 'Economics is very largely concerned with decisions taken by people. When people take decisions, they use free will. Free will, by its nature, is unpredictable. Therefore economic behaviour is unpredictable.'

As you will appreciate, this argument touches on issues which run far outside the realms of economic methodology—indeed, far outside the boundaries of the philosophy of science. The question 'is human behaviour predetermined, or is it to some extent under the control of the individual?' is one of the unsolved puzzles of philosophy, and of religion, come to that.

Luckily, for our purposes in studying the methodology of economics, we do not need to attack this formidable problem: we can simply go round it. We do this by recalling that not even the predictionists in economics are arguing the predictability of individual behaviour; what they suggest is that *mass* behaviour can be statistically predicted.

In other words, the predictionist need not argue that 'people have no free will'. What he does argue is: when groups of individuals act in the way that each person's free will dictates, then the outcome for the group as a whole is predictable within certain limits of probability.

Looking back at the non-predictionist argument with which this subsection began, we see why it has to be called 'inadequate'. In the form in which it's given, it does not specify whether 'economic behaviour' means individual behaviour or mass behaviour. If indeed individual behaviour is meant, then there is no dispute, since predictionists agree that the economic behaviour of an individual is unpredictable. But if mass economic behaviour is meant—and obviously this would be the usual interpretation—then the non-predictionist argument begs the question. All it gives us, in fact, is a flat statement that 'economic behaviour' (implying mass behaviour) 'is unpredictable'. To bring forward the factor of free will as an 'explanation' of this statement is merely to ignore the question which is really at issue—that is, 'does free will carry with it *mass* unpredictability as well as *individual* unpredictability?'

5.1.4 Analogy with physical science

As we have seen, the question at issue between predictionists and non-predictionists is whether mass economic behaviour is statistically predictable. We have just noted that non-predictionists are really begging the question by arguing 'free will'. What is perhaps not so obvious is that predictionists for their part very often beg the question in a different way.

As a matter of fact, predictionists in recent times often have not felt obliged to argue their own position at all, given the climate of methodological fashion that has prevailed in economics for some years past. There are, for instance, very few texts on econometrics that take the trouble to advance any argument in favour of their own methodological position. Instead, most econometric writers simply proceed on the unstated assumption that the methods they describe are indeed capable of predicting mass economic behaviour, given that the needed data are available and that the techniques used are in accord with the right technical prescriptions. But, as we have seen, there is no body of empirical evidence against which this assumption (or 'predictionist hypothesis') can be satisfactorily tested.

When predictionists do advance specific arguments to support their position, they are fond of arguing by analogy with physical science. A quick scan of the literature reveals writers illustrating the predictability of human action by reference to the behaviour of gas molecules, chemical elements in combination, bouncing billiard balls, and a whole flurry of falling bodies—more balls (of unspecified nature), coins, feathers.

As we shall see in the coming chapter, this device of drawing analogy with physical science is very often used not only to support what I am here calling the 'predictionist' view, but also a range of other and related methodological positions.

It is not difficult to see why this style of argument has tempted economists. The procedures of physical science, particularly of physics itself, have traditionally been held up as a model for science generally; and certainly the achievements of these sciences, both in theory and in application, have been vast. How pleasant if economics could get to the same standards of exactness and the same level of achievement! And if at the moment economics cannot do these things, then, it might seem, one thing economics *can* do is to try to get as near as possible to the methods used in these respected physical sciences.

An attractive argument, as I say. But in reality it is open to the same objection as is any other argument by analogy: it only has force if the analogy can be shown to be appropriate. And this is exactly the point, of course, at which the non-predictionists enter their dissent.

Once again, this is not to suggest that the analogy is necessarily 'wrong': simply that when the bare analogy is used, it must be judged an inadequate argument in itself. In fact, in the coming sections we shall look at the appropriateness of this analogy, and try to evaluate how closely the reasoning of prediction in the physical sciences can be compared with that in the social sciences.

5.1.5 *The reasoning of statistical prediction*

First of all: in talking here of 'prediction', we are using the term in the most straightforward of its several senses: namely, a quantitative statement of some future outcome. We have noted that, virtually always, such prediction would be based on inductive observation, perhaps assisted to some extent by theoretical reasoning.

In looking at the general topic of induction in Chapter 3, we have already broken much of the ground for the discussion now to come. We saw that whenever induction is used predictively, the underlying reasoning must be syllogistic: and that the major premise of the syllogism must always be a 'proposition of regularity' (though this premise is most often implied rather than stated). To go back to an old-fashioned example:

1. I have observed that on all past mornings, the sun has risen;
2. what the sun has done in the past, it will continue to do in the future;
3. therefore the sun will rise tomorrow morning.

Another thing we noted from Chapter 3 was that series of past observations themselves can never give any evidence for the proposition of regularity: these past observations refer to the past, and no more.

It is from this position, then, that we can carry on the discussion. Now we are talking, not just about 'prediction generally', but about statistical prediction. And clearly, the crucial question we have to answer is: in what way, if any, does the use of statistical analysis add to our ability to predict the future?

As our first step, let us try to formulate in simple terms what statistical analysis actually set out to do. More exactly: in carrying out statistical analysis on a set of data, we are doing something additional to what we would be doing if we simply looked the data over by eye. What is this extra 'something' added by statistical analysis? Before reading on, perhaps you would like to pause and work out your own answer.

One way of putting it is this: in *any* kind of analysis of data, whether statistical analysis or just simple 'eyeballing', we are arranging the data into a *pattern*. But when we use statistical analysis, we not only work out a pattern; we also work out some measure of *confidence* in the correctness of that pattern. For instance: confronted with a set of measurements of a given characteristic, we would typically work out the mean value of these, and state how likely it is that this mean figure represents the population value. Or if we were looking at a relationship between two (or between several) sets of data, we would work out our 'best estimates' of the various parameters, and add an indication of our confidence that these estimates were indeed correct ones. Again, if we were considering changes over time in some real-world measure, we would work out the trend and give an estimate of our confidence that our calculated trend line did indeed represent the real trend.

Because this notion of 'establishing a pattern and estimating our confidence in its correctness' will come into our discussion often in the next few pages, I will designate it by a shorthand expression, and talk about *establishing a statistical pattern*.

Now, in these terms, how can we word the syllogism that needs to be used in inductive prediction, given that we are using statistical analysis? First of all, it is pretty obvious how the minor premise has to run; as always, it will simply state what our past observations have shown us, so we can say something like this:

I have made a set of observations of situation X, and on the basis of these I have established a statistical pattern in the past instances of this situation.

Turning next to the conclusion we are aiming for: obviously, we want to be able to conclude something about the future. And since we are talking about statistical prediction, we know that whatever we say about the future will be probabilistic, not deterministic—in other words, what we expect to see in the future is not *exactly the same* pattern as we have observed in the past—but, rather, the same *statistical pattern*. We expect our pattern to vary within the same limits of statistical confidence as we have already established for our past pattern.

Minor premise, conclusion—we already know what the 'missing link' between the two must be, namely, the major premise. And we know that this premise must be in the form of a 'proposition of regularity'.

Given all this, you might like now to formulate your own wording for the complete syllogism.

It will be in some such terms as these:

1. I have made a set of observations of situation X, and on the basis of these I have established a statistical pattern in the past instances of this situation;
2. whatever statistical pattern I have observed in the past will also be observed in the future;
3. therefore I conclude that future observations of situation X will continue to conform to the same statistical pattern as they have done in the past.

When in Chapter 3 we were talking about inductive prediction in general terms, we noted that past observation in itself could never provide evidence to support the proposition of regularity. Now that we have brought statistical analysis into the picture, do we have to change our view? In other words, is it the case that the statistical analysis we have carried out on our past data *does* afford us some evidence to support the proposition of regularity?

When we inspect the argument in the full syllogistic form just drawn out, it is clear that the answer is still 'No'. With or without statistical analysis, we have no way of arguing from the minor to the major premise. The patterns we have established from past observation—whether they be deterministic or statistical patterns—still relate only to the past; and if we want to argue from them to future outcomes, we still need to bring in a proposition of regularity.

To spell this conclusion out in full: *statistical analysis of past data can never provide evidence to support a proposition of regularity relating to these data.*

If you have not reasoned this argument through until now, you may well feel some surprise at the idea that statistical analysis is not predictive in itself. Part of the problem here, I think, may arise from the words we use to describe the ideas of statistics. 'Confidence', for instance, is a word that seems to suggest something about the future—but in reality, when we apply this term to the results of analysis of past data, we are speaking only of confidence in the correctness of that *past* pattern. We cannot use these past observations to develop 'confidence' about future outcomes unless we reason via the proposition of regularity, as above. Another statistical term, 'probability', is one that I have deliberately avoided using so far in this section, because it carries such heavy overtones of predictiveness.

5.1.6 Prediction and the 'law of large numbers'

Frequently, predictionists phrase their arguments in terms of what is called the 'law of large numbers' (though the name is not a good one, since the proposition in question has little in common with scientific 'laws'). In reality, this version of the argument is simply an alternative way of expressing the predictionist idea of the persistence of statistical patterns, which in the last section we examined and found wanting. However, since the 'argument from large numbers' is a favourite with textbook writers, let us give it a brief examination.

What the 'law of large numbers' says, in essence, is this: when you start by making only a few observations of some situation, then you cannot place a great deal of confidence in any pattern which these observations seem to show—because, common sense tells you, there might be one or several very untypical observations in those few you have made, which would have a relatively great effect on the overall pattern. As you make more and more observations, common sense likewise tells you that the relative importance of untypical observations is likely to become less and less; furthermore, that where individual untypical observations are free to vary both above and below the normal value, then, for all the observations considered as a group, these extreme values will tend to cancel out.

Now, all this is of course a description of how the 'law of large numbers' plays its role in the statistical analysis of *past* data. But how about prediction? The usual predictionist 'argument from large numbers' simply runs: 'Over a large group of observations, individual deviations from the norm tend to cancel each other out; therefore group outcomes can be predicted, even though individual outcomes cannot.' A very sensible-seeming argument —but also an inadequate argument, as we are able by now to see straight-away. It is inadequate, of course, because it misses out the major premise, and in so doing, begs the question about mass predictability. If we construct the full version of the syllogism, we will see what the major premise (labelled '2' below) would have to be:

1. In past observations of situation X, I have established a pattern in the observed outcomes, and have noted that individual deviations from this pattern have tended to cancel out over large numbers of observations;
2. in the future, individual deviations from the observed pattern will tend to cancel out over large numbers of observations, in the same way as they have in the past;
3. therefore the statistical pattern which I have observed in the past will also apply to the future.

The important point to note is, once again, that the past observations themselves give no evidence for the proposition of regularity. Merely to say that, in the past, untypical observations have tended to cancel out is not to prove anything about whether this will continue to be the case in future. If we want to argue that it will be, then once again we can only do so by bringing in the needed proposition of regularity as our major premise.

I would suggest that if you are in any doubt about the findings we have reached, then you re-read this and the previous section and satisfy yourself that their arguments are in fact watertight. It must be said that in the coverage given to economic methodology in some general texts on economics or econometrics, this fundamental issue fails to get even a mention; too often, the writers concerned merely state the 'argument from large numbers' which we have here seen to be inadequate, and they support it perhaps with an analogy from physical science. This being so, I shall risk being over-repetitive, and state once again what we have now established: when statistical analysis is used on the data of past observations, then the results of this analysis will themselves relate only to the past. There is no epistemological basis for supposing that statistical analysis in itself provides quantitative evidence of future outcomes.

5.1.7 Statistical prediction: physical v. social sciences

In our discussion of the reasoning of statistical prediction, we have opened the way to working out what may be the real differences between prediction in the physical sciences and in the social sciences. I say 'may be' rather than 'are', since the epistemology of this area has not been at all well explored.

As we have seen, when any scientist makes a statistical prediction, he needs to reason along these lines:

> I have made a large number of past observations, and from these I have established estimates of a 'true' value and of deviations from that value. Admittedly, I cannot predict the future variations from this pattern that may be observed in individual cases. *But I am assuming that these future variations will tend to cancel each other out, in the same way as they did in the past* (this is the proposition of regularity), and that therefore my past estimates of the 'true' value, and of the deviations from it, will continue to be correct in the future.

In the physical sciences, it is universally assumed that this proposition of regularity does in fact hold. Physicists do not pretend, for instance, that they can predict the behaviour of individual gas molecules. But by studying the mass behaviour of very large numbers of molecules, they can arrive at an estimate of the 'typical' behaviour of a gas molecule, within certain statistical limits. Though this estimate must be derived from past observations, it is also taken by physicists as applying to the future, since they assume (usually by implication) that variations in behaviour on the part of individual

91

molecules will continue to cancel each other out over large numbers of future cases.

Thus, if we wanted to try to apply the 'law of large numbers' to the prediction of human behaviour, we would have to make the same assumption—that individual variations away from a past 'norm' will tend to cancel out over large numbers of future instances. And this is where the warning bells begin to ring: experience suggests that in many circumstances, variations in human behaviour do *not* follow this rule.

Suppose you are trying to predict the future course of some economic statistic—the growth rate, the level of employment, the production of a farm crop, or whatever. If you decided simply to graph the past trend in that particular statistic, and then tried to predict the future by projecting the trend line, you would be rapped on the knuckles by any competent forecaster. 'Trend projection is naïve in the extreme', he would tell you. And, of course, he would be correct: experience has shown again and again that trends can 'break', and sometimes do so very sharply, with the graph line taking off in some totally unexpected direction—unexpected, that is, from any judgement based on the past course of the trend line.

And yet, what exactly are we doing when we try to aid our prediction by applying statistical analysis? We start by estimating, not just the past trend itself, but also statistical limits of confidence within which the 'true' trend line can be said to fall. And when it comes to projection, we project not simply the observed trend line, but rather the statistical 'band', as it were, within which we have estimated the 'true' trend line to lie. In other words, our projection is now probabilistic rather than deterministic.

Texts on time-series analysis usually leave the matter there, as though the introduction of a probabilistic element into projection had somehow taken care of the fact that the future is uncertain. But of course, as we know from our discussion in this chapter, it has done nothing of the kind. The fact is that in using statistical analysis in this way, we are merely 'extrapolating probabilities'; and from the epistemological point of view, this is almost as naïve as the extrapolation of a simple trend line. It amounts to making the assumption that variations in the economic behaviour of individuals *must* continue to cancel each other out in the future in exactly the same way as they did in the past; and the mere existence of 'trend-breaks' in economic series *shows empirically that this assumption is mistaken*.

In fitting our statistical confidence limits round our trend line, what we have actually done is to give a measure of how closely the past course of the trend line, as judged from the observations we have made, reflects the past 'true' value of the trend. Now *if* it happens that the past configuration of the trend does continue into the period for which we made our predictions, then these statistical limits will continue to be valid in that period. But *if* instead there is a break in the trend, then our projected statistical limits will have served no purpose other than to provide us with a misleading forecast.

As a practical example of the perils of statistical prediction, let us return to the Phillips curve (which we originally met in Section 4.2). As we said, the data originally used by Phillips showed a close correlation between the level of employment and changes in wage rates, and did succeed in predicting the relationship for some years after he published his famous paper; indeed, the Phillips curve was almost accorded the status of an economic 'law'. But as we know, the 'curve' has by now ceased to predict events to any useful degree of accuracy: the reasons for this failure are still obscure at the time of writing.

Examples like these must clearly support the non-predictionist view that in the field of prediction, it is not safe to appeal to an analogy between economics and the physical sciences. But can these be considered *representative* instances? Is there really a fundamental difference between the predictability of mass outcomes in economics and physical sciences? And if there is, have we any idea of the reason for it?

As I have said, this is still an area of controversy, and a detailed discussion of it would take us beyond the aims of this book. But from the point of view of practical economics, we can give a short, sharp, and relevant answer to all three questions that have just been asked: namely, 'It doesn't matter'. What really does matter is that in economics we cannot *always* take it that the assumption of regularity will hold true—even when we mean 'regularity' in a probabilistic sense. The suggested 'analogy with physical science', as regards mass predictability, may sometimes turn out to be a correct analogy—but at other times it may turn out to be incorrect. Further, we have no way of telling in advance whether it will or will not be correct in a given instance—in other words, we can never tell in advance whether a statistical prediction will 'work' or not.

And this is all we need to note for the purpose of real-life economic research or application. For these practical purposes, we need not concern ourselves whether this indicates a difference in kind between economics and physical science, or just a difference in degree—nor, for that matter, whether some day the difference will be eliminated. What does matter is that the difference exists now, in the current 'state of the art'; and that it is a big enough difference to merit being regarded as a difference in kind, whether or not it actually is so.

Before leaving this section, it is worth making a final point about the suggested 'analogy with prediction in physical science'. We have already seen why, from the point of view of economic science, this analogy is inadequate. Some writers on the general philosophy of science have argued its inadequacy for a different reason: namely that in *physical* science, there are in reality many situations in which an assumption of regularity cannot be made, even in a probabilistic sense. More specifically, they point out that the two-way division between social science and physical science is not serviceable for all purposes. What we should really do is split down each of these two classes into two subclasses: 'laboratory situations' and what might be called 'field situations'—the latter being all instances of investigation outside the tightly controlled world of experimental work. As it happens, pretty well all investigation in social science would come under the heading of 'field situations'; the reasons for this are probably obvious to you, and we shall return to this general point later in the chapter. What these writers point out is that it is really only in laboratory situations in physical science that the assumption of regularity is universally made; in field situations, where a whole variety of influences may determine the course of events, then inductive prediction may be subject to very much the same limitations as in social science.

On this reasoning, the proper analogy is not between economics and physical science, but between economics and field situations in physical science. This revised version of the analogy indeed seems a lot more appropriate. But at the same time, we have to remember what conclusion the revised anaolgy points to. Some predictionist writers, by a slightly devious process of reasoning, have seemed to suggest that this analogy *supports* the idea of mass predictability in economics ('Economics *is* like physics; in physics, things are predictable; therefore . . .'). In reality, of course, the revised analogy is aimed at the opposite conclusion—namely, that it is not safe to assume future regularity in *any* field situation, whether in physical or social science.

Throughout our discussion of economic prediction so far, the argument has been carried on in an intuitive way. We have spoken about the proposition of regularity as though it were something quite arbitrary, simply pulled out of the air. Further, we have noted simply as a 'fact of life' that it is safe to make this assumption in experimental science, but that it is not safe to make it—at least, not always—in economics. In the following section, I shall outline an argument that suggests a rather more firm grounding for these notions about the proposition of regularity, and, in doing so, suggests also what may be the genuine 'difference in kind' between prediction in economics and in experimental science. If you are happy with the intuitive version of the argument, then *you should omit the following section*, certainly on a first reading.

5.1.8 The 'proposition of regularity' as hypothesis

We can continue our argument from the position just noted: namely, that in experimental science, it appears safe to make an assumption of regularity (in probabilistic terms)—that is, to assume that past patterns will continue into the future within statistical limits of variability. Now, *why* can we say this? And *why* can we say that in economics it is not safe to make the same assumption, at least, not always? You might perhaps pause a moment and formulate your own answer.

In the most straightforward terms, the answer amounts to this: in experimental science, if we make an assumption of regularity, it *works*; whereas if we make the same assumption in economics, it sometimes works and sometimes does not.

Now, in considering whether an assumption 'works', what are we doing? We are, in fact, *testing* our assumption against real-world outcomes. And if we now recognize the 'assumption of statistical regularity' as a proposition that is to be tested empirically, then we can rechristen the 'assumption', and call it instead a *'hypothesis* of statistical regularity'.

It is essential to keep clear in our minds what this hypothesis says. We are not just hypothesizing that 'future events are predictable', or any other such simple formulation. Our hypothesis is something much more specific: namely, that if a pattern of past events is established by inductive observation, then this pattern can be expected to persist into the future, within limits of variability set by statistical analysis.

Given, then, that this is our hypothesis, what are we saying about it in the separate contexts of experimental science and economics? Once again, we need to be on guard against an oversimplified version of the case: we cannot reasonably say just that the hypothesis is true in experimental science but untrue in economics. We need, instead, to look at the position separately for each of these two scientific areas.

With regard to experimental science: at some risk of oversimplification, we can say that the hypothesis of statistical regularity is accepted as being true in all circumstances. In other words, the *deterministic* version of the hypothesis is accepted as being true. Now of course this hypothesis, like any other hypothesis, is incapable of being proved true by observation; but it can be proved untrue—and, being a deterministic hypothesis, it can be proved untrue by even one contrary observation. What we are saying, then, is that in experimental science, no such contrary observation *has* ever been made. In other words, in experimental science we never come across a situation where statistical patterns established in the past do *not* persist into the future.*

We can now immediately see the difference between the position of economics and that of the experimental sciences. In these latter sciences, the deterministic hypothesis of statistical regularity is universally accepted as being true; in economics, *we know that this deterministic hypothesis is untrue.* We know, in other words, that in at least some situations of economic investigation, statistical patterns established in the past do not persist into

*To be more exact: if a set of observations were ever made in experimental science which seemed to run counter to the hypothesis of statistical regularity, then scientists would be overwhelmingly impelled to appeal to failures in the duplication of experimental conditions, or other disturbing influences known or unknown, rather than allowing the possibility that the deterministic hypothesis of statistical regularity were untrue. And the reason is obvious: if, in any field of experimental science, a set of results could ever be produced which *did* provide convincing evidence against the deterministic hypothesis of statistical regularity, then all experimental results in that field of science would lose their meaning.

the future. It is here, if anywhere, that we find the real 'difference in kind' between prediction in the experimental sciences and in economics.

In fact, we can carry our reasoning further than this. Given that in economics the deterministic hypothesis of statistical regularity is known to be untrue, how about the probabilistic version of the same hypothesis? In other words: we know that past statistical patterns in economics do not *always* persist into the future; but have we any idea of how *likely* they are to persist into the future? The answer is that we do not. We are aware that past statistical patterns sometimes turn out to continue into the future, but sometimes do not; and we do not have any evidence on which to convert the 'sometimes' into a 'how often'.

In this connection, we can bring back to mind the suggested distinction between 'uncertainty' and 'ignorance', which you may recall from Section 4.4.4. In terms of this distinction, we see that economic prediction faces not only uncertainty, but ignorance as well. The uncertainty comes from the fact that in the statistical analysis of past data, we need to allow the possibility that whatever pattern we establish may, in fact, not quite be representative of the 'true' pattern. If we decide to make the assumption of statistical regularity, what we are doing is to project that degree of uncertainty into the future.

The element of ignorance arises from the fact that in reality we do *not* know whether our past statistical pattern will persist or not—we do not know, for instance, whether a trend will 'break' or some past relationship break down. The chance of these things happening cannot be expressed in the terms of statistical probability—or, at any rate, in the current 'state of the art' nobody has found a way of expressing it in these terms. The fault of many predictionist arguments is to recognize the element of uncertainty, which can be dealt with by statistical procedures, but to disregard the element of ignorance, which cannot.

5.1.9 Summing-up

The last few sections have devoted considerable space to arguing out the true nature of the limitations of inductive prediction in economics. The main reason for placing such heavy emphasis on this topic is that, as I have said, general texts on economics and econometrics so seldom give it adequate coverage, if indeed they cover it all. This is all the more surprising in view of the importance attached to inductive prediction as a tool of present-day economic analysis. In Chapter 9, we shall be able to take another look at the problem of prediction in the context of econometric method (though, if you are acquainted with some details of econometric technique, you may already have realized some of the limitations which the arguments of this chapter have implied for the results of econometric studies).

Here, it may be useful just to sum up in the simplest terms what has been argued about inductive prediction in economics. It seems clear, at any rate, that the often-suggested analogy with prediction in physical science (or, more correctly, in experimental science) is one that must not be accepted uncritically when it comes to economic prediction. It is at least plausible to argue that economic prediction faces ignorance as well as uncertainty—in other words, that there is an element of unpredictability about economic events which cannot be dealt with by the procedures of statistics.

Thus it seems reasonable to suggest that when investigators choose to use methods of statistical prediction, they should be expected to justify the use of these methods rather than use them uncritically. By the same token, it is up to us, as readers of research results based on such methods, to take a critical look at the assumptions these methods imply—in particular, of course, the assumption that past statistical patterns will stay unchanged in the future.

5.2 Normative and positive

5.2.1 The distinction

The distinction between *normative* and *positive* statements is one which is easy to grasp in general terms, but very difficult to define exactly. We can perfectly well start from the simple definition which you will find in most economics textbooks: 'a positive statement concerns what *is*; a normative statement concerns what *ought to be*.' Quite often, you will find writers using the phrase *value-judgement* to mean the same as 'normative statement'.

Sometimes a normative statement can be identified simply by the fact that it contains the words 'ought' or 'should'. For instance, the suggestion 'Businessmen ought to try to maximize their profits' is clearly normative. It says nothing about what *is* the case—about whether businessmen do or do not in fact try to maximize profits. Had we said simply 'Businessmen try to maximize profits', on the other hand, we should equally clearly have been making a positive statement.

It is possible to come across normative statements that do not actually contain the words 'ought' or 'should'—but which, instead, merely imply these ideas. Suppose we said 'It is good if businessmen earn profits', or perhaps took an opposing view and suggested 'It is unfair for businessmen to earn profits'. Statements of this kind, once again, concern simply the speaker's own ideas of what *ought to be*, and so are normative.

Contrary to what some textbooks say, it is never possible to convert a normative to a positive statement merely by 'defining your terms'. Once a normative idea has been expressed, it will retain its normative nature regardless of any further definition. For instance, suppose we turned to the person who had said 'It is good if businessmen earn profits', and asked him to make clear why he took this view. He might say: 'What I mean is that when businessmen earn profits, economic activity is sustained and growth is encouraged.' But his implied view would then, of course, be 'Economic activity and growth are good things'. If, dedicated to the pursuit of truth, we went on in turn to ask him why he thought this, he would have to give a further round of explanation; but however many he gave, the fact would remain that in judging a certain state of affairs as 'good' he would be stating his own personal feeling, and no more. Defining the reasons behind a normative statement can certainly often make it easier for hearers or readers to decide whether or not they *agree* with the opinion of whoever is making the statement. It may even help the maker of the statement to decide whether he wants to hold to his stated opinions or to change them. But it can never turn a normative statement into a positive one.

For a statement to be positive, all that is required is that it be concerned with facts rather than with feelings or tastes; the statement in question does not necessarily need to be factually *correct*. For instance, the suggestion 'Businessmen try to minimize profits' is one that very few people would consider to be supported by the facts, but it is still a positive statement.

What is more, the facts concerned do not need to be checkable against *available* data. If we predicted, say, 'In the year 2000, GNP per head in the UK will be 50 per cent above its present level', we should of course have no means of checking our prediction against any data currently available. But our statement is still about a matter of fact—albeit expected future fact—and hence is positive.

5.2.2 Testability and the positive/normative distinction

These references to 'checking statements against facts' will perhaps have brought back to mind our discussion of testability (Section 4.3.4). It is useful to consider briefly how the distinction between testable and non-testable statements relates to the positive/normative distinction.

If, first of all, we recall that a normative statement is concerned purely with the speaker's own feelings, tastes, and preferences, it is clear that such a statement can never be testable, either in principle or in practice. There are no observable data against which we can check statements of 'what ought to be', 'what is fair or unfair', and so on. We ourselves may agree or disagree with the statements concerned, but our tastes are no more objectively checkable than those of the person we disagree with.

In other words, if a statement is normative, it is non-testable. As we know, normative statements are not the *only* kind of non-testable statement: the other kinds were mentioned in Section 4.3.4.

By the same reasoning, we can see that any statement which is testable (either in practice or in principle) must be positive and not normative.

Is it correct to say, though, that 'all positive statements are testable'? In this, there is some disagreement among writers; as we shall see in the next subsection, this disagreement is tied up with differing interpretations of the word 'positive' itself. But if we accept the outline of the nature of the positive/normative distinction in the foregoing section, then it seems reasonable to say that definitions and tautologies are positive statements (since they certainly do not concern 'what ought to be'). Likewise, an ill-defined statement may quite well be concerned with facts, even though it is not expressed clearly enough to allow it to be checked against observation. Such a statement, though non-testable, will be positive. At the same time, other ill-defined statements may be concerned only with the expression of personal tastes, and hence will be normative as well as non-testable.

5.2.3 More problems over words

In this area of discussion, as in so many others which the methodologist deals with, there are squabbles and confusions over the meanings of words. As usual, it will pay us to take a brief look at these, if only to alert ourselves to the difficulties which may arise from these verbal problems as we read further in the literature.

First, as regards the nature of the positive/normative distinction itself: you may find writers suggesting that, while positive statements are about matters of fact, 'normative statements concern matters of opinion'. The problem with this explanation is that the world 'opinion', here, is itself vague. For instance, if I said: 'In my opinion, the majority of businessmen in the UK do try to maximize profits', I should obviously be making a positive, not a normative, statement. In other words, it is perfectly possible to have opinions about what is, as well as about what ought to be—and only the latter class of opinions will be normative.

The same objection applies to the suggestion that 'positive statements are objective, while normative statements are subjective'. Admittedly, in discussions of economic theory, the term 'subjective' is usually taken as meaning exactly the same as what we have here called 'normative'. But in applied economics, we often speak of 'subjective' estimates, 'subjective' forecasts, and so on, meaning simply that the figures in question have been dreamed up according to inspired personal guesswork on the part of the economist, rather than being derived by formal data collection or analysis. Clearly, 'subjective' statements in this latter sense will be positive and not normative.

Going on now to a rather more tricky verbal problem: consider the statement 'If businessmen want to maximize their profits, then they should produce at the point where marginal cost equals marginal revenue.' Is this positive or normative? It certainly contains the word 'should'. But if we accept the explanation of the positive/normative distinction given at the beginning of this section, we must conclude that the statement is positive. It asserts that something *is* so in fact; it says nothing about the personal tastes, preferences, or inclinations of the person making the statement. And, of course, it is testable (though opinions may differ over whether it is testable | No. in practice or in principle).

Unfortunately, a fair number of economic texts can be found using the term 'normative' to describe statements of just this kind. Why 'unfortunately'? Because, if writers choose to stretch the meaning of 'normative' in this way, they must also abandon the clear proposition that 'no normative statements are testable'. And, as will be explained in the following section, most economists would think that there are good reasons to maintain a sharp distinction in economic science between ideas of what is—ideas which can correspondingly be tested against objective observation—and ideas of what ought to be, which can only be attacked or supported by arguments over personal tastes, feelings, or political leanings.

Before leaving this discussion of terms, we should look at one further confusion over the meaning of 'positive'. There is a famous methodological essay by Milton Friedman, called 'The methodology of positive economics'; and at least one currently popular text on introductory economics has also used the last two words in its title. Are the writers concerned trying to stress that the economist needs to keep his own prejudices, political views, and personal tastes out of his practice of economic science? If their titles do mean this, why do they *need* to stress this notion, when, as we have said, the great majority of economists agree with it anyway?

The fact is that 'positive', in the sense in which it is used by these writers on 'positive economics', has a meaning only distantly related to the 'positive/normative' distinction. The writers concerned are in fact proclaiming their belief in one particular view of economic method, which emphasizes the empirical testing of predictions. We shall be looking at this view in some detail in Chapter 6. For now, we need only register that, once again, it can be judged unfortunate that the term in question has been given a double meaning. As the literature tediously shows, economists have argued at great length over the question: 'Is economics a positive science?', without realizing that the bulk of their disagreement arises from the different interpretations they have put on the word 'positive'. This is a pity, since economists have more important things to argue about.

In the following section, the terms 'positive' and 'normative' will keep the meanings given to them in Section 5.2.1.

5.2.4 Economics—positive or normative?

In answer to the question 'Is economics positive, normative, or both?', the only truthful answer we can give is: 'It all depends how you define "economics".' In practice, though, it is certain that the great majority of economists would reckon economics to be a wholly positive discipline.

On this majority view, the economist does not have the task of *setting* economic objectives; his job is simply to explain the economic effects of different possible ways of achieving these objectives, given the means that are available, and using the tools of economic theory and observation.

For instance, it is not up to the economist to say whether redistribution of income is fair or unfair, or to make any judgements about the ethical desirability of income redistribution in itself: these judgements are for the politician. What the economist can say is, for instance: 'Such-and-such a degree of income redistribution is likely to change total consumption by x per cent', or perhaps: 'Income redistribution is likely to produce a disincentive effect among the higher income groups'—both positive statements, though the first statement is probably more easily checkable against available data than the second. To take another example, the economist does not set out to judge what the goals of businessmen *should* be: it is not up to him to say, for example: 'It is better for businessmen to try to maximize their profits than to aim for a more moderate profit level and for less risk.' The sort of thing he can say, instead, is: 'In order to maximize profits, a businessman should follow policy X; to achieve lower profits with less risk, policy Y should be followed instead.'

In reality, of course, it is likely that the economist and the politician, or the economist and the businessman, will sometimes be one and the same person. But most economists would take the view that when the person concerned is making his *normative* judgements about the ethical desirability of income redistribution, say, or about the merits of different aims on risk versus profit, he is 'taking off his economist's hat' for the moment. These judgements rely on criteria about which economic theory cannot comment and is not designed to comment.

All this is pretty straightforward. But there are certain areas of economics in which the division between normative and positive ideas is not so obvious as in the two examples just given. On these vaguer frontiers, according to some economists, normative elements may creep into economic reasoning. For instance, take the process known as 'cost–benefit analysis'. Very often, when a cost–benefit exercise is being carried out on some large public-works project, the economist is called on to quantify such things as amenity value, convenience or inconvenience, and other such 'intangibles'. Sometimes, this kind of thing can be evaluated on the basis of some objective measurement. But more often, there is simply no objective standard that can be used with any degree of reasonableness. At this point, often all that the economist *can* do is to make his own personal judgement—in other words, to think in normative terms. Then again, in the field of welfare economics, since there is no generally accepted standard by which an 'increase in welfare' can be objectively measured, the economist has to define a standard according to his own personal ideas (or, at least, use a standard that some other economist has defined in this way). This personal definition, it can be argued, must entail normative judgement.

There is not a great deal of point in arguing over whether instances like this really do or do not constitute 'normative economics'. You can say, if you like, that when the economist makes his judgements of the value of 'intangibles', or when he is deciding on his own notion of 'increased welfare', he has just for that moment taken off his 'economist's hat', and that these judgements are, therefore, not really part of economics.

Whether you choose to accept this point of view or the contrary one, the really important thing is to be aware that normative judgements *are* being made at points like this, and to realize why this fact is significant for economic policy decisions: because normative judgements can legitimately be challenged on matters of personal taste or political persuasion, whereas positive statements can only be challenged on matters of fact. This is an idea that is very familiar to the 'pressure groups' which may be formed to contest government decisions. To quote an example from a few years ago: the controversy over the siting of the proposed 'third London airport' turned largely on different people's ideas of the valuation of the 'loss of amenity' which would arise from the siting of the airport in various possible places.

Economics, then, is essentially a positive study, at least in the view of most present-day economists. That is, it is not considered legitimate for the economist to let his *own* value-judgements creep into his economic reasoning. It would be totally wrong, however, to say that 'economics is *not concerned with* value-judgements'. Indeed, almost the exact opposite is true. Nearly all the propositions of economic theory speak of human decisions which are connected with *choice*; and these choices consist unavoidably of value-judgements. These may be anything from a government's judgements of desirable policy objectives, to a consumer's judgement on whether he gets more satisfaction from a cabbage or from a lettuce. The fact is, economics is very much *concerned with* value-judgements. But it must take these judgements as given. Economics does not attempt to *make* value-judgements, nor to contest those made by other people.

You may have noticed that in this discussion I have carefully qualified the assertion that 'economics is a positive study' by pointing out that this is the view of *most* economists, but not all. In fact, there are some economists who hold to exactly the opposite view, and say that economic thinking is, and must be, normative. The best-known variant of this view is that held by Marxian economists. They believe that what we know as 'economic theory', though considered by non-Marxians to be objective, really rests on normative presuppositions about economic aims—presuppositions which have been so thoroughly ground into the minds of capitalist economists that they have come to be held at an unconscious level. According to the Marxians, then, the non-Marxian version of 'economic theory' is simply an elaboration of capitalist aims and prejudices masquerading under the guise of positive science.

To examine this case thoroughly, we would need much more space than can be afforded in this introductory book. You may care to assess the Marxian argument here for yourself. The most fundamental objection to it, I believe, is this: we can admit the fact that, in a capitalist economy, many of the economic aims noted by the economist will be capitalistic—for instance, that entrepreneurs will try to maximize profits, will try to negotiate the lowest wage rates consistent with the supply of and demand for labour, and so on. As we have seen, any economist—be he Marxian or non-

Marxian—must observe these normative aims and must take them into account in his objective theories of how the economy works. But that is a very different thing from saying that the economist *himself* need follow these aims, let alone agree with them or disagree with them. Most non-Marxian economists, it is fair to say, do sincerely try to exclude their own normative preferences from their scientific reasoning; they may not always quite succeed, but no one is perfect. The Marxians argue that capitalist economists *must* always be viewing the world through capitalist-normative spectacles, and it is this sweeping proposition in the Marxian argument that seems especially difficult to support.

There is perhaps just a grain of truth in the Marxian case, however. The fact is that there are some goals of economic activity which are widely accepted as standard aims towards which economic problem-solving is expected to work. Typical examples are maximization of profit, maintenance of economic growth, increases in 'welfare' (in whatever way this may be defined). Now, these are, of course, objectives for which there are clear and easily supported arguments. But they are, nevertheless, still normative, not positive; and so when we slip into talking about these goals as being 'economic rather than political'—as if they had wholly objective justification—then we are committing an error, and it is perhaps this which has helped to fuel the Marxian attack.

As a closing point in this section: there are some economists, this time outside as well as inside the Marxian fold, who assert that economic thinking *should* be normative—or, at any rate, that it should contain normative as well as positive elements.

You will realize the difficulty of assessing this point of view: namely, that the statement 'economics should be normative' is itself a normative statement. Thus, there is no objective criterion by which the suggestion can be judged. The best we can do, instead, is to explain the reasons for this normative view and for opposing views, to help us decide whether we ourselves are normatively 'for' or 'against'.

The 'normative economists' have never spelt out in very great detail why they hold to their stated view. But as far as can be guessed, what they are arguing is that the economist, instead of trying to hold himself aloof from the political process of policy-making, should on the contrary plunge into it, becoming an active participator in the job of making the world a better place.

I personally (along with the great majority of economists, I believe) am against this point of view. For argument's sake, let us compare the economist with another professional man, the medical doctor. On the doctor's panel there will be some patients he likes, others he dislikes. If he gives first-rate treatment to those he likes and puts off seeing those he dislikes, does that make him a good doctor? Then again, suppose he examines a patient and realizes that a certain, unpleasant treatment is needed if this patient is to show improvement. Should the doctor avoid recommending the treatment simply because he knows the patient will not like it? And suppose finally that another patient will only get well on a diet of red meat; the doctor himself, for religious reasons, is a strict vegetarian. If he therefore prescribes for this patient a diet of cabbage, has he fulfilled his professional duty?

All this, of course, is argument by analogy, hence is logically inconclusive. But since we are here arguing a normative and not a positive case, conclusive answers can anyway never be expected.

5.3 Experimentation and control

For the physical scientist, a very common form of investigation is the *experiment*. This simply means that the researcher, instead of waiting for nature to throw up an instance of whatever he is investigating, sets it up deliberately. Not all the physical sciences can always use experiment as a technique; astronomy is one obvious example of a physical science that seldom has the opportunity to experiment.

A frequent feature of the experiment is what is called a *control*. Suppose the physical scientist is carrying out an experiment in which he is investigating the result of introducing substance X into solution Y. If he decides to use a control (or, we say, if he decides to make it a *controlled experiment*), then he will construct not one experimental set-up, but two. In both of these solution Y will be kept in exactly the same conditions—of temperature, pressure, and the like. There will be only one difference between one set-up and the other: in one, substance X will be introduced into the solution; in the other, nothing will be introduced. The one in which nothing is introduced is the control.

Another example can be taken from the medical field: whenever a new drug is being tested, it is standard practice to divide the party of volunteers into two groups. One party is given the drug; the other is given some inert substance (or, as doctors call it, a 'placebo'). Elaborate precautions are taken to make sure that the division of the original party into its two groups is done at random, and that nobody in the experiment knows whether he is getting the drug or the placebo. The group receiving the placebo are the control group.

It is obvious why physical scientists place so much importance on the controlled experiment. The notion is to be able to tie up cause with effect in a totally unambiguous manner—or as nearly unambiguous as human ingenuity can make it. For instance, in our first example above, since the only difference between one set-up and the other is the addition or non-addition of substance X, it may be considered fair to reason that if something happens to solution Y when that substance is added, then the addition of the substance is the cause of the effect observed.

It goes without saying that experimentation, let alone controlled experimentation, is very seldom possible in economics. It is occasionally done—for instance, an experiment on the results of a negative income tax has been carried out in the USA. But in general, we are not usually able to apply and remove taxes, throw people out of employment, apply tariffs, and the like, in order to satisfy our scientific curiosity—interesting though the results would be. Still less, as a rule, are we able to split the population into two random groups, impose some economic policy on one group, and leave the other group with no policy.

The idea of trying 'controlled experiments' in economics leaves us with laughable mental pictures of this kind. But there is a perfectly serious conclusion to be drawn. We come back, in fact, to a point that has already been foreshadowed in our discussion of *post hoc ergo propter hoc* (Section 2.5.4): in all practical situations in which we are trying to observe the effects of some economic policy, or to tie up cause and effect in other areas of economic research, we are never able to tell for sure whether what we look on as possible causes are in fact the causes (or the only causes) of what we observe; just possibly, there may be a cause or causes we are not aware of at all.

This notion—that observed events may be brought about, not by just one possible cause, but by several—is sometimes called the *principle of the plurality of causes*.

Strictly speaking, there can never be a perfect control, even in sciences which lend themselves to experimental procedures. For all the ingenuity the scientist can bring to bear, it must always remain possible that there are some causative factors operating which he has omitted to think of—or of which he is ignorant—and that these factors have had an influence on the results of the experiment. To quote a standard example, and a deliberately ridiculous one: suppose, in the experiment on solution Y, the full version of the experiment was carried out by a scientist with blue eyes, while the control was set up by another scientist with brown eyes? It is conceivable, though unlikely by any sane judgement, that it was the eye-colour difference that produced the difference in outcomes, not the addition of substance X.

This question of the effectiveness of experimental control—like all questions about experimental conditions, as we saw in Section 4.4.3—is one to which no standard answer can be found in any epistemological recipe-book; rather, it is a matter for 'gentlemen's agreement' among scientists. In some areas of science, there is little difficulty in deciding whether an adequate control has been set up; in others, the difficulty is considerable. For instance, the notion that the experimenter's eye-colour might affect the results of a chemical experiment is clearly ridiculous. But if we go to our other example: suppose the drug being tested were administered by a pretty, sympathetic nurse, while the placebo was given by her ugly and rude colleague?

This point—that control can never be totally effective—has sometimes been taken up by economic methodologists who have been trying to argue that the methods of physical science must also be the ideal methods for economics. They point out that there is no sharp borderline between totally controlled experiment and totally uncontrolled field situations—rather, you have a continuous scale of 'controlledness' running all the way from the one to the other.

And, of course, this argument as it stands is perfectly correct. But it illustrates a general fault of this kind of 'strictly speaking' argument. The fact is that though there may be no sharp *borderline* between a class of situations *A* and another class *B*, nevertheless there may be a very distinct *difference* between the two classes. For the practising economist, whether in application or research, the situation is clear: there is a well-defined procedure called controlled experiment; he is very seldom in a position to use this procedure; and therefore, if he wants to talk sense, he needs to interpret his results in the light of the principle of the plurality of causes.

Occasionally also, we find writers implying that statistical testing is somehow a substitute for controlled experiment in economics. In an ideally controlled experiment, they argue, we would allow only one possible causative factor to operate, and so any effect observed could be ascribed without doubt to that cause. In an uncontrolled situation, we admit that there may be many possible causes operating; but by making repeated observations of that situation, and using statistical analysis, we can see how closely the presence of each suspected causative factor is related to the presence of the effect in which we are interested. The closer this relationship turns out to be in the case of any given factor, the more grounds there are for believing that that factor is indeed a cause of the effect in question. In other words, according to this argument, the difference between establishing causality in a controlled experiment and establishing causality in a field situation is again just one of degree.

The problem is, given that the difference *is* one of degree, it is a very large degree! In the tightly controlled world of laboratory experiment, we seldom have trouble in connecting cause and effect beyond reasonable doubt. In some other areas of science—for instance, in biological investigations of many kinds—we are not able to set up fully controlled experiments, but we can make up for this to a large extent by using randomized experimental designs; statistical analysis can then attach cause to effect in a pretty unambiguous manner. But in the usual situation facing the economist—when no experimental design is possible at all, when the number of possible causative factors may be very large, and when there may be important factors operating whose presence is not even suspected by the investigator—then it becomes much less sensible to suggest that statistical analysis is somehow 'standing in' for experimental control.

If statistical testing does not provide us with a convincing substitute for controlled experiment in economics, what does? The answer is: nothing does. Economists simply need to live with the knowledge that their results can never be of the unambiguous kind that the physical scientist can get by using controls. It is up to us, in our choice of research methods and the phrasing of our results, to be aware of this limitation on our findings and to make sure that our readers are also aware of it.

5.4 Causal v. teleological explanation

We have already met the argument that 'people have free will, while things do not; therefore investigation in social science must meet problems that investigation in physical science does not.' In the context of economic prediction, we decided that this idea of 'volition' was something of a red herring: what really mattered was to establish the epistemological basis of inductive prediction in physical and social science—and then, if we decided that there *was* a real difference in the predictability of events between these two fields of science, we could put this difference down to free will if we wanted to.

Another question, which will be discussed in this section, is: can human behaviour really be *explained* in the same way as the behaviour of non-human objects? In other words, can the social sciences manage with the same style of explanation as the physical sciences? The answer is, once again, the philosophers' favourite—'yes and no'. In fact, it depends what you mean by 'explanation'.

Let us take it first that we mean the term in its rather specialized methodological sense—that is, we say we have 'explained' something when we can convincingly fit it into the framework of a deductive theory, one which stands the test of empirical evidence. A moment's reflection will show that this kind of explanation is, in principle, no less possible when we are handling propositions about human behaviour than it is when we are dealing with non-human objects. You can construct a theory, for instance, about gravitation, about the transmission of genetic characters, or about the ways consumers maximize their welfare. The last-named will contain statements about human motives, the other two will not. But there is no reason why this feature should make the economic theory relatively any less coherent as a deductive structure, nor any less likely to contain testable statements.

If we decide to adopt the rather wider sense of 'explanation', and say that we have explained an event when we know enough about its causes to be able to influence its future occurrence, then again we see that there is no black-and-white distinction between economic explanations and those of the physical sciences. Given that we admit there is such a thing as free will, and that people have it while objects do not, still nobody would argue that people's behaviour cannot be influenced; and it seems reasonable to suggest that the best way to influence behaviour is to find out what causes that behaviour in the first place. Admittedly, it may be very difficult to find out in practice what *does* cause a certain type of human behaviour—but it is no simple matter, either, to discover what causes the 'behaviour' of a subatomic particle, even though the detailed problems of investigation are very different in the two cases.

In these two senses, then, the explanation of economic behaviour does not differ essentially from the explanation of physical occurrences. However, the operation of free will in human behaviour does bring with it one very distinct and important difference between physical science and economics; one might say that this difference relates not to the structure of explanations, but to the things that explanations talk about.

More exactly, it concerns the nature of the 'causes' that can operate in these two divisions of science. If, for instance, an astrophysicist is investigating changes in the temperature of a star, he would hardly suggest that the star was changing its temperature because it wanted to. Or, to borrow an appealing example from Professor Machlup: if a geologist is enquiring why a particular rock is where it is in the landscape, he does not ask the rock; and he would be very surprised if it spoke up and told him 'I came here because I did not like it up there near the glaciers, where I used to live; here I like it fine, especially the nice view of the valley.'

In other words, we do not try to explain natural occurrences by reference to any purposes on the part of the objects we are investigating. But in explaining human behaviour—or at least, that part of human behaviour that is a matter of decision-making—we often do phrase our explanations in just this way. It is difficult to read a page of any economics text without coming across some reference to purposeful action: businessmen decide to invest more, so as to increase their future capacity; a government raises taxation, with the objective of cutting back economic activity; speculators buy stocks of a commodity, hoping to make a profit on the deal; and so on.

These two different modes of explanation have technical names that are worth knowing. If we explain something without any reference to purpose—that is, if we simply say 'event B happened because event A happened'—then this is called *causal explanation* (or *mechanistic explanation*). If, on the other hand, we do make reference to a purpose—if we say 'event X happened because it was aimed at making event Y happen'—then we are using *teleological explanation.*

It is clear that explanations in the physical sciences can be only causal. But in economics and the other social sciences, we can explain things either causally or teleologically. Come to that, any one economic event can very often be explained in both causal and teleological terms. To go back to the three instances noted above: the businessmen may invest more because interest rates have gone down; the government may raise taxation because tax revenue has fallen short of expenditure requirements; and the speculators may buy because they have been tipped off about a coming shortage. None of these causal explanations excludes the possibility that the teleological explanations may come into the picture as well.

Thus, we see that the economist, like any other social scientist, has access to a whole area of explanation which the physical scientist can never encounter. This can be viewed as both an advantage and a disadvantage: an advantage in that the selection of possible causative factors at the social scientist's disposal is relatively rich; and a disadvantage in that the process of investigation is thereby made relatively complex.

When a physicist sets out to gain understanding of the structure of subatomic particles, nobody would suggest that he should try to get inside the mind of an electron, or put himself in the shoes of a positron. If, by accident, a physical scientist does find himself trying to explain the 'behaviour' of natural objects as though it did result from feelings and motives, he will find himself accused of the error in reasoning called *anthropomorphism*, i.e., arguing as though things were really people.

But, as Professor von Mises has tellingly pointed out, if a social scientist neglects to take account of these very same feelings and motives on the part of the people he is studying, then he is just as much in error: he is, we might say, guilty of 'anthropomorphism in reverse', of trying to argue as though people were really things.

Some years ago, there existed an extremist school of philosophers who argued that social scientists should indeed restrict their explanations to causal features which could be observed by physical procedures, and should abandon altogether any reference to motives, preferences, and other such intangibles. This thesis was directed principally at psychology, and perhaps it did some good in that area by emphasizing the rather mystical nature of some psychological speculation. By now, no methodologist of social science any longer gives house-room to this extremist view. Yet echoes of it sometimes still turn up in the methodological superstitions of social science—and, surprisingly enough, they turn up in economics most of all. Perhaps this is because some economists, as we have said, have hankered after the scientific 'respectability' of the hard physical sciences; or perhaps it is because some aggregate data in economics—national-income figures, for example—seem very much distanced from the actions of real, live, individual people. This hangover from an old extremist philosophical position may help to account for some methodological features in economics that are otherwise puzzling: for instance, the reluctance to put much reliance on investigational methods that look directly at individual motives; or the tendency among some economists to proceed as though motives were nonexistent, or at least closed to empirical observation. These positions have figured quite largely in controversies over the testing of economic theories, the topic which we examine in the next chapter.

Reading guide: Chapter 5

Controversies over the *prediction problem* in economics, are, as we shall see in the next chapter, very much bound up with wider controversies about economic method generally; therefore, you will find various statements of the predictionist and non-predictionist viewpoints when you come to look at the references in the reading guide to Chapter 6. And, of course, the reading guide to Chapter 9, on econometrics, will give you sources for practical detail on forecasting method, as well as citing the results of some studies of its real-world success. For now, read Robbins, *Essay on the Nature and Significance of Economic Science*,[70] Chapter 5, sections 2 to 7; and the opposing view in R. G. Lipsey, *An Introduction to Positive Economics*,[46] pp. 9–11 and 197–99.

Kaplan, in Chapter 14 of *The Conduct of Inquiry*,[36] in my view, burkes some important issues, coming only to the rather feeble conclusion that human action is 'sometimes' predictable (the point, of course, is: how often is 'sometimes'?). For a good discussion of the pitfalls of scientific prediction generally, with some striking practical illustrations from social as well as physical science, read Chapter 7 of J. T. Davies, *The Scientific Approach*.[22]

The 'positive/normative' distinction is thoroughly discussed in T. W. Hutchison, *'Positive' Economics and Policy Objectives*.[31] One economist who believes that economics is (and should be) normative is F. J. B. Stilwell, who sets out his arguments in his book called, boldly enough, *Normative Economics*.[78] In Boulding, *Economics as a Science*,[7] read Chapter 6; and in Krupp, *The Structure of Economic Science*[42] read the essay by Richard B. Brandt, on the problems attaching to the concept of 'welfare'.

For comments on the general problems of interpreting economic data, read Chapter 3 of Robbins, *An Essay on the Nature and Significance of Economic Science*.[70] And if you have not yet read Fritz Machlup's article 'Are the Social Sciences Really Inferior?',[50] cited at the end of my Chapter 1, you will find it even more useful to read now.

Discussion topics: Chapter 5

1. The topic of 'free will' comes up very specifically when we are considering the possible mass reaction to economic forecasts. Think of this situation: in a certain region, there are a large number of producers of a transportable, not easily perishable product (say, pigs). In that region there are several different markets at which the pigs can be sold. Now suppose that an official market-news service is set up, and that it tells these farmers that the price being paid for pigs at one of the markets is expected to be unusually high. Now imagine that you are one of these farmers, and that you hear this market news. Consider:

(a) To what market would you send your pigs?

(b) To what market might everyone else send their pigs, and what would be likely to happen as a result to the price being paid at that market?

(c) Next time you had pigs to sell, suppose the news service once again told you that prices at one particular market were expected to be unusually high—where would you send your pigs this time?

(d) And where do you think everybody else would send their pigs this time? What would be likely to happen to the price at the market which the news service had named as the 'high-price' market?

(Hint: there are several possible answers to each of these questions, especially to (c) and (d). Try to reason through the implications of different sets of alternatives, as regards farmers' reactions to these price forecasts).

2. What difficulties do these possible outcomes pose for the people who are trying to forecast market prices?

3. Consider the following two empirical relationships in economics: (a) the Phillips curve, during the years in which it predicted well; and (b) the long-run ('secular') consumption function. (A reference for the first is in the reading guide to Chapter 4; and for a picture of the second you can consult many macroeconomics texts, e.g., E. Shapiro, *Macroeconomic Analysis*,[76] page 133). As we know, the Phillips relationship has broken down; the secular consumption–income relationship still holds. Can you think of any reason—empirically based or otherwise—for saying that the secular consumption function is less likely to break down *in future* than the Phillips relationship has done?

4. In imagination, set up a *controlled experiment* by which you could judge the effects of increasing direct taxation. (Your specification should include means for observing results, as well as setting up the control.) Now pick out the features of your imaginary set-up which are impossible practically or politically, and review the difficulties which these place in the way of empirical judgement of the actual results of increasing taxation.

6

Economic theory and reality

In Chapter 4, we examined the structure and validation of scientific theories generally. In this chapter we go on to look at economic theory in particular. We discuss the controversial question of whether the structure of economic theory, and the means by which it can be validated, are essentially the same as in the physical sciences, or different in important ways.

There is a large literature on this subject, and it would have been easy to fill the entire book with a detailed examination of the various views that have been put forward. As it is, I shall confine the discussion here to a single chapter. Very largely, this has been made possible by the fact that previous chapters have done much of the spadework necessary for an understanding of the issues involved.

The layout of the chapter is as follows: in Section 6.1, a preliminary look is taken at the various ways in which the reasoning of economic theory can be expressed. In Section 6.2, some differing views on the structure and validation of economic theory are brought together; each of these views is briefly appraised in the light of the general discussion of scientific procedure in earlier chapters. In Section 6.3, various problems and controversies are considered about the specific nature, testing, and uses of theory in economic science; in the course of this discussion the various views put forward in the previous section are further examined. Finally, in Section 6.4 a summing-up is provided, and we consider how each methodological viewpoint can be rated as a convincing account of scientific method in economics.

One of the main shortcomings in the literature on this subject has been the frequent failure to specify exactly what is to be the criterion of 'proper' procedure in economic science. As we noted in Chapter 1, it is of no use simply to call for procedure that is 'scientific', because that term itself is open to many differing interpretations. As we shall see, some economic writers seem to have chosen criteria of 'scientific' procedure which have depended on rather arbitrary philosophical judgements. These may or may not have much relevance to whether the results of economic investigation are useful in real-world terms.

Here, I shall start from the proposition that economics, as a 'policy science', should be oriented towards providing results that are indeed useful in terms of real-world application. This in turn suggests that the best criterion to use in judging 'proper' scientific procedure in the discipline is that of *explanatory power*. As you will recall from Section 4.5, this criterion can itself be interpreted in two different ways. The less stringent definition of 'explanation' implies the ability to control the future course of events. A more stringent definition—which will usually entail the less stringent one—is that we should be able to fit observed events into the causal framework of a deductive theory. For now, let us keep both these criteria in mind, but set the less stringent of the two as a minimum requirement for 'proper' procedure in economics.

6.1 The languages of economic reasoning

Given that, as a reader of this book, you will be familiar with at least introductory economics, there is no need to explain in detail the different ways in which the reasoning of economic theory can be expressed. It can, of course, be stated in words, in diagrams, in numerical terms, or in algebraic symbols, or any combination of these four. The last-named style of expression is what is usually called 'mathematical economics', though of course the use of geometrical diagrams and numerical examples is also mathematical in its own way.

Though the use of mathematics in economics dates back to the very earliest years of our subject's separate existence, it is only very recently that it has assumed the prominent role it now plays. Even two or three decades ago, it is fair to say, the bulk of theoretical reasoning in economics was done in verbal and diagrammatic terms, though often backed up by a mathematical appendix. Nowadays, it is a rare journal of economic theory whose pages are not peppered with algebraic symbols.

Like anything else in this imperfect world, the use of mathematical reasoning has both its advantages and its disadvantages. Not surprisingly, given the recent fashion for mathematical method in economics, its advantages tend to be stressed rather more strongly than its disadvantages, and so it is as well to devote a little space to an unbiased discussion of both.

First, we should register what is the fundamental role played by algebraic reasoning in economics: as one excellent textbook puts it, mathematics provides economists with a useful set of *abbreviations*. By the use of symbols, we can say economically and in a short space what it might otherwise take us a lot of space and a great many words to say. For instance, once we have chosen the symbol M_1 to stand for 'notes and coin together with checking deposits', then we can use the brief symbol every time the idea comes up. We do, of course, have the alternative device of choosing a name to describe this idea—'money narrowly defined', if you like—but this is still a long way round compared with just M_1. When we go on to discuss not just one economic variable, but relationships between several variables, then the total saving in space and effort as compared to using verbal reasoning can be very great indeed. Not only do we avoid having to name the variables in words every time we refer to them, but the manipulations we carry out on these variables can be very concisely expressed in algebraic symbols.

It is largely in this department also that we see one advantage of algebraic as opposed to geometrical reasoning: in a diagram, it is rather difficult to express ideas of relationships between more than two variables at a time. The visual resources of diagrams can be stretched to give some idea of 'three-dimensional' relations. But when it comes to more than three dimensions, we find ourselves unable even to envisage what the necessary diagram would look like; in terms of algebra, on the other hand, this sort of reasoning presents no problems.

Another 'pro' feature of using algebraic reasoning in economics is that symbols, *once defined* (and it is important to note this qualification), are free of ambiguity. For instance, once we have decided that M_1 is to have the meaning given above, then it keeps that precise meaning right through the calculations in which it may be employed. If we use verbal argument, by contrast, there is always some danger that we may allow some overlaps in meaning which can possibly lead to wrong conclusions (what is true of M_1 may or may not be true of, say, 'money' or 'liquidity').

It is often suggested that algebraic styles of reasoning are more 'powerful' than those which use words. The word 'powerful' is usually left unexplained, and it seems to mean several related things. It may refer to the 'shorthand' function of algebra, already mentioned here: the idea being that by packaging many separate ideas into the concise form of an algebraic expression, our mind is left free to take on the full-time job of reasoning, rather than being bogged down in the manipulation of numerous words or figures. Related to this is the point that the operations which can be performed on algebraic symbols are themselves laid out on well-recognized lines; if we can transform an economic problem into one of these established schemes (a set of simultaneous equations, for example), then we can proceed to a solution almost without thinking, or at least without thinking of the mechanical aspects of this particular manipulation.

Perhaps a more fundamental aspect of the 'power' of symbolic reasoning is this: by setting our problems in recognizable shorthand form, it may sometimes enable us to relate our particular problem to an explanatory framework—a system of deductive reasoning—that has been developed to tackle a different range of problems, and hence cast light back in turn on the specific problem we are dealing with. To quote a notable example: the concept of 'marginality' is, as you will be aware, peculiar to economic reasoning. But when this idea is expressed in algebraic notation, it becomes immediately obvious that it is related to a wide-ranging set of topics— including, for instance, the growth of plants and the acceleration of falling bodies—all of which lend themselves to the same styles of algebraic manipulation and problem-solving.

How about the pitfalls of using mathematical reasoning in economics? These result from one fundamental fact. That is: economics can *use* mathematics; but economics is not, and never can be, a branch of mathematics. At risk almost of being over-obvious, one can point out that even if there were no such study as mathematics, people would still be buying, selling, manufacturing, consuming, choosing. When we use symbols or diagrams in economic reasoning, then it must be the economic ideas that dictate what happens to those symbols or diagrams—and not the other way round. If you have ever attended a discussion session among, say, students at the beginning of a course in macroeconomics, you will have come across reasoning which ignores this point:

'Why does equilibrium come at such-and-such a point of national income?'

'Because that is where the aggregate demand schedule crosses the 45-degree line.'

Needless to say, this 'because' is no 'because' at all: in the real-life economy there is no 45-degree guideline, and, come to that, precious little trace of an aggregate demand schedule; both these things are merely explanatory devices which we have brought into existence to aid theoretical reasoning. I attributed this kind of mistake to beginning students; but in more abstruse form, it is a pitfall into which the most high-powered economic theorist is liable to tumble. Not, perhaps, in using elementary diagrams; but in manipulating the complex mathematical apparatus of, say, welfare economics or input-output analysis, it is only too easy to slip into the misconception that the economic world is somehow powered by what happens in the mathematics, rather than the other way round.

There are various specific disadvantages to the use of algebraic reasoning, which are mostly the 'opposite sides of the coin' to some of the advantages I have just mentioned. Take, for instance, the notion that symbolic notation helps to cut out vagueness. In reality, the supposed 'exactness' of symbolic reasoning is of a very special and restricted kind. The fact is that to define symbols, we must use words in the first place; and if there is vagueness in the words—as there usually is—then the symbols defined by means of these words must carry that same amount of vagueness. Therefore, when we speak of the 'exactness' or 'non-ambiguity' of symbols, we mean only that the symbols convey exactly what they have been defined to convey: we are saying nothing about the adequacy, relevance, or clearness of the definitions themselves.

This caution applies not just to the definitions of the meanings of the symbols used in economic reasoning, but to the relationships assumed between them. It is often pointed out that algebraic reasoning makes assumptions wholly explicit, whereas verbal reasoning does not. Again, it is true that algebraic statement of an assumption lets us see exactly what that assumption says—no more, no less—in terms of our symbols as we have defined them. But it does not necessarily follow that we are thereby made fully aware of the economic meaning of what we have assumed. Take, for instance, the standard textbook assumption about the nature of the average-cost function facing the typical firm: namely that it is a quadratic, having the general form $a - bx + cx^2$. In assuming this, we are merely saying that the average-cost curve has the U-shape which will be familiar to you if you have studied of the theory of the firm. In mathematical terms, our assumption is perfectly explicit (and indeed pretty elementary). What is not immediately so obvious is that we are at the same time making some further important, and unstated, assumptions about the economic picture. We are suggesting first of all that there *is* a relationship that can be identified as an 'average-cost function' facing a 'typical firm'. We are assuming also that such a relationship, if it does indeed exist, has the nature of a smooth and continuous function—that is, that it can be graphed as a curve having no kinks or breaks in it. When you come to think of it, these are pretty ambitious assumptions; perhaps you may like to spend a minute or two thinking whether a real-life businessman is likely to perceive his costs in this particular way.

In choosing this elementary example, I am of course not trying to suggest that professional theoreticians are likely to overlook *these* particular unstated assumptions, nor that mathematics is incapable of handling assumptions that are nearer to real-life complexity. At the same time, the instance does show how an assumption which is mathematically explicit may be far from explicit economically.

Admittedly, these criticisms of algebraic reasoning could potentially also be levelled at verbal reasoning. We have just noted that symbols can entail vagueness and can obscure assumptions; but words can do these things as well. The point is, though, that while words usually seem just as vague as they are, symbols seem exact even when really they are vague.

An enthusiast for algebraic reasoning in economics might remind us here that all the statements in a scientific theory—whether they be expressed in symbols or in words—start life in the domain of constructs, and typically do entail some kind of simplifying assumptions. He might argue that if the mathematical theorist wants to assume an average-cost function of the general form $a - bx + cx^2$ for the purposes of his theorizing, then he is quite at liberty to do so; and that there is only one way to tell whether the accompanying 'unstated assumptions' do or do not constitute a real problem—namely to subject his theorizing to an assault by the facts.

This argument is of course correct, so long as the reasoning in question is of a kind that *can* be set against observable data. Paradoxically enough, though, it is relatively easy for the mathematical theorist to come adrift from the world of testable reality—easier, it can be suggested, than for the economist who phrases his reasoning in words. Here, the very crispness and ease of manipulation of symbols may turn out to be a positive disadvantage. Words, by contrast, are awkward and cumbersome—but it may be that the reality we are investigating is also awkward and cumbersome. For instance, the general-equilibrium theorist has no difficulty in setting out reasoning which, using algebraic notation, considers the interrelationships between price, demand, and supply for every product traded in an economy. Needless to say, there is no way in which the real-life data could be assembled which would allow this reasoning to be tested.

In some areas of economic theorizing, it is fair to say, there has almost grown up the feeling that the symbolic reasoning is the be-all and end-all, and that to relate this theorizing to the untidy world of reality is somehow below the dignity of the theorist. But this is not just being impractical: it is being *unscientific*, in the full sense of the word. The economist defines himself as a scientist precisely by his willingness to confront his reasoning with real-life data. If he declines to do this, then he needs to change his own job designation, and call himself logician, mathematician, mystic, or magician.

To sum up: mathematical reasoning in economics is an excellent servant, but a correspondingly bad master. To keep our mathematics firmly in its proper position as flunkey, we need only bear in mind what has already been said: that the economics must always dictate what happens in the mathematics, never the other way round.

6.2 Various views

6.2.1 *Viewpoints and labels*

We now turn to some of the ideas which economic methodologists have put forward about the distinctive features of the structure and validation of the theory of our subject. The approach I intend to follow here is to describe each viewpoint in the terms of the writers who have favoured it, and then to give it some brief criticism in the light of what we have learned in our discussion thus far.

Of all areas of economic literature, this must be one of the most confused and confusing. Admittedly, it is possible to discern several schools of thought, but any attempt to categorize them must be pretty arbitrary. One school of thought shades into another. You find writers who seem to shift position between one school and another as time goes on, or even express seemingly conflicting views in one and the same piece of writing. Writers often seem to misunderstand what other writers are arguing; and accordingly, they put out 'counter-arguments' which are, in fact, attacking something that the other writer never meant to say.

Still more confusingly, it quite often seems as though writers misunderstand their *own* position. If you ask a golfer, even a very good one, to describe to you the action he uses when he swings at the ball, it is likely that what he tells you will be quite out of line with what he actually does (as revealed, say, by high-speed photographs). So it is often with economic method: economists may make methodological pronouncements which, on inspection, turn out to have very little resemblance to what they themselves actually do when they are practising their discipline. Abraham Kaplan neatly expresses this situation by drawing a distinction between 'logic-in-use' and 'reconstructed logic'—in this context, between what economists actually do and what they say they do.

Caught in this crossfire of misunderstandings and counter-misunderstandings, any methodologist trying to make an unbiased assessment of the situation obviously has a hefty job on his hands. And it is made still worse by a chronic problem which we have noted at several points in the book: namely, the proliferation of jargon terms which mean different things to different people. For instance, as we shall see, words like 'assumption', 'realistic', or 'positive' are all used in various differing senses by economic methodologists; but it is seldom made clear exactly what meaning is intended. Sometimes, indeed, it is a fair guess that the writer in question himself has no clear idea on the matter. As the chapter goes on, I hope it will become clear how some long-established controversies can be reduced very largely to arguments over words.

These confusions of meaning attach not only to the ideas that are put forward by the different schools of thought, but also to the names by which the schools are known. Terms like 'positive economics', 'analytical school', and so on, can mean very different things to different people; and often, as we shall see, these phrases themselves are pretty inappropriate as descriptions of the methodological views in question. Ideally, it might be better to drop all such labels. But, while that would certainly reduce confusion, it would mean that the description became unmanageably long; and so, for better or worse, I have attached names to the various schools of thought distinguished below. If you are new to the study of methodology, you should bear in mind that other writers may well use the labels rather differently. I have merely chosen those labels which seemed to me the most appropriate (or least inappropriate) to describe each methodological viewpoint.

6.2.2 Apriorism

Let us start by looking at the account which is furthest of all from the conventional idea of 'scientific method' as it is usually spelled out for physical science. This is the approach known as *apriorism*.

The word comes from the Latin phrase *a priori*. Like several other philosophical terms, this comes up in everyday conversation in a variety of vague usages, implying something like 'from first principles', 'on the face of it', and so on. But in its philosophical sense, it conveys something much more exact: if we say that something is *a priori*, we are asserting that it is inherent in the structure of our thinking, rather than being learned by experience. To put the same idea in another way: if a proposition is *a priori*, then we would be unable to make sense of a world in which that proposition did not hold true.

Needless to say, there are philosophical controversies over whether we are or are not justified in believing that anything is really *a priori*. Clearly, by the nature of the notion of *a priori* truth, it will always remain difficult to think of any conclusive test of this question. For our purposes, we can skirt most of this discussion, and take note only of one or two simple observations. We should recall the distinction between material truth and logical 'truth' (Section 2.4). Without too much heartburning, we may take it for granted that some propositions have logical 'truth' *a priori*; for instance, the fact that 'nothing can be at the same time *A* and not-*A*'; and indeed, the fact that the conclusion of a logically correct argument follows inescapably from its premises. Either ideas like these really are *a priori*—inborn in the way we think—or they are so basic to our understanding of the world that we may take them as *a priori* for all practical purposes.

However, some philosophers have gone much further than this, and asserted that some propositions are *materially* true *a priori*. Among this school are to be found the apriorist methodologists in economics.

Having followed through our discussion in earlier chapters about the picture of the validation of scientific theories, you will have no difficulty in seeing why this suggestion pulls the carpet from under the feet of conventional methodologists. So far, we have adhered to the usual notion that the only way in which science could check on questions of material truth was to engage in a process of empirical testing, the character and problems of which we looked at in detail in Chapter 4. But what the apriorist is saying is that some propositions need not (indeed, cannot) be tested: that we would be incapable of understanding a world in which these propositions were other than *materially* true.

Probably the best-known apriorist account of economics is that put forward by the late Professor von Mises. He went further than merely saying that some of the propositions of economics were materially true *a priori*; he argued, in fact, that *all* the statements of economic theory followed deductively from an axiom that he held to be materially true *a priori*, the so-called 'category of action'. All conscious human behaviour, said von Mises, was aimed at substituting a 'better' for a 'worse' situation, in the view of whoever was carrying out the action. Economists had no right to try to dictate *what* was to be considered 'better' or 'worse', since this would involve introducing their own value-judgements into their reasoning. Nor was there any sense in trying to 'test' this proposition about human action. Given that an action was a matter of conscious choice, von Mises argued, we would be incapable of understanding a world in which this choice was *not* intended to substitute a 'better' for a 'worse' state of affairs in the actor's own estimation. In other words, the 'category of action' had material truth *a priori*. Starting from this materially true axiom, we could reason out all the theorems of economics.

According to this view, the empirical testing of economic theory becomes totally superfluous. If the apriorist talks of 'testing' at all, he can mean only the checking of deductive reasoning to make sure that the conclusions do in fact follow necessarily from the premises. And you will see, by the way, that this view of things carries with it some implications that would startle the textbook-trained philosopher of science. On the apriorist view, because the predictions of theory follow by valid deduction from higher-level state-ments that are themselves materially true *for certain*, then it must follow that these predictions are also certain—rather than being surrounded by the fuzz of uncertainty and ignorance which, as we saw earlier, characterizes empiri-cal findings. Likewise, the fallacy of affirming the consequent is no problem on the apriorist interpretation: since the higher-level statements of theory are seen as being materially true *a priori*, there is no reason to go through the painful and logically problematical process of reasoning up to them from lower-level statements.

In this brief summary, I cannot do justice to von Mises' fiercely argued position, and I certainly suggest that you sample some of his writing for yourself; the reading guide at the end of this chapter will lead you to it. For now, let us consider what we are to make of this apriorist approach from our standpoint as unbiased assessors of methodological views.

Intuitively, a position like von Mises' strikes us as extreme. Given that economics deals with real-world data, can we really accept that the economic scientist is exempt from the need to set his theories against empirical observation? Can it really be the case that the conclusions of economic theorizing are known 'for certain', in terms of material truth? If so, what is so special about our subject matter as to account for these charac-teristics?

Then again, what can we make of the contention that all the theorems of economics can be deduced from the 'category of action'? One obvious objection to this, on formal grounds, is that from just one axiom, you can deduce nothing; you need at least one more proposition to use as a premise before any deduction becomes possible. Von Mises never makes it entirely clear what other premises, if any, he sees as coming into the reasoning of economics. At one or two points in his writing, however, he does briefly mention 'special assumptions' which need to be introduced. If these other premises are meant also to have material truth *a priori*, von Mises does not get round to explaining from where they get this property. If, on the other hand, he means these other assumptions to be empirical, then it follows by implication that they would have to be checked against reality before the economist could use them in real-life application—a point which would bring von Mises' logic-in-use very much nearer to that of the conventional methodologist.

Looking at some of the higher-level statements of economic theory from a commonsense point of view, it becomes difficult to see how they could be deduced with certainty from von Mises' 'category of action'. Given that people always act to bring about a 'better' situation in their own estimation: does this mean, for instance, that businessmen will try to maximize profits? Or does it mean that they will aim for a lower and safer level of profits? Either might be thought consistent with a 'better' situation, as far as we can tell without actually being the businessmen in question. From these and similar examples, it is hard to avoid the conclusion that von Mises' 'category of action' is far from sufficient to provide us with the grounding for all the theorems of economics—quite irrespective of the problem of whether the 'category of action' itself is or is not to be regarded as materially true *a priori*.

Some methodologists from other schools of thought have attacked apriorist reasoning in another way. They point out that the suggested 'category of action' entails a tautology (see Section 4.3.5). If you say that any action taken is, *by definition*, aimed at substituting a 'better' for a 'worse' situation, and that the only person able to judge which is the better and the worse position is the person doing the acting, then you remove any possibility of testing this proposition against reality; it is so, simply because you have defined it as being so. Correspondingly, this criticism goes on, any further statements deduced from this starting statement will themselves have only analytical truth; and because they cannot be set against real-world data, they must be regarded as being useless to science.

Clearly, this gets us into deep water. *If* in fact the 'category of action' is correctly to be regarded as a tautology, then the criticism is justified. But if, instead, writers like von Mises are correct in thinking that statements of 'human action' do say something about the real world that is a matter of material truth, and not just of definition, then the criticism falls down. In this connection, some opponents of the apriorist view have been a bit too optimistic in believing that it is always clear whether a statement is or is not tautological. On the contrary, as we have seen, it becomes difficult to determine this for certain even when we are talking about such abstract systems of reasoning as arithmetic and geometry, to say nothing of the much more practical field of study we call economics. Von Mises himself has pointed out that though Euclid's geometry is formally tautologous, engineers do not hesitate to use it when they are drawing up plans for bridges—and that if you ignored the real-world importance of these 'tautologies', you would finish up with some pretty ramshackle bridges. The implication is that 'formally tautologous' need not by any means imply also 'scientifically useless', in economics or any other field of study.

At this point, we can leave the apriorist view, to be given another look when we have discussed some of the distinctive features of economic theory and its validation. Although von Mises' apriorist account probably goes too far to be acceptable as an entirely credible account of economic procedure, it nevertheless—by the sheer starkness of its contrast with conventional ideas of 'scientific method'—alerts us to the possibility that the conventional account may itself fall short of telling the whole story about economic method; and it contains some guidelines to what these shortcomings of the conventional account may be.

6.2.3 The analytical school

Try asking some of your economist friends: 'Where did Keynes get the evidence for his ideas about the nature of the consumption function?' The usual answer will be something on these lines: 'Well, I suppose he went to the statistics of national income, and compared these with a series for consumption in the same run of years—then did his statistical sums and got his answer in that way.'

But in reality, the great man did nothing of the kind. He simply thought up his picture of the consumption function—and, indeed, the whole of his theory of national-income determination—out of his own head.

At no stage did Keynes appeal to inductive observation, or statistical testing, as a basis for his reasoning. When he made his famous statement that '. . . men are disposed, as a rule and on the average, to increase their consumption as their income increases, but not by as much as the increase in their income . . .', he was putting this proposition forward simply on the basis of what he considered to be common sense. For his evidence, he looked not at books of statistics, but at his own knowledge and judgement of economic affairs.

Indeed, virtually all of the familiar propositions of what we call 'economic theory' were developed in just this way: that is, on the basis of common-sense observation of everyday economic events. Very often, the economist would observe not only what other people did, but what he himself did, or what he would do in a given hypothetical situation. This latter style of commonsense observation—in which one looks at one's own actions and motives—is often called *introspection*, from Latin roots implying 'looking into oneself'.

This school of thought—which accepts commonsense observation and introspection as admissible procedures for the checking of economic theory—has been called by various names; here, I shall adopt what is probably the most often used of these, and label it the *analytical* school.*

Quite often in methodological literature, writers fail to make any distinction between the analytical and apriorist schools, using either one of the labels to describe both approaches. But there is a clear and significant difference between the two. The analytical account does not assert that the propositions of economic theory are materially true *a priori*. What is being argued, instead, is that these are propositions about empirical reality—that they are *capable* of being set against factual observation—but that they are so obvious to common sense that they do not *need* to be 'tested' by inductive-statistical means.

This rather simple point is one that has sometimes seemed to bamboozle methodologists from other schools, whose idea of 'scientific method' inclines more towards the methods of physical science. These writers have sometimes seemed to believe that *either* you validate a proposition by empir-

---

* The potential confusion attaching to this label is, of course, that it seems to imply that economists of this school are concerned only with the analytical truth of economic propositions—that their reasoning is, in Friedman's phrase, a 'retreat into purely formal and tautological analysis'. As argued in this section, this is a wrong interpretation.

ical testing—which, in their terms, means inductive testing aided by statistical analysis—*or* you put it forward as true *a priori*. But, on what I am here calling the analytical account, you can get a halfway house between these two possibilities: your propositions can be empirical, without being based on inductive-statistical testing.

To put the same idea into the more formal terminology of Section 4.6: what the economists in the analytical school are doing is to use *rules of correspondence* which admit common sense, everyday observation, and introspection as proper styles of investigation for the economic scientist to use.

As we also know, there is no epistemological rule-book which will tell us which are the 'correct' rules of correspondence to use in any scientific area. Instead, it is a matter of intersubjective agreement—or, as far as economics is concerned, we should perhaps say 'intersubjective disagreement'. Methodologists from other schools have not been slow to point out that the analytical economists' use of 'commonsense' observation and introspection is out of line with what would be considered admissible by physical scientists. This harks back to a point we noted right at the beginning of our discussion of scientific procedure, namely that some kind of instrumentation is usually expected to play a part in the process of observation. In trying to judge whether liquid A is hotter than liquid B, we said, you do not just stick your finger into each in turn and rely on your personal impression; you use a thermometer. It is just as unscientific, say the critics of the analytical school, to rely on 'commonsense' observation in trying to judge economic situations: you need to use inductive observation and statistical analysis.

The analytical economists' answer is simply that economic data are very different from those of physical science, and that it therefore makes no sense to suppose that methods of observation need meet the same criteria in both these scientific areas. In Chapter 5, we explored the most important distinctive features of economic data, and the discussion will be taken further in Section 6.3.

Going on now to a second prominent feature of the analytical approach, closely related to the first: the analytical economist lays relatively great stress on the notion of the *applicability* of higher-level statements. This contrasts with the textbook version of the hypothetico-deductive account, in which emphasis is placed instead on the falsification (or, if you will, verification or validation) of hypotheses.

Take, for instance, the statement: 'Consumers buy more of a commodity when its price falls.' It is ludicrous, say the analytical school, to try to 'falsify' or 'verify' this statement—since it is obvious from everyday observation that the statement is true of many consumers, at many times and many places; equally, it is obviously untrue of some other consumers, at some other times and places. What matters is whether the statement is *applicable* to the particular economic situation that is being studied. In so far as it does apply to that situation, any lower-level statements deduced from it (with the aid of other 'commonsense' statements and auxiliary hypotheses) will also be applicable to that same situation.

Economists in the analytical school have laid great stress on the deductive aspects of their procedure. Indeed, sometimes—rather overstating their own case—they have called economics a 'deductive system', or used other phrases meaning the same thing. Needless to say, this has been a rich source of confusion in methodological literature, since writers from other schools of thought have taken it to mean that economics was being presented as a totally abstract, tautologous system like algebra or formal logic.

On the reconstruction of the analytical approach which I have here suggested, we can guess at a less extreme interpretation. To analytical economists, the task of inductive investigation of the truth of high-level statements is not important, since these statements are anyway viewed as being obvious, simply by common sense. What really does matter is to work out the deduced implications of these commonsense starting statements. The implications, unlike the starting statements, may not be at all obvious, and it is the economist's contribution to make plain what these deduced consequences really are. Once the implications of a given set of starting statements have thus been thought out, they will be available as a practical guide to decision-making in all situations to which that set of starting statements is applicable.

In this connection, several writers have suggested that it is usually the simplest and most widely accepted statements of economic theory that provide the greatest guidance to real-life policy-making. The point is that while these familiar theorems of economics seem straightforward to us as economists, they do not seem at all straightforward to those who have not had a training in our discipline—who have not had the chance to think through the deductive problem-solving mechanism which, on the analytical view, is the really valuable aspect of economic reasoning.

Let us take just two examples from many possibilities. An elementary supply-and-demand analysis will tell us that, when a purchase tax is imposed on some good, then (except in a few special configurations of the two curves) the incidence of the tax is split between buyers and sellers, not just borne by the buyers. But you try explaining that to someone who is not acquainted with economic theory! Likewise in the macroeconomic field, have a try at explaining to an intelligent non-economist friend why it was that nations could 'spend their way' out of a depression like that between the wars. 'But surely,' your friend will reply, 'if somebody is in a bad way economically, the thing to do is to save, not spend?' If you eventually manage to convey the true situation, it will only be because you have done what the economists in the analytical school see as the central job of the economist—that is, to make clear the implications of economic situations via the deductive apparatus of theory.

How about 'testing' on the analytical view? We have seen already that, according to this school of thought, the starting statements of economic theory do not require to be 'tested' by inductive-statistical observation—either directly or via the testing of deduced 'predictions' in the hypothetico-deductive manner. It is sufficient to use commonsense observation, perhaps introspectively, to arrive at these starting statements. Once this has been done, then the analytical economist—like the apriorist—would argue that the most important 'test' of an economic theorem must lie in the checking of its reasoning for deductive correctness.

At the same time, economists in the analytical school have been well aware that the findings of their analysis needed to be set against real-world outcomes. They have suggested that this can be done in a very direct way: the material correctness of a given piece of economic analysis is to be checked by putting into action the policy recommendations that follow from it. If these recommendations *work*—not just once or twice, but consistently—then we can take it that the analysis has indeed been a correct expression of the real-world situation at the times and places concerned. Though analytical writers have not usually used the term 'testing' to describe this idea, we can very well think of it as a process of 'testing by usefulness'—or, more exactly, 'testing by repeated usefulness'.

Note what happens, though, if the recommendations of the analysis *fail* to work. On the analytical view, this does not mean that the higher-level statements of the reasoning used are 'falsified'; just that they have turned out not to be *applicable* to that particular situation.

For instance: the Keynesian analysis of national-income determination could be judged more 'correct' than pre-existing analyses because the policy prescriptions derived from it *worked*, whereas the policy measures based on these earlier analyses had failed to work. In other words, the success of the policy suggested that Keynes had been successful in thinking up the particular set of starting statements which were applicable to the economic situation existing at the time he published his *General Theory*. Using the same reasoning, we can look at the present-day problems of the economy—where Keynesian prescriptions of cutting back spending now seem to 'work' only very imperfectly as a means of curbing inflation—and reach the tentative conclusion that the starting statements used by Keynes may no longer be fully applicable to the present-day situation. On the analytical account, therefore, the task currently facing economists is to engage in some commonsense reflection until they succeed in arriving at a new set of starting statements that will allow the deduction of some policy prescriptions which do work.

Having thus described the analytical approach in its own terms, we may leave it for further consideration as the chapter goes on. In doing so, we may note that it does seem to be a strong contender as a 'correct' reconstruction of what is actually done in economic science. Quite apart from any philosophical considerations, this assessment could be based simply on the knowledge that virtually all the generally accepted 'economic theory' now existing has been developed in the way suggested by the analytical school.

Yet, at the same time, the methodologist is not free to ignore criticisms from writers of other schools who have argued that the analytical account is too much of a hit-and-miss affair to be regarded as 'scientific'. The whole trouble with common sense, these critics have pointed out, is that sometimes it turns out not to be right. They argue that economics—irrespective of how it has evolved in the past—must now concentrate on the systematic empirical testing which seems to have been so successful in physical science. In the next section, we take a look at the most extreme version of this argument.

6.2.4. 'Positive' economics

Even if you have never previously read any methodological literature, you are very likely to have come across the phrase 'positive economics'. It turns up in all sorts of economic literature, from learned journals right through to general introductory textbooks. But though the term 'positive' is bandied about so freely, its meaning is subject to a great deal of confusion, even by the standards of philosophical jargon. Before trying to assess this approach to economic method, therefore, we need to pause and try to make sure what it is we are assessing.

As we saw in Section 5.2.1, the word 'positive' basically means 'concerned with facts', and is usually contrasted with 'normative', which means 'concerned with tastes'. This, then, is one of the things that we might take people to mean when they talk about 'positive economics'—that it is an approach which is based on facts, not on the economist's own tastes or personal feelings.

But this does not get us very far. Those writers who have described their own approach as 'positive economics' have specifically been trying to bring out a contrast between their position and that of the apriorists and analytical economists. However, these other schools also see economics as a factual study, and not at all as a matter of the economist's own motives or personal feelings; indeed, as we have seen, they have stressed the need for the economic scientist to keep his own value-judgements out of his reasoning.

In fact, the word 'positive', as it is nowadays most often used in the context of economic method, means something much more specialized than simply 'concerned with facts'. It designates an approach spelled out in its most famous form in an essay by Professor Milton Friedman, 'The Methodology of Positive Economics'. Just as nobody can claim any knowledge of economic methodology unless they have read Robbins's *Essay on the Nature and Significance of Economic Science*, so this piece by Friedman —conveying a very different view of economic method—is required reading. You will find some comments on the interpretation of Friedman's essay in the reading guide to this chapter.

Briefly, Friedman's contention is this: suppose you have two competing hypotheses with which you can set out to explain an economic situation.

Then the 'better' of the two hypotheses will be the one which gives the more accurate predictions—and not necessarily the one which proceeds from the more realistic assumptions.

These concepts—of 'testing by predictions' and of the 'realism of assumptions'—have figured so largely in methodological discussions in economics that I shall give them sections to themselves later in the chapter.

You will realize that this interpretation of 'positive' brings us a long way from the general meaning of the word, given at the beginning of this section. Now, it is not just a matter of economics being concerned with facts; not just a matter of these facts being testable, or of their actually being tested; they need to be tested 'by predictions', and not 'by assumptions'. If you feel that what we are now talking about has little to do with the 'positive/normative' distinction, you would (in my opinion) be right.

The use of the word 'positive' to describe Friedman's account may be a rather distorted echo of the name given to an extremist philosophical school of past years, the *positivists*. Even when this school was flourishing, it was by no means agreed—even among the positivists themselves—just what they stood for in the way of scientific procedure. The confusion over the meanings of 'positive' and 'positivist' has grown greater over the years as the terms have been stretched to fit all kinds of different views of scientific method, not only in economics but in other sciences as well. If the original positivist position can be described briefly in such a way as to convey anything at all, it was that unless a statement was such as to yield predictions which were testable against factual observation, then that statement had to be regarded as meaningless from a scientific point of view.

This idea had its origins very much more in the 'strictly speaking' reasoning of academic philosophy than in any requirement of real-life scientific work, and most philosophers of science by now regard this extreme positivist position as having little more than historical curiosity value. Nevertheless, as Professor Machlup has pointed out, there often seems to be a kind of 'cultural lag' in the transmission of methodological ideas from one scientific discipline to another, and it is probable that we find in this the clue to both the name and the nature of 'positive economics', argued by Friedman.

This account of economic method has been widely quoted in general economic texts as being the 'correct' approach for economic scientists to use. Yet strangely enough, there can be few methodological positions that have been so thoroughly demolished in the journal literature. Shortly, in Sections 6.3.1 and 6.3.2, we will have the chance to consider why Friedman's arguments seem so convincing at first sight, and why so many methodologists have rejected them on closer inspection.

6.2.5 *Moderate empiricism*

As you would expect, some of the criticism of the extreme positivist account has come from economists in the apriorist and analytical schools, who feel that scientific procedure in economics need not in any case depend on a process of 'testing' of the kind used by the physical scientist.

However, there have been many other critics of Friedman's position who have in fact agreed with him that economics must systematically test its propositions against reality by means of empirical observation (that is, by inductive-statistical means). What these critics have disagreed with is the positivist suggestion that such testing has to be directed at predictions *only*, and not at assumptions. They have pointed out that in economics, it is often possible to check not only lowest-level statements, but also higher-level statements, against empirical observation. And where this is possible, they argue, it is surely desirable; the direct checking of higher-level statements avoids the problematic business of reasoning up to them in the hypothetico-deductive style. In practice, you are always faced with the need to test a *set* of hypotheses, and no single test is likely to give you a clear-cut answer; therefore the more tests you can use, the better—whether the statements you are testing are 'predictions' or 'assumptions'.

There's no ready-made label to describe this view, widely held though it is. In its own way, it is certainly 'positive', in that it lays emphasis on empirical testing; but we need some label which will mark it off from the more extreme 'positivist' view. In what follows, I shall attach the name *moderate empiricism* to this school of thought.

6.3 Economic theory: structure and testing

6.3.1 'Testing by predictions'

Whatever may have been the origins of Friedman's prescription for 'testing by predictions only', his justification of this methodological approach for economic science ran as follows. The 'assumptions' of economic reasoning, he argued, were quite designedly *not* 'realistic': they were deliberate simplifications of reality. On the basis of a brief acquaintance with economics, you will be aware of some of these simplified theoretical notions: for instance, the 'rational consumer', ever bent on choosing the optimal basket of goods; the businessman who thinks of nothing but maximizing profit; the perfectly competitive market situation where everybody has instantaneous, perfect information about both past and future events.

In fact, went on Friedman, you could say more than this: the more 'realistic' an assumption became, the less useful was it likely to be as theory—because, in order to increase realism, you had to reduce the generality of the concepts you used, and so decrease the range of situations for which they had explanatory power. For instance, instead of some theoretical 'profit-maximizing businessman', we *could* base our reasoning on the actions of some set of real-life businessmen, who might or might not behave like their simplified counterparts in abstract theory. But in that case, the conclusions of our theorizing would apply only to that particular set of real-life businessmen, and we might have to rethink the whole matter if we looked at different businessmen.

In any case, Friedman added, it was impossible ever to make any direct check on the 'realism' of assumptions in economics. For instance, you could not ever say for sure what were the real motives in the minds of business-men, even though their observed actions *seemed* to be consistent with a profit-maximizing aim.

It was all right, said Friedman, for the economist to reason *as if* business-men were profit-maximizers, *as if* firms were perfectly competitive, and so on. This 'as-if' reasoning could be considered serviceable so long as the predictions that followed from it turned out to be right. But it was the predictions only which mattered when it came to the assessment of compet-ing economic hypotheses—because these predictions, unlike the 'as-if' assumptions, could be directly observed in real-world data.

At first reading, this seems a convincing argument—and it seems even more so in Friedman's original article. And yet: if you are reading this book at leisure, you may care to pause, re-read the 'potted' version of the argu-ments just given, and assess them against what we already know about the structure and testing of scientific theories generally, as well as about the distinctive features of the data used in economic science.

What happens when you 'test by predictions'? It is exactly the process which, in Chapter 4, we called 'checking a hypothesis that is not directly testable by reference to directly-testable consequences' (Section 4.1).

You will recall that such testing entailed the use of a hypothetical syllo-gism. The major premise, i.e., the hypothetical statement, included the particular hypothesis we were setting out to test; but it also had to include auxiliary hypotheses, covering things like the conditions in which the test was being carried out, the features which were to remain unchanged during the test, perhaps an assumption of regularity, and so on, for as many features as we thought necessary to specify. The number and nature of these auxiliary hypotheses was a matter for intersubjective agreement among scientists in the particular field of study in which we were working.

Thus we finished up with a hypothetical syllogism where the antecedent consisted not just of one condition, but of many. By way of a reminder, let us draw it out, letting H stand for our original hypothesis; $A_1, A_2, \ldots, A_n$ stand for our indefinite number of auxiliary hypotheses; and P stand for our 'prediction' or deduced consequence. Let us phrase the syllogism in the fashionable 'falsificationist' manner, and ignore probabilistic reasoning. So it runs:

1. If (H and $A_1, A_2, \ldots, A_n$) are true, then P is true;
2. P is not true . . .;

Now, as we know, the conclusion of this argument is:

3. therefore (H and $A_1, A_2, \ldots, A_n$) are not true.

We know also that it is fallacious to try to conclude 'H is not true'; the falsity of the compound antecedent may possibly have come from the falsity of any of the A's—that is, from any of the auxiliary hypotheses—even if the original hypothesis, H, were really true. In other words, you can never test one hypothesis in isolation; you must test it along with all its accompanying auxiliary hypotheses.

So much is a fact of life in *any* kind of hypothetico-deductive investigation. But now let us translate this into the terms of Friedman's prescription for 'testing by predictions only, not by assumptions'.

In fact, Friedman never makes it entirely clear what he means by 'assumptions'. At times, he seems to use the word to signify what I have here called the 'original hypothesis', symbolized H above; at other times, he seems to mean the auxiliary hypotheses, the A's of our syllogism; and at still other points, he seems to be talking about the whole compound antecedent of the hypothetical. However, we can recall the phrasing of his initial argument: that when we compare two competing hypotheses, the better is to be chosen on the basis of its predictions and not its assumptions. So we shall take it that by 'hypothesis', he means our H; by 'assumptions', the A's; and by 'prediction', as before, our P.

Now, in these terms, suppose we take two competing hypotheses and try to find which is the 'better' by attempting to falsify the predictions of each. We realize that we cannot just compare the two original hypotheses; we must compare the hypotheses, *each accompanied by its own auxiliary hypotheses*. Let us call the two main hypotheses H' and H'', the corresponding sets of auxiliary hypotheses A' and A'', and the respective predictions P' and P''. Then our comparison does not just consist of saying:

1. If H', then P'; but if H'', then P''.

What we really need to say is:

1. If (H' and $A_1', A_2', \ldots, A_n'$), then P';
   but if (H'' and $A_1'', A_2'', \ldots, A_n''$), then P''.

Once again, this is a situation in which the investigator in any science must find himself when he is attempting to compare two hypotheses on the evidence of their predictions. But the physical scientist certainly does not react to this simply by ignoring his assumptions. Quite on the contrary, as we have seen, a central feature of the hypothetico-deductive approach is to specify the nature of these assumptions or experimental conditions (the A's in the hypothetical). This can never give the physical scientist a totally cut-and-dried 'yes' or 'no' answer to his testing, because it is never possible to achieve the 'perfect' investigational set-up. But what can be achieved is a high degree of intersubjective agreement about the truth or falsity of the A's, and hence about the validity or otherwise of the supposed comparison of the original hypotheses, the H's.

If one really follows Friedman's prescription and deliberately ignores the assumptions behind one's process of testing, then one abandons the possibility of getting any intersubjective agreement on the appropriateness of the test. Friedman's suggested means for 'comparing' hypotheses thus turns out to be no comparison at all.

What is more, as many critics of Friedman's paper have pointed out, this extreme positivist account must also make it impossible to give a scientific *explanation* of economic events. This is so, whether we adopt the more or the less stringent sense of 'explanation' (Section 4.5). By choosing to ignore assumptions, we are giving up any attempt to fit our observations into the deductive framework of theory. And by saying 'predictions are all that matter', we are denying that our reasoning can give any systematic help in controlling economic events—since, as we have seen, you may be able to predict an outcome without having any idea how to influence it.

Nor does it serve much practical purpose to suggest that the economist can reason 'as if' people's economic motives were such-and-such. The job of the economic policy-maker, whether in government or business, is to influence people's actions. It is clear that the economist can best help in this task by trying to form an idea—however imperfect—of what the motives behind these actions really are.

Where, in any case, do the extreme positivists get the idea that it is impossible to check directly on the higher-level statements of economic theory? Once again, as it happens, it is not made very clear in Friedman's paper exactly why he holds this view. Perhaps it is a result of his enthusiasm for the procedure of physical science, where higher-level statements as a rule really *are* unobservable. It may also be an echo of the old philosophical view that only the lowest-level statements of a theory could be compared with protocols. As we saw in Section 4.6, present-day accounts of the validation of theory raise no objection to the idea that higher-level statements can also be compared with observable events. And certainly, when we come to the specifics of economic work, this wider view seems to be sensible. For instance: consider the lowest-level statement 'Businessman Bloggs is producing where marginal cost and marginal revenue are equal.' This is one possible deduced consequence of the higher-level statement 'Businessmen are profit-maximizers' (along with various auxiliary hypotheses, which you may like to specify from your own knowledge of the theory of the firm). The lower-level of these two statements is directly testable, given that you can get the needed accounting data. But so is the higher-level statement, given that you can carry out the needed survey study on a representative sample of businessmen.

Friedman's essay, already well and truly battered, will come in for more incidental criticism in the following section. If you are new to economic studies, one point may have been puzzling you: given that Friedman's extreme positivist position has been so thoroughly demolished by later methodological writers from every school of thought, why is it that his account of economic method is still quite often quoted as the 'correct' one in general economic texts? The clue, perhaps, comes in something Professor Machlup has said:

> It would be an interesting undertaking to show how little the methodological propositions stated by a writer are related to his own research and analysis. Many do the things they pronounce impossible or illegitimate, and many fail to do what they declare to be essential requirements of scientific method . . . a great economist may, without any consequences for his scientific work, embrace and proclaim the most naive and outdated methodological principles. Students of methodology should beware of the temptation to rely on authority in accepting the methodological pronouncements of a great figure in his field.

I have often wondered whether, when Machlup wrote these words, he had Friedman's paper in mind. Whether he had or not, his warning is well worth remembering.

6.3.2 The 'realism of assumptions'

In discussing the 'realism of economic assumptions', Friedman was touching on a methodological controversy that had been going on for many years before his essay was written, and in fact is about as old as the discipline of economics itself. Today, the controversy still grumbles on. Here, I can give only the briefest glimpse of the wordy broadsides which philosophers of economic science have fired at each other over this matter. And we may be thankful for this necessary brevity, since these exchanges are among the most tortuous and tortured in all methodological literature. In this section I am going to argue that the controversy results almost entirely from confusions over words, to a greater extent even than most methodological squabbles. Painfully following through the literature on this subject, one realizes that the two terms 'realism' and 'assumptions' have each had differing meanings placed on them by different writers, and that this confusion is the source of most of the resulting argument.

In talking about Friedman's essay, we have already noted some of the 'assumptions' that have figured in the controversy: for instance, the businessman bent only on profit-maximization; or the 'perfectly competitive' market set-up. From your acquaintance with economic theory, you can easily add to this list of 'assumptions'—of theoretical pictures of people, markets, or motivations—made in the higher-level reasoning of economics.

132

Historically, perhaps the most famous figure of all is that ever-walking ghost of economic discourse, the 'economic man'. This is the idealized individual about whom economists are said to theorize—a cold-blooded, calculating character, devoid of human error or charitable sentiment, and intent simply on squeezing every drop of satisfaction—monetary or otherwise—out of the economic situation in which he finds himself. He is not only the older-fashioned version of the 'rational consumer', but also shares the qualities of the profit-maximizing entrepreneur and speculator. All in all, he is not an attractive character.

For well over a century, people have been pouring scorn on 'economic man', and incidentally on the economists who (supposedly) theorize about him. In reality, say the critics, no such person as this 'economic man' exists; so, given that economics lets him figure in theory, what use is economics?

Whether we are considering 'economic man' or any of the other notions which the economist 'assumes' for the purposes of his theorizing, the question for the methodologist is: are these notions to be regarded as 'realistic' or are they not? And either way, why does it matter?

In fact, the word 'realistic' is not generally used in methodological writing outside the economic field. Within economics, we find the term being used in two quite distinct senses; many writers, though, have failed to realize the distinction, and it is from this that confusion has developed.

Recall first of all Friedman's assertion that the 'realism' of a hypothesis was somehow inversely related to its power as an explanatory device. To make a hypothesis more 'realistic', you had to hedge it round with more and more specific conditions, which at the same time restricted its explanatory power to a smaller and smaller range of situations. Thinking back to the terminology we met in Section 4.6, we can make a pretty reasonable guess that Friedman is here talking about the *level* of statements in theory. The higher-level the statement, the more 'unrealistic' it is, in the sense that it is likely to be relatively abstract and relatively far removed from specific happenings that can be observed in the real world. Conversely, a low-level statement could be called relatively 'realistic', i.e., not very abstract, and either directly observable or close to direct observability.

The second sense of 'realistic' is much closer to the everyday meaning of the word. In non-technical conversation, when we talk about something as being 'realistic', we simply mean that it is in conformity with what really happens. In the terms of science, we might translate that by saying that the proposition in question was plausible in terms of material truth. And, of course, this latter idea is quite different from the notion of whether the statement is of high or low level.

If this idea needs underlining, it can be done by comparing the following two statements:

1. Businessmen try to maximize profits; and
2. Businessmen try to minimize profits.

Either of these propositions *could* be put forward as a statement in a 'theory of the firm'. Clearly, they are identical in level. But, from whatever school of thought an economist might come, he would certainly consider that statement 1 was more 'realistic' than statement 2, in the sense of reflecting more accurately the state of affairs in the real world.

By registering these alternative meanings of 'realistic', we become able to give two sensible alternative answers to the question of whether a realistic proposition in economic theory is better than an unrealistic one. First, if we interpret 'realism' as indicating the level of a statement in theory, then the question really does not mean much: whether the economist uses a high- or a low-level statement will depend on the problem he has in hand. We could make the obvious point, perhaps, that a higher-level statement should be able to explain a wider range of situations than one of lower level; so, in this very restricted sense, the 'unrealistic' statement might be called the 'better'. If, alternatively, we take 'realism' to indicate accuracy in reflecting the real-world state of affairs, then it is clear that a realistic statement will be better than one that is unrealistic.

Going on to consider the confusions over the meaning of 'assumption' in economics, we find, once again, that there is confusion between an everyday sense of the word and a more technical usage. In normal conversation, when we say we 'assume' something, we mean simply that we take it to be the case in reality. If I say 'I assume the train comes at 4 o'clock', I mean just that I expect to see the train rolling into the station, large as life, at that time or thereabouts.

Give a thought now to the ways in which we use the verb 'to assume' in economic contexts. It should not take much thinking to bring home the fact that when we 'assume' something in economics, we often intend the word in something very different from its everyday sense. If we 'assume' the economy to contain only two goods and two consumers, for instance, we are hardly setting out to suggest that the real-life economy actually does so. If we 'assume' perfect knowledge on the part of sellers in a market, we are not suggesting that there ever really can be such a market. And when we 'assume other things remaining equal', as we so often do in economic theorizing, the last thing we are saying is that in reality things *will* actually remain equal.

Here again, we can turn to the terminology of Section 4.6 for some help in clearing up the confusion. The fact is that when we use the word 'assumption', we have no means of making it clear whether we are talking about the contents of the c-domain or those of the p-domain—about the world of theory or the world of observed reality. We have, in other words, no way of indicating whether we are attributing logical or material truth to the statements we are 'assuming'.

When I made my 'assumption' about the time of the train, I was making a statement about the p-domain; I was predicting what the real-life train would be observed to do. But in making the economic 'assumptions' given above, we had no intention of describing any specific object in the p-domain; we were referring to constructs. As we noted in Section 4.6, a construct may be directly observable, but is not necessarily so. In other words, for any construct in the c-domain, there may be an object in the p-domain that is immediately identifiable with it, but there may equally well not be. This does not mean for a moment that propositions about constructs which are not directly observable need be nonsensical, useless, or closed to empirical checking, for reasons that we considered in Chapter 4.

In the light of this distinction between the two meanings of 'assumption', let us look back at the 'economic man'. We see straight away how misguided is a lot of the scorn that has been poured on him—because, of course, the poor old 'economic man' is a construct. It is pointless to cry him down because he 'does not exist'. It may well be that he 'does not exist' in the real world, in that there is nobody who behaves in quite the way that the 'economic man' is supposed to behave, at least not all the time. But he 'exists' all right in the c-domain, at least if the economist wants to construct him there. Exactly the same is true of the 'rational consumer', the 'perfect market', and all the rest of those economic constructs which are not directly observable.

Again, take the much-contested 'assumption' that 'businessmen are profit-maximizers'. Is the economist entitled to make this 'assumption', or not? The fact is that in terms of *logical* truth, he is entitled to adopt this assumption, or any other he chooses. But before he is entitled to assert its *material* truth, he must subject it to an 'assault by the facts' in some way or another, whether this is by subjecting the statement to direct observation or by reasoning up to it in the hypothetico-deductive manner. If he 'assumes' it as materially true, and not just logically true, without the benefit of factual checking, then he is certainly worthy of criticism.

And this leads us on to the next stage of the confusion. Because, of course, your interpretation of 'factual checking' will depend on what school of thought you belong to. The hard-line positivist would insist that such checking can only be done via 'testing by predictions'. Moderate empiricists would also allow the empirical checking of observable higher-level statements directly. The analytical school would say that the statements concerned are obvious to commonsense observation; and the apriorist would say that material truth attaches to these statements *a priori*.

When you recall that, for instance, the hard-line positivist would not look upon 'commonsense observation' as being a legitimate means of factual checking, you can appreciate why such a vast amount of confusion has marked the literature on economic 'assumptions'. In this circumstance, the positivist might well accuse the analytical economist of making an unfounded 'assumption' in the sense of giving a statement not just logical truth, but material truth as well, without any evidence to back this up. The analytical economist would consider that he had all the evidence that was necessary, on the basis of his commonsense observation and introspection.

In view of the confusion over the meanings of 'realistic' and 'assumption', it would be a great deal better if we could drop both words out of economic usage altogether, and use instead the perfectly good technical terms that are available to express what we really mean. Some writers have used 'postulates' rather than 'assumptions' to describe the constructs from which economic reasoning starts; and to my mind at least, 'postulate' is by far the better word, since it conveys that only logical truth, and not material truth, is being attached to the statements concerned. However, by now there is no hope of sorting out this usage; writers of all schools of thought use 'assumption' and 'postulate' interchangeably. When they say 'postulate', you can be fairly sure they are talking about the c-domain, but when they say 'assumption' you have to look at the context in order to try to make out which domain is being referred to. Often, you will correctly come to the conclusion that the writer in question is not clear in his own mind *which* domain he is talking about.

I hope I have given you at least some idea of the reasons for the confusion that exists in the literature over this question of the 'realism of assumptions'. Here, we need not concern ourselves any further with this battle of words. Our time is better spent in looking at some of the special features of structure and validation which mark out economic theory in particular, as opposed to 'scientific theories' in general. These insights will in turn throw further light on the problems that have been discussed in this and the previous section.

6.3.3 'Inductive theory' v. deductive theory

Several writers have pointed out that as a science develops over time, its development seems to follow a typical pattern. They have suggested that, broadly speaking, we can distinguish three stages in this process.

When a certain discipline is just beginning to emerge as a separate study in its own right, the scientists concerned with this discipline typically spend a great deal of their time just collecting and classifying facts. They may not have a very clear idea of what these facts will eventually be used to explain, and just be going on a 'hunch' that there is, indeed, something there to be explained. This first stage is christened the 'taxonomic' stage, the adjective simply meaning 'concerned with classification'.

Next in this suggested three-stage process comes the 'nomological' stage. The name this time implies 'concerned with discovering laws'. Here, various sets of observations made by scientists in the discipline have been related to each other in the form of empirical generalizations. In other words, whereas at the taxonomic stage our time was taken up with sorting out observations into classes $A, B, C, \ldots$, in a way that we thought might be most useful for our scientific purposes, now we are able to say that events in class A are closely related to events in class C, less closely related to events in class B, and so on. Here, of course, we are talking in terms of inductive observation, usually backed up with statistical testing. We may still have no very solid ideas about the explanatory framework into which these observed relationships are to be fitted.

In fact, the elaboration of such a framework marks the third of the suggested stages of development—this one being known as the 'theoretical' (or 'hypothetical') stage. Once again, the derivation of the names tells the story: this is the stage at which we have a framework of theory—of linked hypotheses—which we can use to explain the relationships we have observed in our particular bit of the p-domain, and to help in predicting further relationships in it.

As with all such neat 'check-list' pictures, this one needs to be taken with a pinch of salt. In so far as the 'three stages' do describe the development of scientific disciplines, they obviously merge into one another rather than being separated by sharp dividing lines. Further, of course, within any one science there may well be some areas of subject matter that have got as far as the theoretical stage, while others may still be at the nomological or even the taxonomic stage. And even when a science, or part of a science, has got to the theoretical stage, it has still by no means arrived at an end-point. As we have seen, no science has yet developed a theory that can conclusively be tied up in deductive terms with a specific set of starting postulates (we say that no scientific theory has yet been fully *axiomatized*.) And on the side of empirical validation, as we also know, it can well be argued that a science can never arrive at the end of its task, since no set of hypotheses can ever be conclusively verified or falsified by reference to observed data.

Where does economics come into all this? In fact, the main interest of the three-stage checklist from our point of view lies in the fact that economics seems *not* to correspond to it. Several economic writers, notably Professor Machlup, have pointed out that economics is a 'hybrid', in a way that no other science seems to be.

Right from the earliest days of the existence of economics in the form in which we now know it, there has been a recognizable body of deductive 'economic theory'. For the same length of time, there has also been empirical investigation going on in economics: in earlier times, the emphasis was on the taxonomic aspect, though a nomological side to things began to emerge very early on. In more recent years, needless to say, the picture of empirical investigation in economics has been very much in the nomological image, with great emphasis placed on statistical analysis as a tool of investigation.

Economists, then, have both a well-elaborated structure of deductive theory and a solid base of inductive observation as the constituents of their science. Thus, according to the suggested three-stage development scheme, economics *should* qualify, on the face of it, as a fully fledged theoretical science, on a par, say, with physics or mechanics.

But, writers like Machlup have suggested, there is an important difference between economics and these other scientific areas. In the physical sciences, there are clear links between the deductive and inductive sides of the picture; in economics, these links are vague or nonexistent. Despite the vast effort that has been put into empirical investigation in economics, this work seems to have succeeded only in building up a body of inductive generalizations, which cannot readily be related to the deductive theory already existing in the c-domain. Some writers have expressed this idea by saying that, on the empirical side of the economic picture, we have built up an accumulation of 'inductive theory'—that is, a set of inductive generalizations which may tie in with each other to some extent, and which can sometimes be used to try to make 'predictions' based purely on past inductive evidence, without back-up from any explanatory framework.

In the pictured three-stage scheme of development of a 'typical science', the establishment of this 'inductive theory' is a necessary forerunner to the elaboration of deductive theory proper. The content of the deductive theory is largely suggested in the first place by the inductive evidence previously built up; and, as the deductive theory is further developed, it is continually checked back against further inductive observation. In economics, by contrast, 'inductive theory' and deductive theory seem to have followed more or less separate paths of development. Economic theory and observation, far from being closely interwoven with one another, seem to have a gulf between them.

We shall shortly discuss how far it is sensible to suggest the existence of this gulf between 'inductive theory' and theory proper. For now, let us take it that such a gulf does exist. What will be its methodological consequences?

Recall the positivist suggestion that economists should 'test by predictions only' (Section 6.3.1). In a science like physics, which has pretty clearly reached the theoretical stage of development, this idea of 'testing by predictions' means that the low-level implications of deductive theory are set against real-world data; and according to how well these 'predictions' fit the data, we either regard the relevant higher-level statements as being better substantiated or less well substantiated than before. This is just the familiar 'hypothetico-deductive' story. But now consider, by contrast, the process of 'testing by predictions' in economics. Suppose you make a prediction on the basis of 'inductive theory'—that is, on the basis of past empirical evidence you have built up that relates to the situation you want to predict. The time comes when you can compare your predictions with real-world outcomes. Have you thereby made a check on the strength of any higher-level statements of economic theory? The answer, of course, is 'no'. Your prediction was not in fact a deductive inference *from* any higher-level statements, and so clearly it cannot serve as a check *of* any such statements.

Apriorists and analytical economists have been quick to point out the methodological trap which lies in wait here: namely that when economists check empirical predictions against outcomes, they may *think* they are somehow thereby 'testing' propositions in economic theory, when in fact they are not.

Admittedly, if we take the idea of a 'gulf' literally, then the deductive side of the picture seems to be in a pretty serious plight as well. If there really are no connections between the c-domain and the p-domain in economics, then what we call 'economic theory' is doomed to float for ever in a theoretical no-man's-land: it has to be regarded as a 'wholly deductive' abstract system, like algebra or formal logic. We have already noted (Section 6.2.2) that this picture seems intuitively wrong as a description of economic reasoning. In the simplest terms, if economic theory *is* totally abstract, then why does it work when it is applied to real-life problems? If we admit that the prescriptions arrived at by means of theoretical reasoning *do* 'work' in reality more often than could be expected from mere chance, then we are saying, by definition, that there *are* links between the economic c-domain and reality.

As I shall suggest in later sections, there are indeed such links, though their nature may not be quite the same as the philosopher of general science would normally envisage. At the same time, the suggested gulf between theory and observation in economics does exist; the next section explores the reasons for its existence.

6.3.4 *The problems of validation*

The pictured 'gulf' between economic theory and economic observation reflects features of the economic p-domain which pose special problems for the economic scientist if he tries to 'validate' his theoretical propositions in hypothetico-deductive style. In Chapter 5, we looked at some distinctive features of economic data. What significance do these have when it comes to the attempted validation of economic theory?

We have seen, for a start, that not all the special features of economic data need cause particular problems in validation. Though explanation in economics can be either mechanistic or teleological, this need not in principle make for any special difficulty in relating the c-domain to the p-domain; it will simply mean that the contents of both domains, and the rules of correspondence by which they can be related, will be different from those met with in physical science. Likewise, we have noted that though the economic scientist must deal with other people's normative views and choices, there is no convincing case to show that thereby his *own* scientific reasoning need be tinged with normative notions. We have registered also that the 'fuzziness' sometimes attributed to economic data is not really any more a characteristic of economics than of any other scientific field.

But there are two fundamental features of the economic p-domain that do pose problems when we try to apply the physical scientist's ideas of validation. They are, first, the inability of the economist to make controlled experiments, except in very unusual circumstances; and second, the fact that in economics there seem to be no long-standing constant relationships between observed variables.

As we already know (Section 5.3), the effect of the economist's inability to make controlled experiments is that he encounters great difficulty in tying up cause and effect in his observed situations. We saw that in physical science, though strictly speaking the scientist can never set up a 'perfect control', and hence can never be entirely certain of his cause–effect relations, nevertheless it is usually possible to get a high degree of intersubjective agreement on the matter. But the economist—faced with a multitude of possible 'causes' for what he observes, some of them possibly unknown and unsuspected—has to resort to the dubious substitute of statistical testing in order to get any idea at all of cause-and-effect relations. Intersubjective agreement on the interpretation of data may be difficult to come by, and the element of ignorance attaching to the results may be the most significant feature of the empirical scene.

It is easy to see how this problem hampers attempts at the validation of theory. The economist, far more than the physical scientist or even the biological scientist, has difficulty in knowing exactly what set of hypotheses he is testing. Suppose he is trying to test a hypothesis 'H causes P', given conditions $A_1, A_2, \ldots, A_n$.' He goes on to establish the provisional truth or possible falsity of his prediction P. But he will usually have great problems in establishing convincingly whether the success or failure of his prediction was caused by the truth or falsity of the suggested causal link between H and P, since it could have been that he was mistaken about the fulfilment of conditions $A_1, A_2, \ldots$; or, indeed, there could have been another cause or causes operating as well as cause H (or instead of cause H) to bring about the prediction P.

In other words, the process of reasoning upwards in the deductive structure of theory is much more hazardous for the economist than for the experimental scientist. Different methodologists have attached differing degrees of importance to this difficulty, according to the school of thought to which they belong. 'Positive' economists and moderate empiricists argue that, despite the admitted problems resulting from lack of experimental control, economists should still try to follow the copybook version of hypothetico-deductive testing as closely as possible; they suggest that future improvements in statistical method may help to reduce the problems of tying up cause and effect. Analytical economists and apriorists, on the other hand, might argue that the lack of experimental control in economics virtually disables any attempt at reasoning upwards in the structure of theory. The only workable way you can proceed, they might suggest, is to start from higher-level statements which themselves need no testing, and reason downwards from these to arrive at 'predictions'.

Let us turn now to the second feature of the economic p-domain which hampers the straightforward application of hypothetico–deductive testing: namely, the lack of constant relations between economic variables. In Section 5.1.7, we noted that views differed on whether economic relationships were somehow *inherently* unstable (perhaps because of some feature of human free will) or whether it was simply a matter of the inadequacy of current statistical predictive techniques. What was certain, however, was that in the present state of economic science, no constant relationships between variables had yet been discovered—none, at least, with a degree of stability remotely resembling those found in physical science.

Once again, it is not difficult to see what problems this presents for any attempt at hypothetico-deductive testing on the basis of predictions. The whole notion of 'testing theory', as recounted by philosophers of physical science, hinges on the idea that there *are* permanent (or at least very stable) relationships in the p-domain, which can be brought into contact with the constructs in the c-domain. Recall Professor Margenau's notion of testing as being a series of 'circuits' from p-domain to c-domain and back again (Section 4.6). Now suppose that you try to start one of these 'circuits', by making a set of observations of the p-domain which give you a particular relationship between your observed variables. You reason upwards to the higher-level statements in which you are interested. In the usual hypothetico-deductive manner, you see whether these are in accord with the empirical evidence; perhaps revise them a bit; then reason back down again to get to further directly testable consequences, i.e., 'predictions'. But suppose that while you were doing this, the configuration of things in the p-domain changed, in such a way that the relationship which you first observed no longer holds? If so, you would discover that your 'predictions' turn out not to fit the empirical evidence as it now exists. But you would usually have no means of knowing *why* this is. You would be left guessing whether the relationships in the p-domain *had* changed since your original observation; or whether your original observation, or your subsequent observation, were thrown out by observational error; or whether you made a mistake in the deductive reasoning by which you arrived at the prediction.

Here, once again, the different schools of methodological thought interpret this difficulty in different ways. The positivist or moderate empiricist would hold that, while these problems do exist in the current 'state of the art', nevertheless it is only by keeping on trying that we can ever arrive at a point where economics *can* discover stable relationships in its p-domain—it is just that as yet, we have either not succeeded in discovering what these relationships are, or that the methods we are using to investigate them are not good enough. The analytical economist or apriorist would counter this by saying that any further search for stable relationships in economics is futile anyway, since so many years of concentrated effort have failed to bring any to light.

In trying to appraise these differences in methodological attitudes to the two 'problems of validation' discussed in this section, we come up against the usual difficulty—that these attitudes concern not just what economics *has* achieved to date, but what it may potentially achieve in future. It *may* be defeatist to suggest that the problems of validation can never be eliminated by future improvements in knowledge and in techniques. On the other hand, it *may* be unrealistic to say that economists should go on trying to beat these problems, given that so far they have had so little success in this direction. These are matters of opinion. What is a matter of fact is that to ignore the importance of these problems *now*—in the current state of the economic art—is an undoubted error. As things are at the moment, empirical investigation in economics—particularly the notion of 'testing by predictions'—meets hazards which are on a totally different scale from those encountered by the experimental scientist. In so far as there is a 'gulf' between the economic c-domain and p-domain, these problems of validation must largely account for it.

But, if this well-developed body of deductive reasoning that we call 'economic theory' has not been elaborated in the way pictured by philosophers of physical science, then how has it been elaborated? And given that it is not just an abstract structure, but does have some links with reality, how are these links forged? Various writers have made suggestions on these questions; in discussing them, we move into an area of economic methodology which is still very much in process of development.

6.3.5 Theories v. models

Several writers have suggested that the economist meets his particular problems by dealing, not in theories, but in *models*. What is a 'model', in this sense of the word, and how does it differ from a 'theory'?

Straight away, we need to note that in the context of economic studies, there is an unfortunate double meaning attached to the term 'model'. If you have been studying economics for any length of time, you will undoubtedly have come across the word in its econometric sense. (In fact, 'econometrics' and 'model-building' are very often taken as meaning one and the same thing.) Though this econometric usage is related to some extent to the sense in which I will be using the term 'model' in the present section, there are nevertheless some basic differences in the two ideas, and for now I invite you to take it that we are here talking about something entirely different from an econometric 'model'.

Philosophers of science, in fact, use the word 'model' in a sense very close to the one it has in everyday conversation: a 'model', in the simplest terms, in a scaled-down, simplified version of a real-life situation.

In physical and applied science, scientists sometimes make use of models in a quite literal sense: for instance, a scale model of an aircraft may be tested in a wind-tunnel to find out its aerodynamic properties. By extension of this approach, scientists often use 'mental pictures' of models as an aid to explanation and understanding of the real-life phenomena they are investigating. To quote an often-used example, you can picture the collisions between molecules in a body of gas by comparing them with the collisions of billiard-balls on a billiard-table. In this case, of course, the imagined billiard-balls are the models for the actual gas molecules.

Taking the process of abstraction a step further, the scientist could give up bothering to picture his billiard-balls, and instead draw up a set of equations which described the interactions of the balls as they bounced off one another. Then this set of equations would in its turn act as a model for the equations which described the movements of the gas molecules.

Having reasoned this far, you should have no difficulty seeing how economic reasoning can likewise be envisaged as using models. The well-known supply-and-demand diagram, with its clear-cut schedules and its equilibrium point, can be seen as a model of the complicated interactions between buyers and sellers that take place on a real-life market. Those ghostly figures of the 'economic man', the 'rational consumer', and the 'profit-maximizing businessman' appear as models of real-life people, whose motives and actions may not be so clear-cut nor easily identifiable. And so on, for many more instances of economic reasoning.

Since, as economists, we are so familiar with this kind of mental device, we will have little difficulty in working out what are the purposes of using models; and likewise we will find it relatively easy to see what may be the shortcomings of reasoning in this way. The point of thinking in terms of models, of course, is that by simplifying a real-life situation, we hope to be able to understand more clearly the nature of that situation—to work out how we might best intervene in that situation to bring about the real-life results that we want, and how events might develop if we do not intervene in that way. For instance, to return to an example we have already met: suppose a government is contemplating putting a purchase tax on a certain product. Someone has suggested that, 'This means that the entire burden of the tax falls on the consumers of that good.' To try to check this assertion, you *could* wait until the tax was imposed, then go out and laboriously collect statistics of prices to consumers, returns to producers, and amounts bought and sold. You might succeed in producing some convincing conclusion; more likely you would not, because of all the possible disturbing factors and errors in data collection that would bedevil the exercise. (And what is more, by the time you had finished all this, people might well have lost interest in the original question.) Far more readily, you could use the well-known supply-and-demand model to show straight away that, given 'normal' shapes of the supply and demand schedules, some of the tax burden would be transferred to the producers.

Even if you have only just begun to study economics, you will have no difficulty in coining many similar examples. In doing so, you will also easily see the pitfalls which attach to reasoning in terms of economic models of this kind. We said that a model is a simplified picture of the real-life situation. In simplifying anything, we need to drop some of its real-life details—and this is where the problem arises. In choosing what he thinks is an appropriate model by which to explain a given real-life situation, the economist needs to make a choice of *what* features of that situation to leave out of the model. Needless to say, he will try to keep in the features which he thinks are relevant to the solution of the problem in hand, and leave out those which he judges to be irrelevant. If he gets this choice wrong, then the chances clearly are that his analysis of the problem and its solution will be wrong as well.

Recall, for instance, that we have just used a straightforward supply-and-demand model to make our deduction about the incidence of the purchase tax. As you will know, one of the things usually 'assumed away' in the simple model is the fact that the expected 'equilibrium' is not always attained very quickly—or indeed, may sometimes not be attained at all. This in turn is due to all sorts of factors that are likewise simplified out of the model—ignorance or inertia on the part of buyers or producers, brand loyalty, rigidities in pricing arising from uncertainty, and so on. If any of these possible influences really turns out to be operative in the market you are considering, then your simplified model may give you a wildly wrong answer. To name just one of the many things that could happen, suppose consumers, instead of reacting to the purchase tax by cutting the quantity they bought, felt that even greater price rises were on the way, and so started buying up stocks of the product? If they were still doing this during the time in which your 'solution' was meant to apply, then your reputation as an analyst would suffer.

What has been said so far in this section is pretty familiar to most economists. In our discipline, we do talk quite often of reasoning in terms of 'models', using this term (outside econometrics) as a sort of vague equivalent of 'theories'. It is only relatively recently that some economic methodologists have begun to explore the formal differences between theories and models, and to try to bring out the implications of these for economic reasoning.

If we are looking for a cut-and-dried explanation of how models differ from theories, we will not find it in any reference book of the general philosophy of science. Physical scientists mix up the terms 'theory' and 'model' just as indiscriminately as economists do; and philosophers have not yet established full agreement on what the distinction between the two terms should be. However, there are some distinguishing features which are quite well agreed, and we have these to go on in the discussion which now follows.

We have seen that a model has the characteristic of being a simplification of reality. Is it this feature that marks out a model from a theory? The generally accepted answer, as we shall now see, is: yes and no, depending on what exactly you mean by 'simplification'.

We do not determine the essential characteristic of a model merely by noting that it uses simplified pictures of key concepts. For a start, according to the usual textbook account, theories simplify in just this way. Their high-level statements are about clearly defined constructs which 'simplify out' the fuzzy edges of ignorance and uncertainty that apply in the real world. As you move to successively lower levels of a theory, so you introduce more and more qualifications—which just amounts to saying that you progressively drop your initial simplifications. And turning now to look at models, we see that these may also contain varying degrees of simplification; as we have just noted, the choice of how much simplification to retain in a model is a matter for decision by the analyst. In the example on which we have been working, for instance, we could perfectly well have dropped the simplifying assumption that consumers' behaviour is not modified by expectations. We would still have been using a model, though the degree of simplification would have been less than in the basic form of the model concerned. Nowhere is there any rule-book which says: 'At *this* degree of simplification, your reasoning ceases to have the nature of a model, and becomes a theory instead.' A theory can incorporate as many or as few simplifying assumptions as the economist likes to consider, and so can a model.

The distinction between theory and model does not turn just on *how much* is left out, but rather on *what* is left out. To be more exact: a *theory* always includes statements specifying exactly what part of the p-domain the theory applies to; a *model* does not include this set of statements, or at least, it only includes them incompletely.

It is useful to translate this suggestion into the formal terms of Section 4.6. We noted there that, in checking a hypothesis against observable 'predictions', you had to employ a number of auxiliary hypotheses before you could deduce your needed prediction. Thus, if H is our hypothesis, and P our prediction, the hypothetical we use as the basis for our 'test' was seen to be not just:

If H, then P;

but rather

If $(H$ and $A_1, A_2, \ldots, A_n)$, then P;

where the A's are, of course, the auxiliary hypotheses.

Now, we have said that a 'theory' always includes a set of statements specifying the theory's applicability. This merely means that, somewhere among the A's, there will be a particular set of auxiliary hypotheses which do this job of specification—which tells us the places, times, and conditions in which the theory is meant to apply. In symbolic terms we could re-christen these statements S's, leaving the rest of the auxiliary hypotheses labelled A's. Thus our hypothetical would now become:

If $(H$ and $S_1, S_2, \ldots, S_n$ and $A_1, A_2, \ldots, A_n)$, then P.

On the suggested distinction between a 'model' and a 'theory', therefore, a theory must specify fully the nature of the S's, while a model does not do so.

In these terms, the testing of a theory can be split into three phases. The scientist will have to establish convincingly, first of all, that he really is investigating a situation in which the theory is supposed to apply—that is, he has to gain intersubjective agreement on the material truth of the S's at the time and place of his investigation. Then he has to gain similar agreement on the material truth of the other auxiliary hypotheses, whatever they may be; and finally, he must gain agreement on the material truth or falsity of the prediction—that is, the consequent of his hypothetical. Only on the basis of all three of these phases can he justifiably argue back to his higher-level hypothesis. If his prediction turns out false (to an acceptable degree of intersubjective agreement), *and* if he has also established agreement on the truth of his S's and his A's, then he must regard his hypothesis—the 'H' in the syllogism—as having been falsified, or at least seriously weakened. But if he has not managed to establish agreement on the truth of any one of his S's or of his A's, then he becomes unable to make a convincing link between his prediction and his original hypothesis.

If we accept that in a 'model', the nature of the S's is not fully specified, then it follows that it will *never* be possible to reason convincingly from the truth or falsity of predictions to the truth or falsity of the model's higher-level statements—because we will never be able to be sure that the conditions of applicability, our S's, have or have not been fulfilled at the time and place of our investigation. To put it in the formally preferable language of falsificationism: if our prediction is falsified by observation, we can never convincingly reason that the higher-level statements in our model are therefore false, because we can never be sure that the situation we have been studying was really one to which our model was meant to apply.

It is not difficult to see why this suggested distinction between models and theories has held immediate appeal to those economic methodologists who have been trying to fit the pattern of economic method into the context of the philosophy of general science. By suggesting that the economist deals in models instead of theories, we get a ready-made rationalization of the 'gulf' that exists between deductive theory and inductive observation in our discipline. The economic c-domain is pictured as being occupied not by a theory, but by a multiplicity of models. These may be linked deductively to some extent, and they may be of greater or lesser degrees of abstractness, according to the number of 'simplifying assumptions' that each one retains or drops. But what they all have in common, according to this account, is that they lack the sets of statements that would be needed to specify fully the conditions for the applicability of each model—and which of course, by that token, would transform the 'model' in question into a 'theory'.

Satisfyingly enough, this story also accounts for the fact that in economics, 'competing' hypotheses seem to co-exist happily for long periods of time, rather than being 'weeded out' in the manner of the physical sciences. Suppose, for instance, you take these two contradictory statements:

1. Businessmen try to maximize profits; and
2. Businessmen aim not at maximum profit, but at a lower and safer profit level.

In the conventional account of the validation of a theory, these would be

146

'competing' hypotheses about the behaviour of businessmen, and it would be the aim of the scientist to test them against observation (either directly, or indirectly via their competing predictions) so that, eventually, the 'better' of the two hypotheses could be identified.

But if we reconstruct economic reasoning, not as a developing theory, but as a collection of models, there is no reason why we should expect to identify either of the two hypotheses as being the 'better'. We lack complete knowledge of the conditions in which either hypothesis is supposed to apply, and so empirical testing can never bring about intersubjective agreement on which of the hypotheses is the 'better' of the two.

So much for this account of the nature and use of 'models' in economic reasoning. Briefly, what can we make of it in our role as assessors of reconstructed logic?

Perhaps it can best be seen as an extension of the methodological approach which I have called 'moderate empiricism' (Section 6.2.5). It provides an attractive explanation of why this approach—sensible-seeming in itself—has so far been notably unsuccessful in closing the gap between economic theorizing and empirical observation.

Certainly the 'models v. theories' distinction, by stressing the notion of the *applicability* of higher-level statements, must represent a considerable advance on any reconstruction of economic reasoning which fails to do so. Some positivist writers, in particular, have seemed to be unaware of the problems of establishing applicability, speaking as though 'competing hypotheses' in economics could unambiguously be identified, and could one day (given only some improvement in observational methods) be weeded out in the 'textbook' hypothetico-deductive fashion. In this view they have been more optimistic than philosophers of general science, who have drawn attention to the difficulties of specifying and testing applicability, even in a 'hard' science like physics.

In following this section through, you may have recalled that we first met the idea of applicability, not when we were talking about moderate empiricism, but in relation to quite another school of methodological thought—that of the analytical economists. In fact, long before the 'models v. theories' distinction had come in for detailed discussion by economic writers, the analytical school had established the concept of applicability as a central feature of their reasoning.

6.3.6 Models and the analytical view

Analytical economists have not usually used the term 'model'; more often, they have spoken of the 'theorems' of economics. But if we allow for this and other small differences in wording, we see at once what a striking similarity there is between the analytical view and the moderate-empiricist view, once the latter view has been modified to take account of the 'models v. theories' distinction. The analytical economist speaks of his theorems as deductively linked sets of statements in the c-domain, and stresses that a given theorem may or may not be applicable to a particular real-life situation; the moderate empiricist says exactly the same of his models.

When the analytical economist is formulating his theorems, he uses common sense to try to choose sets of starting statements that are likely to be applicable to the real-world problem he is investigating. The moderate empiricist, in choosing the initial assumptions to incorporate into his model, is doing exactly the same thing.

Both schools, as we have seen, also hold that both the 'assumptions' and the 'predictions' of a model should be subjected to direct factual checking wherever possible. To be sure, the analytical economist believes that the best way to 'test the predictions' of a model is to put into practice the policy prescriptions that follow from it. But this, if you like, can be seen as just one variation of hypothetico-deductive testing. The prescribed policy measure is itself the 'hypothesis' (or, more precisely, one of the set of linked hypotheses) under test, and the expected economic outcome is the 'prediction'.

Further, as we have also noted, the failure of policy prescriptions need not lead the analytical economist to regard the higher-level statements in his theorem as having been 'falsified'; he may suspect, instead, that he has made a mistake about the applicability of that particular theorem to the real-world problem under study. The moderate empiricist, in very much the same way, holds that the failure of predictions need not 'falsify' his model—because, once again, the question of applicability remains in doubt.

Have we now come round to realizing that the analytical and moderate-empiricist schools are in fact saying exactly the same thing about economic reasoning, only in somewhat different words? The answer probably is: not quite.

In suggesting what may be the real differences between the two approaches, we need to engage in a fair amount of 'reconstruction of logic'. Indeed, unless we are careful, our 'reconstruction' will go too far beyond the bounds of what actually has been written by economists in the two schools. But without too much guesswork, we can sketch out fairly clearly the ways in which the two methodological positions diverge from one another.

Recall, first, what moderate empiricists see as the defining feature of a model: namely, that the conditions for its applicability are not fully specified. As we know, this means that a model can never be falsified on the evidence of false predictions. Now, looking at the other side of this coin: suppose the predictions from a model turn out to be correct? It is obvious that this does not 'verify' a model, any more than false predictions 'falsify' it. It does give us some reason to suppose—subject to the usual logical problem of testing—that the model *has been* applicable to the situation in which we applied it. But, because the conditions for the model's applicability are not fully spelled out, we have no way of estimating how likely it is that the same model will be applicable to any *future* situation. If we do attempt to judge a model's future applicability, we face *ignorance*, not uncertainty: we are unable to express our judgement in probability terms, but must speak only of a possibility.

We saw that some moderate empiricists have recommended that economists should try to convert their models into theories, by working out more precisely the conditions of applicability of higher-level statements. Admittedly, they have never made it very clear how this is to be done; but if it could be achieved, it would mean that ignorance over the applicability of models could be replaced by uncertainty. If the auxiliary hypotheses defining applicability were fully specified, then it would become possible to try to establish the probability of the material truth of these auxiliary hypotheses by means of inductive-statistical investigation, just as with any other hypotheses. Economists would thus be able to estimate in advance how probable it was that a particular set of higher-level statements would apply to a given real-world situation.

On the analytical view also, economists face ignorance about the applicability of their theorems to future events. But the reason for this ignorance is not seen as lying necessarily in incomplete specification of applicability conditions. The analytical account would suggest, instead, that *whether or not* these conditions are fully spelled out, it must remain impossible to convert the ignorance over a theorem's future applicability into uncertainty by means of inductive observation. This interpretation hinges on the acceptance by analytical economists of a proposition which is no stranger to us: namely, that in the economic p-domain, no stable constants have been identified.

It is clear what this implies for the notion that the future applicability of models might be judged by inductive observation, as the moderate empiricists have suggested. Suppose you do succeed in fully specifying the applicability conditions for a given model (or theorem, call it what you will); and suppose you then carry out inductive testing to try to determine the applicability of that model. Suppose also that you get a set of results which is convincing in statistical terms. That set of results, like any empirical data, will relate to a certain time, place, and configuration of the economic p-domain. Now suppose that you try to apply the same set of higher-level statements to another time, place, or configuration of economic events. It *may* be that your model is still applicable to this new situation. On the other hand, it may not; and given that in economics—in contrast with the experimental sciences—no stable constants are to be found, you have no means of knowing in probability terms whether your model *will* be applicable to the new situation, no matter how much inductive testing you do of its applicability to past situations.

Indeed, as writers like Robbins have pointed out, attempts to use inductive testing in this way are not only to be regarded as a waste of time, on the analytical interpretation; they may be positively undesirable, in that they may give the economist a false sense of security about the applicability of a particular model. A model may indeed have applied very accurately to a past configuration of events, according to the evidence of statistical testing. But by the time you come to try to apply the model in policy terms, the configuration of things may have changed—and your statistical testing can give you no indication of the probability of such a change.

In short, then, we see that the analytical school's denial of inductive-statistical testing as a correspondence rule is not merely wilful abandonment of scientific rigour. On the contrary, it is a purposeful response to the premise that in the real world of economics, there are no long-standing stable relationships.

6.4 Various views revisited

Of the various views of economic method which we have discussed in this chapter, we have noted that the most extreme—at each end of the spectrum—fail to stand up under investigation as being convincing reconstructions of economic practice. The extreme apriorist view fails to make out a case for its suggestion that all the theorems of economics can be deduced from starting statements that are materially true *a priori*. We can modify this extreme view by admitting—as apriorist writers have themselves occasionally hinted—that other, empirically derived, statements are needed to complete the deductive structure. In doing so, we certainly achieve a more credible reconstruction of economic reasoning—but at the same time, we rob the apriorist view of its own identifying feature.

At the other end of the scale of views, we have also had cause to reject the extreme positivists' suggestion that an economic hypothesis should be judged purely on the success of its predictions. We saw that even in the philosophy of general science, this extreme position had long ago been discredited: by denying the relevance of the material truth of the antecedents of higher-level hypotheses, it makes it logically impossible for the scientist to explain the phenomena he investigates. We noted, too, that despite the inadequacy of this position, it persists in some general economic literature as the 'ideal' method for economic science to follow. In reality, not only does the extreme positivist account provide a faulty reconstruction of economic method, but there are signs that it fails to correspond to what is actually done by the economists who prescribe it as the desirable procedure of economic investigation.

As regards the possible harmful effects which these extreme positivist ideas may have exerted on the actual practice of economics, one of course can only speculate. But, as Professor O'Brien has pointed out, much current work in economics seems to be running into two methodological dead-ends. On the side of theory, elaborate structures of reasoning are built up on theoretical assumptions which are openly admitted to be wildly 'unrealistic'—which, that is, could not conceivably be made applicable to any real-

150

world problems. On the empirical side, complex statistical procedures are used to try to arrive at 'predictions', which give us little or no practical insight into the economic causes operating behind events. Whether or not these two ills actually result from the influence of extreme positivism, they certainly correspond to the positivist prescription of 'judging by predictions, and not by the realism of assumptions'.

What is more, this emphasis on the importance of predictions has come to be reflected in a strange view professed by quite a number of economists who follow the positivists' reconstructed logic: namely that unless economic reasoning yields predictions which are testable in practice, then that reasoning can have no relation to reality. Here is Professor Lipsey, for instance:

> What has always seemed ludicrously inconsistent to me is that some economists should hold the view that economic theories cannot be tested empirically while at the same time vociferously advocating particular economic policies. [We should] . . . recognise as inconsistent the economist who gives strong advice to governments on how to run their economic affairs while at the same time denying that economics can make predictions about the world that are precise enough to be testable.

In taking up this position, Lipsey seems to be dismissing out of hand not only the apriorist approach, but also the 'commonsense' procedure of the analytical school; and, as we have seen, this is quite a sweeping dismissal, since the analytical view is just as much empirical—concerned with reality—as is the positivist school. Furthermore, to dismiss analytical reasoning in economics is to dismiss the whole of 'theory' as it now exists—or at least to write it off as a second-best, pending the time when 'testing by predictions' will provide us with something better.

Rejection of the two extreme views—apriorist and positivist—leaves us with the two more moderate positions: those of the analytical economists and the moderate empiricists. It seems clear that the latter two accounts are the real contenders for the title of the 'correct' reconstruction of economic method. Recalling first the moderate-empiricist account: we saw that while it calls for systematic empirical testing of economic propositions, it admits that this testing can be directed not just at 'predictions', i.e., lowest-level statements, but also, wherever possible, at higher-level statements as well. Indeed, it recognizes that unless we can give some idea of the material truth of the antecedents of our predictions, then the predictions themselves tell us nothing that can help us in our task of economic explanation. In a recent and still-developing modification of this position, it is suggested that what we call economic 'theory' is really a collection of 'models'—systems of higher-level statements which lack a complete set of auxiliary hypotheses specifying exactly the circumstances in which the higher-level statements are meant to apply. This, as we saw, is one way of accounting for the 'gulf' between deductive reasoning and inductive observation in economics. On this account, the path of development for economic theory must lie in the clearer and clearer specification of the applicability rules for the existing models, hand-in-hand with improvements in the methods of inductive-statistical analysis which will allow the applicability of the models to be judged—the eventual objective being the conversion of this network of models into a recognizable theory, in the sense in which this term is used by the philosopher of physical science.

Though the older view, which I have here called 'analytical', does not use the language of 'models', and has sometimes been seen both by its opponents and its advocates as representing an approach totally at variance with that of the physical sciences, we have seen that the difference between it and the moderate-empiricist position is less than might appear at first sight. It, too, sees economic 'theory' as being a collection of theorems, which can be brought into play in assessing real-life situations in so far as a particular theorem is judged to be applicable to a given real-life problem. On the analytical view, however, whether or not the conditions for the applicability of theorems are well enough specified to be testable, there is no need to test them, since it is judged obvious at a commonsense level that the starting statements used will be applicable to a very wide range of real-life situations. Formally, this means that the analytical economist admits to his rules of correspondence the procedure of commonsense observation. By so doing, he accepts the permanent presence of ignorance as regards the future applicability of his theorems—not just as an anti-scientific whim, but because of the premise that economic events anyway fail to exhibit the stable constants which appear in the physical sciences. The analytical view therefore emphasizes, not attempts at 'validation' of higher-level statements, but rather the process of deduction *from* these statements which allows the economist to arrive at real-life policy recommendations.

Is there any way of saying which of these two moderate approaches to economic reasoning is to be considered the 'better'? It would be rash to attempt any such judgement, given that the journal literature contains more controversy and confusion on the subject than it does agreement. In fact, the aim of this chapter has been to take you to the stage where you can begin, if you like, to follow this literature through, and thereby build your own opinion of the road ahead for economic method.

Perhaps the real answer to this problem is that there *is* no one answer. Rather than trying to set up either approach as the 'right' one and the other as 'wrong', it may be more fruitful to stress that neither has sole call on the title of 'scientific method' in economics—just as neither can be dismissed as 'unscientific'. It may well be that the analytical approach is relatively well suited to some subject areas of economics, the moderate-empiricist approach to others. Advocates of either view have, perhaps naturally, tended to ignore the multiplicity of topics covered by economic studies, and to talk as though *all* economic propositions were clear to common sense, or alternatively as though *all* economic propositions had to be established by inductive-statistical means before they could safely be entertained. It seems fair to guess that the real situation is somewhere between these two extremes.

Certainly, as we know, the past track-record shows the analytical view as by far the more important contributor to the existing body of knowledge that we call 'economic theory'. But we know also that no stable constants are to be found in economic studies, and there seems no reason why the realm of economic methodology should be any exception. The analytical approach may continue to provide economics with the bulk of its useful rationale in the future, as it has in the past; or the moderate-empiricist approach may take over the leading role. If we try to gauge how likely is either outcome, we meet that familiar component of most real-life economic reasoning—namely, ignorance.

Before leaving this discussion, I should briefly add that my aim has been to review economic reasoning in terms which could be directly judged against the yardstick of the 'hypothetico-deductive account' of general science. In doing so, I have deliberately left out any reference to some other views of the progress of economic science, and I invite you to turn to the reading guide for information on these. (At the same time, I apologize to any advanced readers who feel that these omissions are unforgivable).

One such approach is that which sees scientific advance as being a sociological process (approximately speaking) and which is exemplified by the work of Kuhn and Lakatos, already referred to in Chapter 4.

Another view, this time peculiar to the social sciences, and indeed to economics especially, is that of *historicism*: the doctrine that history evolves according to ascertainable patterns, and that the main job of the economic scientist is to try to discern these patterns, so that the policy-maker can be guided in his long-term efforts to achieve the kind of economic change he desires. This view underlies Marxian thinking, as well as being held by various schools of modern non-Marxian economists. As with the approaches of Kuhn and Lakatos, so with historicism: I personally feel that their emphasis on the longer-term development of economic science takes them rather far from the day-by-day process of investigation and research which it has been my main job to describe in this book. Hence their banishment to the reading guide—in sources, however, which I hope you will find time to follow through.

Reading guide: Chapter 6

There is a very wide choice of texts which will introduce you to the methods of mathematical economics. The one I mention in Section 6.1 is by R. Morley, *Mathematics for Modern Economics*.[60] For discussion of the role and limitations of algebraic language in economics, see the essays in Krupp, *The*

Structure of Economic Science[42] by W. J. Baumol and by E. Rotwein; and read Chapter 5 of Boulding, *Economics as a Science.*[7]

As you will realize, the controversies over method which this chapter has covered are so wide-ranging that even a selective bibliography would run to cumbersome length. What I shall do in this reading guide, therefore, is first to give some leading statements of each of the methodological viewpoints described in Section 6.2; then cite a few key articles which discuss these viewpoints. In the bibliographies of these latter articles, you will find ample material with which to pursue methodological controversy through the journals in as much detail as you wish.

One book by von Mises, *The Ultimate Foundation of Economic Science,*[58] gives the most condensed statement of his extreme apriorist view. Alternatively, try Chapter 1 of an earlier book by the same author, *Epistemological Problems of Economics.*[57] Von Mises does not suffer fools gladly, and he sprinkles his pages with philosophical jargon. Also, his discussion is occasionally interrupted by passages of what one can only call Right-wing diatribe. But do not be put off by any of this; you will be rewarded with a view of some thought-provoking perspectives on economic method.

To appreciate Robbins's classic presentation of the analytical view, you should now simply read the remaining sections of his *Essay on the Nature and Significance of Economic Science,*[70] or, preferably, read the whole book straight through, including the parts already cited. (Just to illustrate the difficulty of putting sharp dividing lines between schools, you may also detect tinges of the apriorist and moderate-empiricist in places.) Read also the essay by Frank H. Knight, 'What is "Truth" in Economics?'[41]—a short and witty piece of demolition work on the overambitious claims made by some economic 'positivists'. By the way, J. M. Keynes never bothered to spell out his own reconstructed logic at any length, but to confirm him as a member of the analytical school, simply look at the wording on the very first page of *The General Theory of Employment, Interest and Money.*[38]

Passing on to the 'positivist' view: having read the critical assessment of Friedman's methodological stance, you should now certainly check it out for yourself at source, in his essay 'The Methodology of Positive Economics'.[27] Beware, however: it is my view (and one shared by some other writers more distinguished than myself) that the controversy over Friedman's famous article has arisen quite largely because Friedman himself is not entirely sure what he is arguing. So before tackling his essay, make sure you understand the groundwork laid in Section 6.3, to minimize the possibility of getting into a mental tangle when you are reading Friedman's persuasive prose. Be alert, in particular, for his ambiguous use of words: we have discussed the various meanings of 'assumption' and 'realistic' (Section 6.3.2). Also, the first few pages of his essay make it appear as if he was about to discuss the positive/normative distinction, when in fact he does nothing of the kind; apart from these few pages, his essay does not set 'positive' against 'normative', but rather sets 'positive economics', in Friedman's own formulation of 'testing by predictions only', against other ideas which correspond more or less to what I have here called the analytical view.

The moderate-empiricist position is set out in a splendid article by D. P. O'Brien, 'Whither Economics?'.[63] The journal in which the article appears is, perhaps, not one of the most widely available, but do your very best to get your hands on it. This article, in fact, also doubles as one of the 'key articles' which I mentioned at the beginning of the reading guide, since it contains discussion of a range of methodological views and has a truly encyclopaedic bibliography.

Now the other 'key articles': look first at the essay by Martin Bronfenbrenner which begins the collection in Krupp, *The Structure of Economic Science*[42] and in that same book, read Fritz Machlup's paper. Machlup has been a prolific writer on methodology: read also his journal article 'The Problem of Verification in Economics'.[49] (For another slant on the same problem, read also the essay by Kenneth Boulding in Krupp, *The Structure of Economic Science*[42]—though this cannot be called a 'key article' for our purposes, since it contains no bibliography.)

For a specific lead into the controversies arising from Friedman's 'positivist' declaration, read two articles by Eugene Rotwein, 'On "The Methodology of Positive Economics"'[73] and 'Empiricism and Economic Method: Several Views Considered'.[75] I personally think that Rotwein writes with a toe in the positivist camp himself, but see what your own view is on this. There is one article in Rotwein's extensive bibliography which I shall cite here also, since it makes out a particularly concise and clear case against Friedman's 'testing by predictions only': it is D. V. T. Bear and D. Orr, 'Logic and Expediency in Economic Theorizing'.[3]

So much, then, for the 'key articles'; their bibliographies, as I have said, will keep you reading for some considerable time. It remains to mention a few references to more specialized topics covered in this chapter. The most fully developed statement of the nature and use of epistemological models in economics is by Andreas Papandreou, *Economics as a Science*.[64] Papandreou sets out his argument in highly condensed symbolic language, so that it becomes quite a struggle for those (such as myself) who are not used to expressing themselves in this language to extract what is actually being said; if you are prepared to fight your way through this barrier, you will find a great deal of food for thought—and original thought at that, since no one has yet got very far in coherent development of Papandreou's ideas. To gain a perspective on these same issues as they have arisen in the context of physical science and of social science generally, see Caws, *The Philosophy of Science*,[10] Chapter 19, and Kaplan, *The Conduct of Inquiry*,[36] Chapters 30–33; you will still find open questions rather than conclusive answers.

As regards the interpretation of economic science in the light of T. S. Kuhn's account of 'scientific revolutions', see the article by B. J. Loasby, 'Hypothesis and Paradigm in the Theory of the Firm'.[47] The alternative interpretation according to Lakatos's 'methodology of scientific research programmes' is thoroughly covered in a volume of symposium proceedings edited by S. J. Latsis, *Method and Appraisal in Economics*.[45] In that book, the papers by S. J. Latsis, A. W. Coats, and M. Blaug are of particular interest from our point of view, since they discuss not only Lakatos and Kuhn, but also some of the other methodological views examined in this chapter.

It seems strange at first sight that probably the best description of historicism is to be found in a book which argues *against* this viewpoint, namely that by Karl Popper, *The Poverty of Historicism*.[66] But Popper's method is always to set up his opponent's case as strongly as possible before proceeding to criticize it; and in so doing, he gives a crystal-clear explanation of the meaning of historicism. (In my opinion, he has historicism in ruins by the end of the book; but judge this for yourself.)

Finally, for a comprehensive discussion of the topics covered in my Chapters 1–6, but in the context of 'social science generally' rather than economics in particular, read the book by Alan Ryan, *The Philosophy of the Social Sciences*.[75]

Discussion topics: Chapter 6

1. As everyone knows, in Keynesian terms the symbol Y means 'national income'. List (by reference to your textbooks if you have not already learned this) the various different real-world measures of national income which can be used to stand in for the general symbol Y.

2. Likewise, everyone knows the textbook version of the equation for the simple consumption function, $C = a + cY$ (though the intercept and slope coefficients, which I have here called a and c, will probably be called by different symbols in your own textbook). List as many as you can of the unspoken *economic* assumptions which are implied by this simple algebraic expression.

3. Consider (a) the supply-and-demand model, and (b) the Keynesian model of income determination. (If you had a go at topic 4 in the list of discussion topics for Chapter 4, you will already have thought out the starting statements behind the former model.) Among the propositions of each model, which do you think *are* 'obvious to common sense', in the sense of obviously applying at most times and in most places? Which other statements in each model do you think need to be checked empirically on each occasion that economists wish to apply the model concerned?

4. Hark back to the two economic theorems which came into the discussion of the fallacy of composition in Section 2.5.3, namely the 'paradox of thrift' and the demonstration of the difference between individual and mass results of increasing output in agriculture. Review your economic understanding of these theorems, confirming in particular how they use common-

sense starting statements to reach *unexpected* conclusions—unexpected to non-economists, that is. While you are at it, you might also review (if you need to) the economic reasoning behind the two findings which, in Section 6.2.3, I suggested you might 'try explaining to an intelligent non-economist friend'—namely, why it is that a purchase tax usually does not fall completely on the buyers of a good; and why nations could 'spend their way' out of depression.

(The final two discussion topics relate to economic instances which, if you are at the beginning of your studies, you may not yet have met. If this is so, then hold these discussion points over until you come to learn the economics.)

5. Consider the 'competing hypotheses of the consumption function' (the absolute-income, relative-income, and permanent-income hypotheses, plus one or two variants of these according to the text you use). Review your economic understanding of these; and from an epistemological point of view, confirm how they show the difficulty which economists face in validating any one particular set of high-level statements by reference to real-world observation—even when, as in the case of consumption and income, the real-world aggregate data required are readily available and there is a high degree of intersubjective agreement on their appropriateness as measures of the concepts concerned. (These thoughts will come up again in Chapter 9.)

6. Consider the Keynesian and the classical models of the macroeconomy. List (a) the high-level statements which they have in common, and (b) the high-level statements in which they differ. Looking now at the statements in which they differ, how far do you think these can genuinely be viewed as 'competing hypotheses' in the textbook sense of the philosophy of general science (that is, as contradictory statements about the world, each of which is asserted as applying at all times and all places, so that it is inconceivable that both statements could be materially true)?

7

The job of the applied economist

The theory of any science, as we have seen, consists of the assembled patterns of thought on which that science is based. Application consists in using these patterns of thought to unravel specific problems which arise in the course of events, and on which the scientist is asked to advise.

Having followed the discussion in earlier chapters, you will realize that there is no sharp distinction, epistemologically speaking, between the development of a theory and the application of that theory. If the economist advises on a specific policy problem, what he is in fact doing is to work out the likely consequences of different policy choices. In the language of Chapter 6, then, he is setting up alternative models—incorporating the alternative policy choices—and working out the predictions (or implications) of each model. Or, to put it in another way, the economist, in giving advice on policy, is engaging in scientific explanation. Needless to say, of the two definitions of 'explanation' that we know, the one most relevant to applied economics is that which hinges on the idea of being able to *control* events. As we have seen, this may entail *understanding* the events in question—that is, being able to fit them convincingly into a deductive framework—or it may not, since we can sometimes control events in some measure even though we do not understand them fully.

We have discussed various views of the structure of theoretical reasoning in economics and of ways in which it may be checked against reality. We now go on to look at the specific methods which the economist may use to carry out this checking, in the context of real-life economic investigation.

That is *not* to say that the chapters which follow are intended as a 'cook-book' of empirical economics. There are plenty of texts available which will tell you about the methods of econometrics, survey investigation, statistical presentation, and so on, and the reading guides will lead you to a selection of these. What I am setting out to do here, instead, is to take a critical look at the epistemology of the various methods and the results gained from them, and to appraise what these features mean to the practical task of the applied economist.

7.1 The economist as adviser

As we noted in talking about the 'positive/normative' distinction, most economists would agree that it is not their job to choose economic goals, nor to take the action by which these goals are to be attained. These things are up to politicians, managers, consumers, and all the other actors on the economic scene. What the economist does instead is to give *advice*: advice on the economic consequences of aiming for one goal rather than another, or on the alternative means of reaching a given goal.

To put the same idea in a different way: in the course of decision-making—whether in everyday life, in business or in government—the decision-maker may be confronted with a situation in which he is unsure how to reach a desired goal, or unsure which goal to aim for among several alternatives. He then has a job of *problem-solving* on his hands; and to help in solving his problem, he may call on an adviser.

The advisory function is just one aspect of a much more general economic phenomenon—namely *specialization*. Human beings cannot develop all possible abilities in their lifetime—time and ability are both scarce resources—and the tasks of the community are therefore better performed if the individuals specialize in particular occupations. The adviser is a specialist, in that he accumulates the knowledge, skill, and experience that are most relevant to the kind of advice he is called upon to give. In calling for advice, we do so in the expectation that the expert adviser will be able to save us time and effort in problem-solving, and that this will more than outweigh the payment we have to make to him for his services.

To help us understand what the adviser's job entails, we can split the problem-solving process down into four phases—which, in fact, characterize the advisory task not only in economics, but in every other professional field as well. They are:

1. problem formulation;
2. data collection;
3. analysis;
4. recommendation.

Note that I have listed the final phase as 'recommendation' rather than 'solution'. This is because of the rather obvious fact that the problem-solver's assessment of a situation may or may not be right first time; and as far as economic problems are concerned, we usually find that the only way to check the correctness of the recommendation is to act on it. Once we have been able to observe the results of the policy action taken (as far as we can identify what these may be) then we may be called on to re-assess the situation—to add this new knowledge into our data, perhaps rework our analysis, and finally come up with an amended recommendation. In fact, in economics, it is the exception rather than the rule that we should be able to arrive at a once-for-all solution to a problem, for the reasons that we have considered already. More often, the process of recommendation, action, amended recommendation, is repeated indefinitely. What may appear to be the 'solution' of an economic problem will usually turn out to be a temporary solution only, as economic events develop and change around the problem-solver and policy-maker.

The implication of the first of the four headings, *problem formulation*, is this: quite often, one of the adviser's most useful contributions is simply to work out precisely what the problem *is* in the first place. In economics, this may often mean translating a vague political brief into an objective which is as well defined as the economist can make it. To give just one example, a typical brief given to the applied economist by policy-makers is to 'improve the efficiency' of an industrial sector, a marketing process, or what have you. In fact, the term 'efficiency' (as you will either know or will shortly be finding out from microeconomic studies), is a word that means a great many different things to different people. So the economist's first step must be to try to find out what the policy-makers actually have in mind when they talk of 'efficiency'; if he finds out (as he rather often does) that they have no clear idea *what* they mean by the word, he has to supply some appropriate economic maximand. Only then can he go on to work out ways—if any—in which policy intervention might help to bring about the aimed-for 'improvement'.

It is worth adding that this initial stage of problem formulation may sometimes make the economist stop short, go back to the policy-maker, and say: 'The problem you asked me to solve is not really the one which needs solving.' One recent example comes from the controversy over the siting of London's proposed 'third airport'. The government asked economic advisers to determine which of several suggested sites would be the best one economically. But some economic critics suggested that the right problem to have posed initially would have been, not 'Where should the airport be?', but 'Do we need a third airport anyway?'. As subsequent history showed, there was weight in their criticism: following a long and expensive cost–benefit appraisal of the suggested sites (and the rejection of the economic first choice because of local pressure), the final result was that *none* of the sites was used. This was for the very reason which the critics had initially suggested—the current need for a third airport, wherever it might be, was decided by the policy-makers not to be great enough to justify the cost.

The second stage of the problem-solving process, *data collection*, will obviously follow closely from the initial stage of problem formulation—because, until you know what your problem is, you are in no position to start thinking what data to collect or to choose the investigational method by which you are going to collect them. Having made this commonsense point, we can temporarily leave these two questions, since they are thoroughly discussed in later sections of this chapter, as well as in subsequent chapters.

The key to the nature of *analysis* lies in a peculiarity of the human mind: namely that we cannot 'understand' more than a certain amount of data at one time. By 'understanding', here, I mean the ability to take in a mass of data in a way that we find meaningful and useful as a basis for subsequent action. There is a limit to the amount of detail we can handle at any one time if we are to make sense of the data concerned. If the data which come in from our investigations contain more than that limited amount of detail, we must *summarize* them in some way: as Professor Boulding has put it, we must 'gain knowledge by the orderly loss of information'. In using the word 'loss', Boulding does not mean that we throw away some of the results we collect. Instead, we 'boil down' the raw data into forms which are meaningful to us, rather than trying to work with the entire body of detailed information which we originally collected. For instance, if you were presented with a pile of ten thousand Census forms and asked to draw some economic conclusions from them, you would hardly read through each form separately and then go straight on to write your report. You would, instead, draw up tables of family size and age distributions, maps of geographical location of population, average figures for numbers of people per household, and so on. All of these procedures have the aim of putting the raw data into an easily understandable form.

7.2 The nature of economic advice

The job of the adviser, then, is to take data, analyse them—that is, draw them up in patterns which are meaningful in terms of the theory of his own particular specialized discipline—and use the results in advising on practical problems. Each kind of adviser, naturally enough, will pick out data which are appropriate to his own specialization.

It is for this reason that the advice given on any particular problem by advisers from different disciplines may differ or even conflict. When a conflict does take place, it need not be because one or other of the advisers is wrong: rather, it is just that each will view the problem in terms of the patterns thrown up by his own particular discipline. To give a couple of instances, suppose the problem is: 'What kind of storage should farmers be encouraged to install for their produce?' The technical expert on storage will advocate the method of storage which minimizes losses from wastage, pests, and so forth. The economist will point out that storage has costs and returns, and that the type of storage installation which is most effective in minimizing physical loss may also be more costly than simpler storage methods—so that, at the end of the day, these simpler methods may possibly give the farmer a greater return.

Or suppose you ask your accountant: 'Should I buy and run a car?' He will work out what the car will cost you per year in terms of fuel, repairs, and other running costs, plus depreciation and the interest charge on the money you spend in buying the car. But what if you were to put the same question to an economist? From your own knowledge of economic thinking, you will know how his answer would differ from the accountant's. He would point out that money costs are usually different from economic costs: that against the accountant's cost calculations you would have to set off the costs saved on alternative forms of travel, plus savings in time, and the imputed returns in the form of greater convenience, pride of ownership, and so on.

Many economists would be bold enough to say that, in most problem situations in real life in which some practical action is aimed for, economic advice can *add* something to the advice given by other advisers. For instance, to go back to the question of the best storage for farmers to install: the economist can suggest that, despite the technical expert's advice, what really *matters* is not that physical loss should be minimized, but that the farmer should maximize his net return. In this particular case, the economist would probably be right—simply because most farmers, once the nature of the problem had been brought to their attention, would probably agree that they *did* prefer to maximize their net return rather than necessarily minimizing physical loss of produce. And in reality, there does seem to be a fair number of practical situations in which the economist can contribute this kind of extra advice, by bringing out features of the situation which were not obvious to more technically oriented advisers.

At the same time, we need to be cautious about taking self-assurance too far here. Suppose the farmer in question had listened to us making our economic appraisal, and had then said: 'Thanks. But personally, I prefer a method of storage that will minimize physical losses, even if it does not necessarily maximize my net returns.' We should not have the slightest grounds for saying he—or his technical storage adviser—was 'wrong' in this preference. Here, we are reminded of the basic nature of the adviser's job—to attempt to guide action in order to achieve stated objectives, but not to choose those objectives, nor to take the necessary action.

7.3 The choice of investigational method

The economist, then, has been given his problem to solve by the policy-maker. He has formulated the problem in a way that seems to make sense to him economically; and he has chosen the economic model which he thinks may be most closely applicable to the real-life situation he is investigating. How does he then go about choosing the investigational methods—of data collection and analysis—by which that model is to be applied to reality? (Let us take a wide methodological view, and say that 'application', here, may mean checking applicability of his model's higher-level statements; or checking the outcome of the recommended policy action, i.e., the prediction of his model; or both.)

When it comes down to it, the choice between methods can be viewed as a cost–benefit problem. Any method of investigation entails costs—of the economist's own time, of staff employed, of equipment, and so on; and it also (we hope) provides benefits, in the shape of advice which enables the policy-maker, businessman, or other decision-taker to act more effectively than he would have been able to do without the benefit of the economist's advice.

This commonsense point having been made, however, we come up against a difficulty which arises in any cost–benefit comparison: how should we go about putting a value on the costs and on the benefits?

In fact, in the task of choosing between methods of economic investigation, it is usually a lot easier to evaluate relative costs than relative benefits. For instance, you could make a fairly good stab at working out comparative budgets for a survey study and an econometric study of a given economic problem—in terms of supervisory hours, wages of clerks or interviewers, computer or card-punching time, and all the rest of it. But when it comes to the benefit side of the comparison, you would be hard put to it to estimate the amount by which the results of one method are 'worth more than' the other as far as the policy-maker is concerned.

This latter point, again, is pretty obvious. But it is worth briefly tying it in with what we know about the structure and testing of theories. We noted in Section 6.3.1 that you could never test one hypothesis in isolation: what you had to do was to test a whole set of interlinked hypotheses, consisting not only of the hypothesis in which you were primarily interested, but also of a number of auxiliary hypotheses. When you set out to 'compare two hypotheses', therefore, what you unavoidably had to do was to compare these hypotheses together with their respective sets of auxiliary hypotheses.

Now, in looking at the comparison of two different investigational methods, we see that exactly the same difficulty applies the other way round: each investigational method consists of a particular set of *auxiliary* hypotheses, and in comparing the two methods against real-world outcomes, you necessarily also test the higher-level statements of whatever model you are using as your basis for policy recommendation.

Whichever way round we choose to apply the argument, the outcome is the same: testing can never be a once-off process. Instead, by means of many real-world checks, carried out in as wide as possible a range of problem situations, we may be able to build up more or less confidence in the strength of any given hypothesis. Recall Professor Machlup's idea of 'testing by repeated usefulness': just as it applied to the higher-level statements of economic theory, we now see that it applies to the evaluation of means of investigation. We need to ask: does this method of investigation lead to better policy recommendations than that other method, not just in one or a few economic situations, but consistently? And, needless to say, convincing answers to this question are as difficult to come by as are answers to the same question when it is asked of economic hypotheses themselves.

However, the economist can cut at least some corners by using a device which again is common to all scientific practice: he can rely, at least to some extent, on *intersubjective* judgement of the relative benefits of different investigational methods (see Section 4.4.3 for the notion of intersubjectivity). In other words, he can look at particular features of the alternative methods he has available, and suggest that in the opinion of any reasonable economist, these features are likely to lead to results that are more useful or less useful for the purpose to which that method is to be put.

It will be very seldom that the intersubjective comparison of methods will be able to provide any quantitative comparison of usefulness. At most, what we may hope to do is to get a qualitative ranking of methods in order of their likely usefulness in a particular task (though agreement even on *that* is by no means certain), and compare this with what we know of the relative costs of each method.

What qualitative criteria might be brought into the intersubjective appraisal of methods? Here is one list of questions that could be asked about the methods under comparison; like all lists, it consists of headings which are arbitrary to some extent, and this way of compiling it is merely my own suggestion. The methodologist might ask, considering each method:

1. Is its reasoning sound, and appropriate to the problem and the available data?
2. How accurate are its data and its results?
3. How quickly are the results available?
4. How well can the results be understood?

These are simply commonsense 'plus' features on the benefit side of the cost–benefit appraisal of methods.

In talking of the 'reasoning' of an investigational method, I am referring both to its logic and its epistemology. Self-evidently, the reasoning used in any method of investigation needs to make good sense deductively. As regards the epistemological features which we need to take into account, much of the groundwork was laid in Chapter 5 for the discussion which is to follow in coming sections and chapters. Two questions, we shall see, are of particular importance: by what reasoning is a given method of investigation supposed to aid the economist in prediction? And does the method in question take full account of the fact that the economist usually gathers his data from people, rather than simply by observing inanimate objects?

The question of *accuracy* (and its obverse, error) in economic investigation is one that seems much more simple than it really is. Because of the importance and difficulty of the topic, the whole of the next chapter is devoted to it.

As regards *timeliness*, an obvious point is that if the results of economic investigation are to be of any use in application, they must be made available quickly enough to allow them to be acted on. The maximum permissible timelag will naturally vary with the subject that is being investigated and the use to which the results are to be put. The choice of a 'best' method, in this respect as in others, will depend on balancing the *cost* of greater timeliness with the benefit that one thinks will be derived from achieving it. One needs to beware of falling into the trap of assuming 'the quicker, the better'; if we bear in mind the 'cost–benefit' approach to the matter, it is clear that this is not necessarily so. It is possible to conceive of results which are *more* timely than they need be from the policy-maker's point of view.

The question of *intelligibility* is one that really comes into its own when the economist is aiming at practical policy applications, rather than just engaging in pure research or theorizing. The researcher or theoretician need only ask whether his results will be understood by other economists—and indeed, he usually only bothers about other economists in his own specialized area of the discipline. But the policy adviser runs into grave danger if he takes it for granted that the meaning of his results, to say nothing of economic terms and economic concepts, will be understood correctly by the people he is supposed to be advising.

The degree of intelligibility of economic results will mainly be a function of the economist's skill in presenting those results. The craft of statistical presentation is an essential one for the applied economist; there are excellent texts available on this subject (including those cited at the end of this chapter) and I refer you to these rather than try to cover the topic here.

7.4 An overview of methods

Since this book, as I have said, is not intended as a manual of practical research methods in economics, I shall make no attempt here to give factual chapter-and-verse on the various methods of data collection and analysis that are available to the applied economist. Instead, in the rest of this chapter, I shall merely itemize the main kinds of investigational method which the economist can use, principally so that if you are a relative newcomer to the subject, you can gain some idea of what methods we are talking about in our appraisal of costs and benefits.

There is not much scope for formal description or appraisal of the ways in which economists formulate problems. This may remind you of the general methodological point that we have no rules by which we can formalize the invention of *hypotheses*. Though problem formulation in applied economics may not always entail the *conscious* formulation of hypotheses, this is nevertheless what the applied economist is necessarily doing at the stage of problem formulation. This stage, therefore, remains a matter of inspiration, experience, common sense, and knowledge of the field.

The same is partly true also of the fourth stage of the advisory sequence, recommendation. Most practical economists would probably admit that 'flair' plays a big part in successful recommendation of economic policy; in the present state of the art, it is seldom that a single clear and obvious recommendation will follow mechanically from the three earlier stages of the problem-solving process.

At the same time, it is obvious that successful recommendation will be made more likely if the other three stages of the process have been carried out competently. And of these stages, the second and third—data collection and analysis—do lend themselves to objective dissection and appraisal. It is these two stages, then, which we shall be talking about from now on in this overview of methods.

We may note four major styles of economic problem-solving which have their own formalized procedures. They are: econometrics; survey method; linear programming; and cost–benefit analysis. Of these four, econometrics and survey method are of very wide application, and are of particular interest to us, because in many ways they represent opposing views on the epistemological character of economic data. For these reasons, we shall be looking at each of them in detail, in Chapters 9 and 10 respectively.

The other two approaches are much more specialized in the range of economic problems they are designed to deal with. *Linear programming* is a term applied to certain computer procedures which are used in finding solutions to problems of resource allocation and related topics. For instance, it has found a good deal of application in aiding advisory work on farm management: the farmer has to decide on the most profitable combination of crop and livestock enterprises to employ on his farm subject to the constraints he meets in such features as weather conditions in his part of the country, the kind of soil he works, and so on. As you will realize, even if the farmer deliberately restricts his range of choice to only a few enterprises, he still faces a mammoth task in deciding how to allocate his resources—his land, labour, fertilizer, and so on—between them, since there are so many possible permutations and combinations, each of which will have its own results in terms of profitability. The role of linear programming is to let the computer—with its inhuman disregard for mental tedium—take over the solution of puzzles like these.

Cost-benefit analysis is a somewhat ill-defined method, or set of methods, for appraising the economic desirability of capital projects. It is applied most commonly to large public-works projects, and sets out to take into account the costs and returns on these over a long period in the future, trying to make allowance not only for the obvious monetary sums paid and received but for 'intangibles' like convenience, pollution, amenity, and so on. To mention a well-known example: if economists are asked to choose between several possible sites for an airport, their cost–benefit analysis would not only work out the relative costs of each site in terms of the price of the land required, labour costs in each area, and so on; they would go on to try to establish what 'spillovers' might arise in terms of, say, possible traffic congestion arising because of transport movements to and from each possible site; and they would necessarily need to tackle even more difficult problems. For instance, if the choice of one possible site would mean knocking down some historic churches, using another site would mean spoiling the view from a famous beauty spot, and using a third site would mean disturbing some unique wildlife—how do you go about trying to establish which of these alternatives is the most 'costly' to the community? And when you have worked out all these problems, you must go on to compare these 'costs' with benefits which can be just as much of a headache to calculate: given, say, that the different sites provide different amounts of convenience in terms of travel time to some major city—how do you evaluate this convenience? And how do you go about estimating what the relative order of convenience might be in a decade's time, when patterns of road and air transport may well have changed? The biggest computer in the world is helpless to handle problems like these.

As it happens, linear programming raises many problems on a technical level, but has no special epistemological quirks other than those which arise in any investigation which uses economic data, and which are thus discussed in other chapters and sections of this book. Cost–benefit analysis, as you can guess from the thumbnail description just given, does raise many of its own epistemological problems, but these have been very thoroughly discussed by other writers. The reading guide at the end of this chapter will lead you to these discussions, and it gives a selection of literature on the technicalities of both linear programming and cost–benefit analysis.

7.4.1 Aggregated v. disaggregated data

As regards the stage of data collection, one basic point to make is that the economist has two ways of getting his data: he can either collect them specially for the study he is doing—getting the information he wants directly from the people who are concerned in the economic situation he is investigating—or else he can use data already collected by someone else. Very often, of course, this 'someone else' who does the initial collection of data will be the government or some official body working on the government's behalf.

When the economist is using data of this latter kind, he will get the figures ready-made on the page, and these figures will usually be totals or averages for *groups* of people, certain sectors of industry, certain agricultural producers, and so on, or indeed they may relate to the whole of the economy (as, for instance, do the balance-of-payments accounts or national income figures for a country). These figures—relating to groups of economic actors, not to individuals—are often referred to by applied economists as *aggregate(d) data*, or sometimes as *macro data*, among a selection of alternative terms. (The opposites, not so often used, are *disaggregated data* and *micro data*.)

From the point of view of the individual economist, this distinction between aggregated and disaggregated data is a very necessary one to make. For a start, if the economist decides that he can investigate a problem using only data already collected and published by someone else—if, we say, he decides to run his investigation as a *desk study*—then he must realize that virtually all the ready-made data available to him will be aggregated data. Conversely, if he decides that only disaggregated data are suitable for his study, it will usually follow that he will have to collect these data himself, or at least pay someone else to collect them. The implications of this for the 'cost' side of the cost–benefit appraisal of economic methods are clear. As regards the relative benefits of using aggregated and disaggregated data, we shall be looking at these in some detail in Chapters 9 and 10, where the capabilities of econometric method and survey method are compared.

However, one should not forget that the initial collection of *all* economic data must be in disaggregated form. Official figures of national income, balance of payments, money supply, and all the rest of these familiar economic measures do not just jump fully-fledged on to the page; they must always have been collected by someone and from someone. This fact, an abundantly obvious one when it is set out as baldly as this, has significance when it comes to the appraisal of the accuracy of these figures and the way in which the economist can interpret them. This point will be taken up again in the next chapter.

7.4.2 Ad hoc *enquiry*

A vast amount of the economic advice given in real-life economic application is based on data which have not been collected by any formalized 'objective' method. Instead, the economist will make his own qualitative observations of the problem situation under study; judge what economic 'model' (in the sense of Section 6.3.5) to apply to that problem; and produce qualitative recommendations on the basis of this reasoning. As we saw in Chapter 6, this way of proceeding has a long history in economics. It goes by various names: *'ad hoc* enquiry', 'casual observation', and 'casual empiricism' are three of them.

This last term, in particular, is sometimes used as a term of disapproval by some economists who feel that this kind of data collection is somehow not worthy of scientific procedure in economics. From your reading of earlier chapters, you should have no difficulty in recognizing the weakness in this criticism. The fact is, of course, that we can apply 'testing by usefulness' to this method of data collection, as to any other aspect of scientific application. Put simply, we want to know whether it *works* or not. Or, to be more specific in the context of cost-and-return which we are at present discussing, does it seem that formal methods of data collection and analysis consistently produce more useful economic recommendations than do the methods of 'casual empiricism'? And if the formal methods do produce consistently better results, do these improved results justify the extra costs which are almost certain to be incurred when the formal methods are used? There is no ready-made general answer to this question; it needs to be looked at in the particular context of each task of investigation.

It is worth bearing in mind that in very many situations of real-life economic problem-solving, the most important part of the economist's expertise is his factual knowledge of the detailed 'nuts and bolts' of the workings of a particular economic sector, market, industry, or what have you—knowledge, that is, of what economic jargon usually calls 'institutional detail'. If someone asked you: 'Why is the yen going up against the dollar at this moment?', adding that he would like the answer by three o'clock that afternoon, you would not get very far by taking out a textbook of exchange-rate theory. Nor would you get much further by looking up the statistics for recent fluctuations in the yen and the dollar, and running a regression between the two series. Admittedly, both these items of knowledge (particularly the first) might provide some helpful background to your answer. But the really important things to know would be: who, and where, are the people who at this moment are buying yen and selling dollars? Why are they doing so? What rumours are going round the markets, and what are the facts (if any) behind these rumours? Is government intervention going on, or being planned?—and so on.

Knowledge of this kind, of course, is gained by long experience and day-by-day study of economic events: in other words, by continuous *ad hoc* enquiry.

7.4.3 The 'Royal Commission' method

There is one particular style of data collection that is very often used by governments when policy-oriented economic questions are being looked into. Despite the fact that this method finds frequent usage in official work, it has no formal name of its own; so I shall christen it 'the Royal Commission method', for reasons that will become obvious. In this procedure, the investigators call for statements to be provided by bodies and individuals who have an interest in the problem under study. Typically, these statements will be delivered either verbally or in writing; they may be made out in reply to a set list of questions prepared by the investigators, or may be left to the choice of whoever makes the submission. Often, the submissions may be backed up by more 'objective' investigations—survey studies, visits to firms by the investigators, and so on. In the UK, this style of investigation has been used to tackle economic problems ranging all the way from the marketing of meat to the workings of the monetary system, with just about every other conceivable topic in between.

Though this approach is so often given the sanction of official usage, it is clear that it is no more objectively 'scientific' than is simple *ad hoc* observation. For all the reasons which have already been mentioned in connection with qualitative observation generally, this need not imply that the 'Royal Commission' method is necessarily somehow inferior to more formally 'scientific' approaches. One needs simply to register what are the likely costs and benefits of the method as compared to other methods of exploring the same policy problems.

An immediately obvious point is that normative arguments are likely to figure in the submissions sent in to the investigating body, to a much greater extent than they would in qualitative observation made by the economist on his own behalf. However, it is doubtful how far this can be seen as a disadvantage of the 'Royal Commission method'. Indeed, it might in some ways be viewed as an advantage: in so far as policy choices are matters of normative preference rather than of objective measurement, then it becomes important for investigators to be able to ascertain what that preference is.

One problem which the investigators must face is that of bias: that is, the fact that the views expressed in submissions may not be representative of the bulk of the people concerned in the economic situation. This is obviously likely to be a danger when there are 'pressure groups' operating. The notion of the 'Royal Commission' approach over this problem is that by inviting submissions from all interested parties, the investigators should be able to see all sides of the argument, and make a reasoned choice between them. Whether they always succeed in doing so is, of course, another question. One difficulty which may arise is that the investigators *themselves* may have normative views on the matter they are studying. Again, this is supposed to be counteracted by the fact that the team of investigators should include representatives from all sides of the argument; but, here again, the practice does not always come up to the ideal. There is, of course, no reason why investigators on a team of the 'Royal Commission' type need *necessarily* be subject to normative bias on their own part, any more than an economist or any other scientist need be. But politicians and people in public life, unlike scientists, are not usually trained to separate normative from positive features of an argument.

The 'Royal Commission' approach has the practical advantage that it can be set in motion rapidly, and the investigation can be made as searching or as superficial as the sponsoring body decides. Likewise, the cost of the investigation will be very much at the discretion of the sponsoring body (unlike, say, a formal survey study, which needs to attain a minimum coverage in terms of representativeness and sample size, and so has to take a certain minimum time and cost a certain minimum sum). The cynic could perhaps add another practical political advantage: if necessary, the investigation can be made to take as *long* as possible, with the aim of ensuring that by the time results are produced, most people will have forgotten what the original problem was anyway, so that any politically inconvenient recommendations can safely be pigeonholed.

It is probably true to say that economically speaking, the main shortcoming of results of the 'Royal Commission' method is not any tendency to bias, in the sense of lacking statistical 'representativeness'; but rather that, often, the investigating panels are composed of members who have no economic knowledge or training, even when the problem being investigated is an economic one. The result of this has sometimes been that the nature of the economic problem itself has been misunderstood; or that the economic meaning of the information collected has not been interpreted correctly; or that the recommendations of the enquiry have led to economic results different from those intended, or to no economic results at all.

7.4.4 Accounting

Since the accountant and the economist both concern themselves with money and its management, you might think that accounting procedures would be a widely used way for the economist to collect the data he needs. It is 'strange but true', however, that the data collected by the accountant are usually of very little direct use in *economic* application. This harks back, in fact, to the nature of the advisory job performed by accountants and by economists; the two disciplines are not usually concerned with the same concepts, and so the data they collect are also different. For instance, the ideas of marginal cost and marginal value product, so central to economic reasoning in the theory of the firm, do not figure in business accounting in the normal way of things. The accountant is concerned rather to draw up a picture of an enterprise's assets and liabilities at a given time; when this is done for the beginning and end of a year, the familiar 'balance sheet' of the enterprise is the result.

(It may occur to you to wonder: if concepts like those of marginal cost and marginal value product are so essential to the reasoning of the economist's theory of the firm, why is it that the business accountant—who, above all, should be concerned with informing the businessman about the profitability of his enterprise—seems to pay no attention to them? Two conclusions are tentatively possible: first, that the accountant needs to learn the theory of the firm; or, second, that the theory of the firm has no practical relevance. This, in fact, is one of the classic controversies of economic methodology; there is no space to review it in detail here, but the reading guide at the end of the chapter will lead you to it.)

In some specifically economic investigations, accounting data *are* drawn up in such a way as to be economically useful. For instance, accounts are collected each year from a sample of farmers in the UK in order to furnish data for the policy discussions on farm prices.

Economists, of course, also talk about 'national-income accounting', 'balance-of-payments accounting', and so on. Macro data of this kind, though, are a different kettle of fish from 'accounting' data in the traditional sense of the word. The national-income or balance-of-payments 'accounts' are drawn up in the 'double-entry' style familiar to the business accountant. But the figures on each side of the 'account' are in fact aggregates collected by survey methods, and not by the means used by the business accountant.

7.4.5 'Eyeballing'

Finally, we may note a few points about the analysis of data: it is obvious, for a start, that analysis will not be independent of the means of data collection used. In fact, all four stages of the problem-solving process are necessarily interrelated: the data you collect and the way in which you collect them will be determined by your view of the nature of the problem in hand; and the analysis you apply to the data will likewise be decided on the basis of problem formulation—as well as being affected, often, by the nature of the data you have actually succeeded in getting; these may or may not be the same as the data you would ideally have liked to get (most usually, they are not). In talking about *ad hoc* observation, we have already noted that the qualitative data used by the economist in this approach will be subjected to qualitative analysis, according to the model of the situation which the analyst reckons to be most applicable.

Very often in real-life applied economics, even when the data being used are quantitative—when, that is, the economist actually has figures to look at—the kind of analysis done will be of an informal, intuitive kind: the economist will simply assess how the figures look, and come out with what is essentially a qualitative rather than a quantitative prediction or recommendation. The Americans have an expressive term for this kind of analysis: 'eyeballing'. Here again, we need to beware of assuming that the informality of the method need make it somehow 'unscientific'. What matters is to take a cost-and-return view of its relative usefulness in any given task of economic problem-solving. The fact is that the ability to look through a large array of figures and to spot, by eye inspection, the most telling ones among them is an important skill for a practical applied economist or statistician. Like the ability to come up with 'good' hypotheses, the knack of successful 'eyeballing' seems to be one which cannot readily be formalized by reference to any epistemological rulebook; instead, it is a matter partly of native ability and partly of practice.

Reading guide: Chapter 7

In the text of this book, I had originally planned to say a lot more about the practicalities of *how* economic policy is applied—about all the things that can happen to the economist's recommendations before they ever reach the stage of being converted into policy moves. But this was one of many parts of the original which bit the dust because of length restrictions: and the main reason I finally decided to leave it out was that the subject matter has been so well covered by other writers. My favourite reference of all is Ely Devons, *Essays in Economics*. [24] Though all the essays are well worth your time, read in particular the two called 'Applied Economics—the Application of What?', and 'The Role of the Economist in Public Affairs'. Read also the article by Alan Coddington, 'Economists and Policy'. [18] If you have a bit more leisure, read W. A. Jöhr and H. W. Singer, *The Role of the Economist as Official Adviser*. [35] In Boulding, *Economics as a Science*, [7] read Chapter 4.

For more general perspectives on the economist's activities, you can turn to another book by Kenneth Boulding, *The Skills of the Economist*, [5] or try R. Hough, *What Economists Do*. [28]

On the craft of statistical presentation, read D. Huff, *How to Lie with Statistics*, [30] or more briefly, Chapter 3 of M. J. Moroney, *Facts from Figures*. [61] If you have back numbers of *The Economist*, look at the article called 'Charts for Every Occasion'.[26]

Going on to the specific methods of enquiry covered in Section 7.4: on cost-benefit analysis, a classic article is by A. R. Prest and R. Turvey, 'Cost-Benefit Analysis: A Survey'.[68] Of the many texts available, try the one by A. M. Dasgupta and D. W. Pearce, *Cost-Benefit Analysis: Theory and Practice*.[21] Their Chapter 9, by the way, looks at the 'third London airport' wrangle.

On linear programming, first try Chapter 7 of Edwin Mansfield, *Micro-economics*;[53] this is a good introductory explanation of the economic role of linear programming without any mathematical detail. A general text, this time including the mathematics, is A. Chung, *Linear Programming*,[15] and a comprehensive reference book is R. Dorfman, P. A. Samuelson, and R. M. Solow, *Linear Programming and Economic Analysis*.[25]

For a discussion of the limitations of accounting data in economic application, see Chapter 4 of Oskar Morgenstern, *On the Accuracy of Economic Observations*.[59]

There is a sizeable literature on the real-life relevance of the theory of the firm, and so, in the manner of the reading guide to Chapter 6, I shall give here just one key article: it is by Fritz Machlup, 'Theories of the Firm: Marginalist, Behavioral, Managerial'.[52]

To get an idea of the flavour of results of the 'Royal Commission' style, skim the 'Radcliffe Report'[69] and the 'Verdon-Smith Report'.[81] For heaven's sake do not try to read these from cover to cover: merely try to get an idea of the ways in which each committee went about its investigations, then have a look at the recommendations made, and consider how far the recommendations actually follow from the investigations. If you are a glutton for punishment, try the same exercise on the 'Roskill Report',[71] which is an amalgam of Royal Commission method and cost-benefit analysis.

8

Accuracy and error in applied economics

In this chapter we shall be looking at the concept of *accuracy* in economic results. We shall look also at *error*. In a certain sense, it is correct to say that accuracy and error simply form 'two sides of the same coin'—that accuracy just means the absence of error, error the absence of accuracy. Nevertheless, here we shall look separately at each of the two concepts, because in economic usage, the two raise somewhat different problems; in particular, 'error' is given some specialized meanings which need to be examined specifically.

8.1 Accuracy

8.1.1 The meaning of 'accuracy'

Let us suppose that you, as an applied economist, were given the job of answering the question: 'how *accurate* is that economic statistic?' (By the way: in case you are not familiar with the use of this word 'statistic'—in the singular—it just means what we would more often call a 'figure'. Or, to be a little more exact, it means a figure representing some real-life economic measure—a price, a cost-of-living index, a production tonnage, what have you.) You might think at first sight that the answer to this question would be simple: all you would need to do would be to compare this statistic with the actual value which it was supposed to represent. Then, the nearer the statistic was to this actual value, the more accurate it would be.

A moment or two's thought, however, will show that things are usually not so simple. The most obvious reason for this is that there may very often be no way of finding out what the 'actual' figure really is. To take one of many possible real-life examples: suppose we are looking at press reports of price figures at various markets for a given commodity, and we want to check their accuracy. Often we find that the figure reported in the press for the price at a given market is the *only* figure available anywhere. In other words, we simply have nothing against which we can check the figures we are examining.

You could suggest: 'Why could we not go back to the merchants or auctioneers, or whoever, who were doing the deals at the markets concerned, look through their books, average the prices given, and see whether the averages we get tally with what was reported in the paper?' Again, this seems simple enough in principle—even though, clearly, it would be a costly and slow operation; and, equally clearly, it would depend on the fact that the market operators concerned actually *kept* records of the prices at which they dealt. But in fact, even if records were available, our checking operation would not only be costly and slow, but would most likely be futile in any case. This is because more often than not, we have no way of knowing on what *basis* the published figure has been compiled. Was it meant to apply to *all* the deals done in the market that day? Or just to a sample of the deals, and, if so, how was the sample chosen? Did the figure apply only to deals over a certain size? Of what average quality was the commodity with which we are concerned?

To form a complete picture of the *basis* of any economic statistic, we need to know the answers to numerous questions such as these. Unless we know the answers to all such questions—and often, in looking at practical economic statistics, we know very few of the answers—then we have no way of knowing whether any estimate we draw up as a 'check' on our figures is really constructed on the same basis as the figure we are supposed to be examining.

And consider even a statistic for which we do know the basis of compilation in some detail, and which *is* available from two or more alternative sources. Many important macroeconomic figures come under this heading—for instance, balance-of-payments figures, estimates of national income per head, and growth rates. As a rule, statistics of this kind are produced by government sources; and other versions of the same figures may be produced by, say, employers' or trade union organizations, independent economic research institutes, and so on. From what has already been said, it will be clear that not even this wealth of sources—all of them specifying their basis in complete detail—need make it any easier to say, 'Yes, that statistic is more *accurate* than that other.' The fact is that, since all the figures are likely to have been produced on slightly different bases of compilation one from another, the different estimates will not be directly *comparable*, and hence a comparison of 'accuracy' as between them will have little meaning.

Note, by the way, the applied economist's use of this term 'comparable': if we take a set of figures estimating a given economic statistic at various places or times (for instance, a series of price indices, or a table of prices of a certain type of produce on a given day at various markets), then the figures in the set are comparable with one another if they are all drawn up on exactly the same basis of compilation; if not, they are non-comparable.

If you look through even a few pages of any government-produced volume of macro statistics, you will see breaks in the graphs, and perhaps lines drawn across the tables; and the footnotes will contain the warning of a 'basis change', resulting in non-comparable figures for the years before and the years after the change. Sometimes an entire series will be revised, including the figures for past years, and once again the new series will not be comparable with the old.

For detail on the size, significance, and justification of basis changes in real-life statistics, you can do no better than turn to the background documentation prepared by the UK government's statisticians to accompany their yearly and monthly volumes of statistics; there, the details of compilation are discussed with vast professionalism. Since these and other sources are available (see the reading guide at the end of this chapter), I shall simply mention one recent example of a basis change. Early in 1977, the series showing percentage changes in the effective exchange rate of the pound sterling was revised on to a new basis (in brief, the nature of the change was that the shopping-bag full of foreign currencies bought by the statisticians' pound was altered). The effect was quite startling to anyone who had been familiar with the old series, particularly as the statisticians decided to revise the entire series back to the year in which the pound was first floated, rather than show a break between old and new series. Thus it was that, in the last volume in which the old series appeared, the effective exchange rate of the pound in January 1977 was shown to have fallen to just 56.9 per cent of what it had been in 1971. But if the reader turned to the following month's volume, he found that same January figure showing an effective exchange rate equal to 61.8 per cent of the 1971 value! All that had happened, in reality, was that the change in the basis of compilation of the series had made the percentage decline in the rate work out as rather more gradual than in the original series.

When a basis change is made in this way, the revised figures clearly cannot be called 'more accurate' nor 'less accurate' than the non-revised figures: both sets of figures mean just what they are stated to mean, according to the details given of their compilation, if the reader takes the trouble to check up on these details.

8.1.2 Spurious accuracy

You may well have come across the concept of *spurious accuracy*—though perhaps not under this name—in mathematics courses. We say that a statistic has spurious accuracy if it is *presented* in a form which leads the reader to think that he can have more confidence in its accuracy than is really justified. (Thus 'spurious accuracy' is not really accuracy at all, but, if anything, the opposite.)

Alarmingly enough, several economists who have examined the official statistics available in the UK and the USA have suggested that these figures very often do incorporate spurious accuracy. Here is just one example, quoted from the article by Alan Coddington which was cited in the reading guide to Chapter 7 (the 'CSO' is the Central Statistical Office):

. . . national income is quoted to five digits, even though on the CSO's own estimate that the figure is good to about 3 per cent, only the first two of the digits are significant. It would have to be good to about 1 per cent or better for the third digit to be significant. Thus, the 1966 estimate of 1964's national income was quoted as £26,593 million, rather than, as it should have been, £27,000 million. The other three digits do not embody information; they waste the time of typesetters and proof-readers, and give a misleading impression to all those—in industry, government and the universities—who make use of the statistics.

It is quite true, of course, that the misleading quality of figures like these in official sources could be neutralized if their users took the trouble to check back on the 'small print' which indicates how much confidence *can* be put on them. (We may add that the relevant print is sometimes very small indeed, and *may* not appear in the same volume as the statistics themselves, though UK government statisticians are generally pretty good on this point.) But the point which Coddington correctly makes is this: why should the responsibility for this checking be left with the users of figures, when a more punctilious style of official presentation would save them the trouble?

From the discussion in the previous section, we may briefly add an additional quirk of interpretation: namely, that because we are hardly ever able to tell for sure what the 'actual' value of a statistic is, it follows that we can very seldom say precisely just *how* 'spurious' a given level of presentational accuracy may be. Coming back to Coddington's example, we saw that the CSO had 'estimated the figure to be good to about 3 per cent'. But any such estimation—even by so authoritative an office—is very largely a matter of sensible guesswork (and, as we shall see in Section 9.3, this guesswork can be only *partially* aided by statistical analysis). Nobody could ever measure objectively just what degree of confidence could really be placed on the quoted figure. For all we know, UK national income in 1964 *was* in fact £26,593 million, to well within the nearest million, which would mean that we had been wrong in judging the published figure to be spuriously accurate. For all we know (though sensible guesswork would seem to make it much less likely this time), actual national income was so different from the published estimate that the spurious accuracy extended to the second or even the first digit. The point is that we do not know, and never can know, what the 'actual' figure was.

8.2 Error

Error can arise at any or all of the separate stages which the economist works through when he is performing his advisory role in problem-solving. As we have seen, these stages are: problem formulation, data collection, analysis, and recommendation. As regards the first and last of these, it will be obvious that although there is plenty of scope for error in-specifying the nature of a problem or in presenting recommendations, it is not very helpful to try to make out a systematic list of the specific errors which may arise at either stage—since, as we have seen, these stages themselves do not depend on the economist's following a given set of rules. It may be mentioned that the stage of problem formulation is particularly vital, since it will largely determine what is done at all the successive stages. Thus if mistakes *are* made in problem formulation—or in more straightforward language, if the problem is not well enough thought out at the planning stage—then all three of the remaining stages are very likely to land in trouble.

With regard to the two central stages, data collection and analysis, it is possible to be more specific about sources of error. Our first task is to bring out the distinction between two fundamentally different kinds of error which are met with in economic work, namely *sampling error* and *observational error*; the coming two sections discuss each of these in turn.

8.2.1 Sampling error

In the discipline of mathematical statistics, the word 'error'—like several other important terms—is given a very special meaning, which is quite distinct from the way the term is used in ordinary non-technical conversation and writing.

In everyday speech, of course, the term 'error' simply means something like 'mistake'. In this sense, we can talk about the 'error' attaching to a particular figure, meaning just the amount by which the figure differs from the true value which it is meant to represent. In this everyday sense, then, 'error' is just the converse of 'accuracy'—the more of one, the less of the other.

Statistical analysts use the word 'error' as part of various technical phrases ('standard error', 'error term', and so on), all of which have their own precise meanings. But generalizing from these, we might express the specialized statisticians' usage in this way: 'error' attaches to any statistic which is estimated from a *sample* of the population under study (rather than being ascertained for the whole population). We know from our discussion of induction (Chapter 3) that unless we can perform a 100 per cent enumeration, we can never be sure that results gained from observing some cases in a group do or do not also apply to the other cases in the group. In so far as the results for the observed cases (the sample) do differ from the overall result which could be gained by observing the entire group of cases (the statisticians' *population*), then error attaches to the result we have gained from our observed cases. To underline the nature of this kind of error, we often call it by the more explicit name of *sampling error*.

The whole point of statistical analysis in this context is to work out some quantitative measure of sampling error. Clearly, this cannot simply be done by finding the difference between the result for the observed cases and the result for the whole population, for the very good reason that the latter result is not known. What statistical analysis does, instead, is to use the sample data to make an estimate of the range within which the population result is likely to lie, and to add an indication of probability that the true population value does, indeed, lie within this range.

A full description of the ways in which this can be done will be found in any text on statistical analysis, and it is not my job to pursue this detail. The purpose here was merely to make clear, in the briefest possible terms, the specialized meaning which statistical analysts give to the term 'error'.

If you look back at the wider everyday usage of the word, you will realize that the statisticians' 'error' is just one of the ways in which a figure representing some economic measure could come to differ from the 'actual' value of that measure. In other words: *sampling error is only one of many sources of 'error' in the everyday sense of the word*. All these other sources can be lumped together under the collective name of *observational error*, and their nature is described in the next section.

It will be useful first, though, to sort out one further incidental point of terminology. In the opening paragraphs of this section, I have talked about 'statistical analysis', meaning the application to economic data of the branch of mathematics which we call 'statistics'. But, as we know from Section 8.1.1, the word 'statistics'—the plural of 'statistic'—can also be used more straightforwardly to mean 'figures representing some observed set of economic events'. Correspondingly, a 'statistician' can be someone who studies or uses mathematical statistics; or he can be someone who collects and presents observations of data in the form of figures. From now on, I shall distinguish between the two ideas by a piece of printing trickery: when the mathematical discipline of statistics is being talked about, it will be written with an initial capital letter (Statistics) and so will the Statisticians who practise it. The more down-to-earth pursuit of collecting and presenting figures will keep the small 's'.

8.2.2 Observational error

The many different kinds of mistake collectively making up observational error are conceptually much simpler than the idea of sampling error—in that their *nature* is obvious at a commonsense level, without the need for long-winded technical explanation. But it needs to be added straight away that the conceptual simplicity of these sources of error does *not* mean that they are necessarily easy to spot nor to deal with on the many occasions when they turn up in the applied economist's in-tray. Quite the contrary, as we shall see: in many ways, observational error can be more difficult to counteract, or even to identify, than sampling error.

Let us start at the simple end, and run rapidly through a brief list of the sources of observational error. *Recording error* just means that people filling in forms make mistakes in doing so. The people in question may be members of the public to whom forms are sent asking for information (like the

Income Tax return or the Agricultural Return form, to name but two out of very many). Or, in enquiries using interviewers, the interviewer may make the mistake. The mistakes may just be 'slips of the pen'; or they may be arithmetical errors; or they may happen because the person filling in the form has misread explanatory notes. Where a form is being filled in from records kept by the person doing the form-filling (like a businessman reporting features of his trade for the year, say) the original records themselves may contain mistakes; alternatively, he may have kept no record at all of whatever figures are required, and have to rely on fallible memory.

Concealment and *lying* are two sources of observational error of which the names fully describe the nature. Like recording error, they may originate either with respondents (the technical word used for whoever is being asked to give the information) or with interviewers in interview studies.

Respondent bias and *interviewer bias* are the errors which arise when personal views or attitudes held by the respondent (or the interviewer) cause answers to be recorded which differ from the objectively correct answer. The difference between this and lying, of course, is that lying is done consciously, while bias makes people unconsciously distort the truth. At a fair guess, respondent or interviewer bias poses less of a problem for the economist than for his colleagues in other social sciences, who may have to ask questions on 'touchy' subjects like political and sexual attitudes. We have to remember, too, that we can only talk of error arising from respondent bias if we have reason to believe that a respondent's attitudes have caused him to mis-state matters of *fact*; there are many studies when a statement of attitudes is exactly what we are after (e.g., in an investigation into the siting of an airport), and in this case we want to record those attitudes, 'bias' and all.

The next source of observational error, *sampling bias*, needs to be carefully distinguished from sampling *error*. When investigators are selecting the sample of people, households, businesses, or whatever, from whom they are going to collect information, they usually do so using a selection procedure which is essentially random—that is, the selection is done on a chance basis (you could do it by tossing a coin or rolling a dice, though in real-life investigation there are other means of random selection which are much more practical: the sources named in the reading guide will give you details). The purpose of choosing the members of the sample in this chance manner is clear: it avoids any possibility that the choice could be even unconsciously influenced by the investigator's own preconceptions or by other sources of interference—such as the geographical location from which the investigation was being carried out, the investigator's personal preferences as to the kind of people he likes speaking to, and so on. If any such sources of interference do affect the choice of the members of a sample, we say that the sample suffers from sampling bias. You will see that although a sample may be free from sampling *bias*, its results will still be open to sampling *error*. That is to say: even though a sample is chosen in a way in which is quite free from sources of interference like those mentioned, its results will still only relate to the members of the sample itself. If we want to generalize these results to apply to the *population* from which the sample was drawn, we run up against the epistemological problems of induction with which we are now very familiar.

So far, all the sources of observational error listed arise at the stage of data collection; but there are still further chances for error at the analysis stage. *Clerical error* may arise for any of the reasons causing recording error; and the more stages of analysis that the data pass through, the greater is the chance of error creeping in. (When the economist is being his own clerk, he makes his own clerical errors.) It is partly to counter clerical error, of course, that machine analysis has become so important in recent decades. But ironically, the introduction of machine analysis immediately opens the way for a whole new set of possible *human* errors—namely, those which may arise when data are being transcribed on to machine records (as, for instance, punching computer data on to tape or cards).

Once the data have passed this hurdle, they become subject to *machine error* itself. This can, first of all, include all the various mechanical ills that machines are heir to (and anyone who has had data to analyse, with a deadline to meet, and has had to struggle with an ailing computer, will know just how troublesome these ills can be).

But not all machine error is necessarily a matter of mechanical malfunction. The use of the computer brings extra dangers, which can arise even though the computer is working perfectly in a mechanical sense. The whole point of the computer is that it can rapidly carry out vast numbers of operations, which would be extremely tedious and costly if they had to be done by human labour. Fair enough thus far. But another feature of the computer is that it frequently must approximate—'round off'—numbers as it goes through its calculations. For any one of the individual numbers involved, the degree of approximation thus introduced is negligible. But in certain circumstances, these individual approximations can add up cumulatively over large numbers of calculations in an analysis, giving a final result that departs noticeably from the true figure (that is, the figure that would have been obtained in the absence of 'rounding off'). To make matters worse, since the computer is just doing what it has been built to do, the person carrying out the analysis does not necessarily have any indication of the error that has arisen. He can only check it by laboriously carrying out the calculation again, using numbers which are not rounded, or allowing for rounding errors as the calculation proceeds. This has actually been done on economic data in a few studies; and they show that rounding error can be very substantial on some kinds of calculation. In practical work, though, time and resources seldom allow such double-checking; more often, it is a case of knowing that some such error may be present, but simply ignoring it in the hope that it may not be too great.

The sources of observational error discussed in this section have all related to the collection and analysis of 'raw data', from sample enquiries and the like. In reading them through, you may perhaps have felt that these points were a bit irrelevant to the work of the very many economists who never engage in such fieldwork, but simply use aggregate statistics from published sources. Since there is nothing the user can do about the accuracy of these figures, might he not as well just take them on trust?

In reality, exactly the opposite is true. The more the economist relies on ready-published figures, the more important it is for him—if he wants to avoid reaching misleading findings—to keep in mind the kinds and magnitudes of error that may affect his data. Economic statistics, as we noted in Section 7.4.1, must always start life in disaggregated form: they have in the first instance to be collected somewhere, by someone, and usually *from* someone. Thus, they are liable to all the potential errors that we have been looking at in this section. The fact that a figure is down on the page in official black and white does not absolve it of all possibility of error. On the contrary, it makes possible error all the harder to spot; because the user of published figures, not having himself had anything to do with collecting or analysing them, is 'distanced' from all the possible sources of error we have been discussing. He has no direct way of acquiring a 'feel' for the sources of error in the data he is using. Human nature being what it is, he tends all too often just to dismiss the possibility of these errors from his mind. But he is never right to do so.

8.3 Ignorance, error, and Statistical analysis

In the coverage of sampling error and observational error in the foregoing sections, I have deliberately kept the description as brief as possible, with the sole objective of making clear the character of each of these main kinds of error and the distinction between them. Many applied economists and statisticians spend the greater part of their working lives trying to spot, isolate, and deal with these error sources, and if you have the slightest intention of pursuing an economic career yourself—even if you think at the moment that you want to be a 'pure theorist'—you should certainly turn to the sources in the reading guide for further detail on how this is done. You will find it much easier to come by guidance on sampling error, among the books you find on your library shelves, than on observational error: the first topic comes into all econometrics texts, while for the second you usually have to turn to manuals of survey method. Make sure in any event that you read the classic by Oskar Morgenstern.

There are two main things you should note during such further reading. They are, first, the sheer frightening *size* of some of the potential errors in widely used economic statistics (and having noted this, cast your mind round what it means for economic policy direction, as well as for the 'positivist' directive that the quantitative testing of predictions is the only right way to proceed in economics). Second, register the ways in which practical economists go about trying to detect and counteract error—and, once again, pay special attention to observational error.

Here as elsewhere in the book, I have decided that my limited space is best used, not by reproducing these factual details, available anyway in other sources, but by discussing some epistemological features of accuracy and error that you will not as a rule find being talked about in practical manuals of economic method. Which is not to say, by the way, that the epistemological features in question are merely of abstract interest; on the contrary, as we shall see, they are central to the economist's practical task of identifying, in Coddington's words, 'the division between what we really know and what we think we know but don't'.

Let us begin, then, by returning to some epistemological ideas with which we are already familiar. We know that 'error', in its everyday sense, usually entails two components: sampling error and observational error, the latter arising for any or all of the reasons which were listed in Section 8.2.2. We may go on to ask: in what circumstances, if any, could each of these two main categories of error be eliminated from observed data? Sampling error could be eliminated, as we know, only by carrying out a genuine 100 per cent enumeration of the cases under study. Observational error could be eliminated only by using procedures of data collection and analysis which were entirely proof against mistakes.

It need hardly be said that, in real-life investigation, it will be extremely seldom that either of these conditions is satisfied. Admittedly, the problem is eased by the fact that the economic scientist need only achieve a high degree of *intersubjective* agreement on the fulfilment of each condition, rather than trying to go to some unattainable 'logical conclusion'. For instance, as we know, it is strictly speaking impossible to be sure that one has ever achieved a genuine 100 per cent enumeration, but there are some cases in which the economist can justifiably take it that he has done so. For instance, suppose we wanted to collect data from all the firms in a given industrial sector. By checking with the relevant trade association, it might be possible to make sure—for all practical purposes—that we did indeed have the names and addresses of all these firms.

It is, if anything, rather more difficult to imagine what kind of observational exercise could be set up in economic work such that the investigator could claim with intersubjective credibility that all observational error had been avoided, though it is perhaps just within the bounds of possibility. Remember that the real 'protocol data' of economics are *not* the figures in official publications, nor even the figures entered on survey questionnaires or trade returns, but the economic events themselves: the housewife buying a can of beans; the businessman installing a new machine and selling its products; the trade unionist considering the reasons for his next wage claim. If we try in imagination to set up a totally mistake-free investigation, then our precautions against observational error must extend right back to the stage of initial observation of these events—our true 'raw data'.

Leaving aside these exceptional (or imaginary) cases of investigation, we may return to the realization that in all normal circumstances economic data will be subject to both sampling error and observational error. Thus, as I have said, we can never know what the 'true' value of a statistic may be. The next main point in our reasoning is this: the nature of 'not knowing' is different as between the element of sampling error and the element of observational error.

To deal with sampling error, Statistical analysis can be brought into play. By its use, we can make an estimate of what our results would be if there were no sampling error, and attach to this a measure of confidence in our estimate. In other words, though we can never be *sure* what the results of our observations would be in the absence of sampling error, we can express our unsureness in terms of *uncertainty*.

Note that in this last paragraph, I carefully used the phrase 'make an estimate of what our results would be in the absence of sampling error', and not 'make an estimate of the true result'—because, of course, the 'true result' on our terminology would be free not only of sampling error, but of observational error as well.

Can Statistical analysis, in fact, do anything about observational error? All too often in Statistical and econometric texts, observational error fails to get a mention; or it may be given a quick sideways look in an introductory section, as in this splendid example:

> Even if behaviour were exact, survey methods are not, and our statistical series . . . contain some errors of measurement. Throughout this book we pretend that all variables are measured without error.

And, indeed, the writer concerned maintains his chosen 'pretence' throughout some 200 subsequent pages in which complex and ingenious techniques of Statistical estimation are minutely detailed.

When Statisticians do face up to the existence of observational error, they try to deal with it by making various assumptions about its Statistical nature. The simplest and most widely used of these is that observational error is *random* in its incidence. Unfortunately, while this assumption may make reasonable sense in the context of the physical sciences, it will hardly do as a general proposition in applied economics. Thinking back over the various sources of observational error listed above, you should have no difficulty in seeing that many of them are as likely to be systematic in their occurrence as to be random. To give just one practical instance: it is well known to survey researchers that seemingly innocuous changes in the wording or even the position of a question on a questionnaire form, or in an interview, can bring about startlingly large changes in the totalled result for that question. Just *why* this happens is seldom easy to discover; nor is it usually possible to make any sensible guess in advance about whether any such effect is likely to take place, let alone how big it is likely to be. For our purposes, what matters is this: when we find *ex post* that this kind of swing in results has indeed happened, this is enough to show that the change in the question has not had its effects randomly: instead, it has caused a *mass* swing in one direction or another.

Some complex Statistical procedures have made valiant efforts to attack the problem more realistically, by modifying the simple assumption of randomness in observational error. But as one leading econometrician (L. R. Klein) has admitted, these efforts so far have faced 'intractable problems'. It is safe to say that, in the present state of the Statistical art, the headway made in this direction has been negligible—certainly as regards any practical economic application.

What reasoning, then, *do* we use in trying to estimate and deal with observational error? Let us imagine an applied economist 'eyeballing' a batch of forms he has just received, on which respondents have entered information. In seeking out errors in these returns, the economist's basic reasoning consists simply of inspired guesswork. Some of these guesses will be so soundly based that, to all intents and purposes, he can be 'sure' of the quantitative gain in accuracy that will come from correcting them. For instance, a frequently encountered recording error is for the respondent, when entering a total at the end of a column of figures, to put it one line too high on the form, giving an astonishingly high figure at whatever item that line refers to: it is obvious how this would be identified and corrected.

Even without such a clear giveaway, there are very many other ways in which errors can be spotted. It may be pretty clear that a respondent has simply forgotten to fill in a section on the form; or there may be arithmetic discrepancies in the figures as they stand. Then again, there are certain features of data which, though they do not infallibly indicate recording error, at least make the economist suspect it strongly: for instance, a particular figure may seem impossibly high or low by any sane estimate; or the year-on-year change in a particular item may seem suspiciously large.

In circumstances like these, the economist is on pretty firm ground *if* he can check back with his respondents—particularly if he or someone else can go along to the respondent to put the query and note the revised answer. Here again, the economist would be pretty well justified in saying he knew quantitatively what gain in accuracy had resulted from the correction.

But in many or most practical investigations, checking back is *not* possible; it is prevented by expense or by pressure of time. Then the economist has some much more unsatisfactory ways to proceed. He can make his own commonsense estimate of what the correct figure in question would be, perhaps following some rule of thumb like entering the average for that item worked out from the remainder of the forms, making a standard percentage adjustment from the previous year's figure, and so on. Or, if the suspected error is thought important enough, he may simply throw the offending form out of his sample. (By the way, this latter choice will certainly *not* give him an exact quantitative measure of the amount of error which he has thereby excluded from the sample, for commonsense reasons which I leave you to work out).

In this example, I have greatly oversimplified the many ingenious techniques of identifying observational error that applied economists have available to them, particularly with the aid of computer checking. But, ingenious techniques or not, the *reasoning* used in checking for error is as I have described it. At the end of the day, the economist will be pretty sure that he has guessed right over a certain number of queries; and he will be aware that some of his other guesses are more questionable. He will admit also that in certain cases he knows there is error (shown up, say, by an arithmetic discrepancy) but that he is unable to make any reasonable guess at the cause of the error or at the size of the needed correction.

And there is one more thing which the economist must admit: namely that it is likely—though *how* likely, nobody can tell—that on at least some of the returns there will be errors which do not give away their presence in any arithmetically detectable way. Thus, these errors will not only fail to be corrected, but will fail even to be recognized.

By this stage of our discussion, it should be pretty clear what the epistemological consequences of all this will be. The economist's unsureness over observational error cannot be converted into *uncertainty*; instead, he faces *ignorance*. He is ignorant about the size of observational errors in his data, and usually also about the size of the reduction in this error which may be brought about by any corrective measures.

These difficulties do not stop us from using economic data, nor do they make it pointless to try to reduce the incidence of recording error in any qualitative ways that seem open to us. But they do underline the vital fact that *in economic data there are elements of error which are not open to Statistical estimation or correction.*

As usual, in order to be entirely fair, we have to add 'at least, not in the present state of the art'. My own guess is that, because of the essential nature of observational error in economics, Statistical analysis will never make much more headway than it already has in dealing with this kind of error: time alone will tell whether this guess is right.

In most applied economic work, then, the economist simply has to live with the realization that while his data are open to error, he cannot ascertain quantitatively what that error may be. In large measure, the skill of the applied economist in this situation lies in presenting his results in such a way that his readers are not given any false ideas of accuracy where it does not exist. To do this, of course, the economist needs to keep on reminding *himself* of what he does *not* know, as well as of what he does know—or thinks he knows.

Reading guide: Chapter 8

The classic text in this subject area—and a book which is required reading for any economist—is by Oskar Morgenstern, *On the Accuracy of Economic Observa-*

tions.[59] In addition to the chapter on accounting, already cited in the reading guide to Chapter 7, now read the remainder of Morgenstern's Part One, together with his Chapter 8 and 16. Though the rest of the chapters go rather deep into technicality for our introductory purposes, you may care to skim them. More briefly, read Chapter 15 of the survey-method text by Moser and Kalton, *Survey Methods in Social Investigation*,[62] discussed in the reading guide to Chapter 10.

If you have not already read all the essays in the book by Ely Devons, *Essays in Economics*,[24] (cited in the reading guide to Chapter 7), read now the essays called 'The Language of Economic Statistics', and 'Statistics as a Basis for Policy'. Also, it is well worth while to look up back numbers of *The Listener* to read the article by Alan Coddington, 'Are Statistics Vital?'[17]

Turn out also *The Times* where, in an article called 'Putting a New Face on Things',[34] Peter Jay examines the effects of a major basis change in the UK's balance-of-payments accounts.

If you have not yet been introduced to real-life official statistics, make a start by looking up the UK Government's monthly *Economic Trends* and annual *National Income and Expenditure* (the latter is more familiarly called the 'National Income Blue Book'). Skim through them to try to get a feel for the figures, and look out for explanations of basis and basis change.

The explanatory 'small print' on the basis of compilation of UK Government statistics is to be found in the HMSO series called *Studies in Official Statistics*.[13] In particular, No. 13 of this series explains the basis of compilation of the National Income accounts (the detail has been updated in the 1977 Blue Book).

9

Sense and nonsense in econometrics

These days, it is not uncommon for econometric method to be taught in even the introductory stages of economics courses, and so you may already be familiar with some of the empirical procedures known collectively as 'econometrics'. There are, in any case, numerous textbooks which will give you full detail of the nuts and bolts of econometric method. In this chapter, as elsewhere in the present book, I shall avoid any attempt to reproduce this detail. Rather, we shall be looking at some of the logical and epistemological characteristics of econometrics. To allow us to do so, the nature of econometric method needs first to be spelled out in very brief detail, for the sake of those readers who have not yet had any econometric teaching. If you are confident in your knowledge of these factual details of econometric practice, you may wish to skip Section 9.1.

9.1 Basic detail

Exactly what *is* econometrics? In fact, textbooks on the subject do not agree on a definition. Some take the term very broadly, to signify any method of economic investigation that applies Statistics to economic data. Others say that 'econometrics' is a narrower concept than this: that a method should only be called 'econometric' if it entails the building and testing of 'models'—a term which, as we shall see, is used by econometricians in a sense notably different from that which is familiar to epistemologists. Still other texts maintain that the name 'econometrics' should be applied only to methods that introduce an 'error term'; this phrase also will be explained below.

Here, I shall adopt the widest of these definitions, taking the two narrower definitions as special cases of it. In fact, most of what can be said about economic Statistics generally, from the logical and epistemological points of view, can also be said about the two narrower definitions of 'econometrics'.

Before leaving the topic of definitions, it is worth pointing out that 'mathematical economics' does not mean the same as 'econometrics'. A distinguishing feature of econometrics is that it uses mathematical-statistical techniques to examine *empirical* economic data of one sort or another. By contrast, the purpose of mathematical economics is to put *deductive* economic theorizing into mathematical formulation (recall Section 6.1). As we shall shortly see, though, mathematical economics does enter into econometric practice, at the initial stage of model-building.

We go on to take a brief look at the factual detail of econometric method. At the simplest level conceptually, you find methods of regression analysis being used to try to discover trends in economic variables over time, or relationships between sets of economic data. Regressions can be simple (plotting just one set of data against another) or multiple (examining the relationship between several sets of data). The methods of carrying out the analysis can become very complex; but the basic idea is always the same—namely, that given a set of real-world data which lie around a diagram in a scattered way, you try to 'fit a line' by some Statistical means in order to express a summarized notion of the trend or relationship you are examining. (Recalling Section 7.1, you will realize that this is just one way in which the analysis of data entails a 'gain in knowledge by the orderly loss of information'.)

To take a couple of well-known examples of this approach from macro-economics: it was by this kind of 'line-fitting' that Phillips derived his famous curve; and one of the straightest of straight-line relationships in empirical economics is the long-run relationship between national income and total consumption.

'Model-building', in the econometrician's sense, also depends essentially on regression analysis. But the model-building approach includes an additional element which distinguishes it from line-fitting. The model-builder does not just start from a set of data and try to 'fit a line' to them on some purely Statistical basis. What he does, instead, is to turn to the ideas of deductive economic *theory* first of all, in order to construct a 'model'—expressed in algebraic terms—which he thinks on theoretical grounds may express the economic relationship which he is investigating.

The econometrician pays particular attention to the details of setting up this model—that is, choosing what variables to include and what relationships to put them in. This is the *specification* stage of the model-building process.

Only when the model-builder has completed his specification does he go on to *test* his model against his data. The process of testing consists essentially in computing the data together to find the numerical values of the unknowns in his model which give the 'best' fit in Statistical terms; and then considering how 'good' a fit this 'best fit' actually is. Very often, after the first try at testing, the econometrician may respecify the model to try to give a 'better' fit, and this process may be repeated several times over. With the same idea in mind, the econometrician may also try varying the sets of data which he uses to express the various theoretical notions included in his original model. The specification and set of data that give the 'best' fit are then judged to be those which give the 'best' model of the economic process under examination.

This initial description of model-building can best be reinforced by taking a simple example—one that is far too simple to merit the attention of practical model-builders, but which nevertheless brings out the essentials of the procedure. We are investigating the relationship between national income and total consumption, and as our first step we want to build a model. From Keynesian theory, we are aware of the postulate that consumption varies with national income; in algebra

$$C = f(Y)$$

using the symbols for consumption and national income.

Needless to say, a model as generally stated as this would be of no use for empirical testing; but we can be more specific about the relationship. In our model, let us suggest that the relationship between national income and consumption is positive, and has the form of a straight line. So our model becomes the familiar textbook equation of the constant-slope consumption function,

$$C = a + bY$$

Since we are going to test this against yearly data, let us incorporate into the model the suggestion that the level of consumption in any given year varies with national income in that same year, showing this by adding a subscript t to the symbols:

$$C_t = a + bY_t$$

Now, this version of the model, as it stands, is *deterministic*. It hypothesizes that in each year observed, consumption will vary with national income in an *exact* straight-line relationship. From our earlier discussion, we are already familiar with the idea that real-life observations cannot be expected to throw up this kind of exact result, and that real-life hypotheses are therefore usually phrased in *probabilistic* terms. The econometrician recognizes this, and makes it explicit in his model by introducing a modification which is central to econometric thinking (indeed, some writers view it as defining econometric analysis): he adds an *error term* to his equation. In our example, the probabilistic version of the model would run:

$$C_t = a + bY_t + u_t$$

where u_t is the error term. Very broadly speaking, this term signifies the amount by which the observed value of C in year t has been 'thrown out' by the chancy nature of real-world observation. In Section 9.4.5, where the general topic of error in relation to econometric method is discussed, we shall come back to look more closely at the nature and role of the error term.

Having completed the specification stage, the econometrician would turn to the statistics for national income and consumption for the run of years he was examining, and would run his regression so as to attach those values to the a and b in the equation which give the 'best fit' in Statistical terms.

The econometrician would then judge whether this best fit is 'good' enough to be acceptable. In making this judgement, the criterion used is provided by various *tests of significance*. Essentially, these give an idea of the probability of the observed relationship arising by mere chance: the less this probability, the more likely is it judged to be that there is a genuine relationship between the variables in question. Conventionally, if the probability of a relationship taking place by chance is less than 1 in 20, the variable concerned is christened 'significant'; while if the probability of chance occurrence is less than 1 in 100, the term usually applied is 'highly significant'.

If the fit given by the initial model and set of data is not acceptable in Statistical terms (or, very often, even when it is, but the econometrician thinks it could be improved still further), the next step will be to respecify the model, and perhaps to use different data. The ways in which the respecification can be done are suggested by the investigator's own views about the possible form of the economic relationship (which, in turn, may be dictated by his theoretical reasoning, or may depend purely on commonsense appraisal of the ways in which economic relations may work in practice). For instance, the econometrician in our simplified example might think it possible on commonsense grounds that the level of total consumption in any one year depended on the level of national income in the *previous* year, i.e.,

$$C_t = a + bY_{t-1} + u_t$$

and he would then run his calculation in this modified manner, with a 'lag' between national income and consumption data, to see whether the fit turned out to be better or worse—in terms of Statistical significance—than that given by the first model. The model could be respecified in many other ways: the form of the suggested relationship could be altered from a straight line to a curve (for instance, one could set up a model which showed a downward 'droop' of the consumption function at higher income levels); or another variable or variables could be introduced, entailing a change from simple to multiple regression analysis.

Then again, the econometrician might try several different choices of data to express the terms in his model. For the Y showing income, he might use series of figures for GNP, NNP, gross domestic product, and so on. Likewise, there are various series which may be pressed into service as a measurement of C, consumption.

Typically, the model-builder will juggle around with all these various styles of respecification; each time, he will calculate how 'good' a fit he gets according to his Statistical criterion.

When one version of the model has been identified as the one which gives the 'best' fit, the econometrician will often check it out by using it for *prediction*; that is, he will take values of his independent variable for years as yet unobserved, and see how well his 'best' model succeeds in predicting the values of the dependent variable in these years. In our example, this would mean that given values of national income in years as yet unobserved, the econometrician would calculate the corresponding values of consumption in those years according to his model, and then see how closely these calculated figures approached to the observed figures for the years concerned.

This would seem to imply that the model-builder would have to wait several years from the time he specified his model until the time he could test it against predictions. In fact, what is usually done is to use the device which we remember from Section 4.2 as being employed by Phillips in testing his famous curve—that is, 'predicting the past'. The econometrician will deliberately leave a few recent years out of his data set when he calculates the values of the unknowns in his model, and will then use the figures in these years as his 'predictive' testing-ground.

This account of the factual detail of 'model-building' simplifies the process as much as it possibly can be simplified. There are thick volumes of literature which detail all the technicalities and difficulties of carrying out this kind of analysis on economic data. Very largely, these technicalities arise from the fact that the data available to the econometrician are usually very different from the physical and biological data which Statistical methods were originally devised to deal with.

Frequently, for instance, economic data do not fall into the pattern of the 'normal distribution' which characterizes so many data sets in physics or biology. If you measure the distribution of height of a population, or of its intelligence, you get a spread of results with most of your observations falling around the middle ranges—it is more usual for a person to be of moderate height or intelligence than to be a dwarf or giant, idiot or genius. But, to quote one of many economic counter-instances: if you record the size distribution of a number of business enterprises in a given sector, you typically find that they 'cluster' towards the lower end of the size scale, with only a few very big firms at the high end. In Statisticians' parlance, the size distribution is 'skewed', and so are very many other distributions of data in economics.

Here once again, you should turn to a text on econometrics if you want to look through the complete rogues' gallery of Statistical problems which attach to economic data. For our present purposes, the point to note is this: in the most straightforward styles of Statistical analysis, designed as they were originally for the relatively neat data of the physical and biological sciences, these data problems of economics are ignored or 'assumed away'. The econometrician thus has two choices: he can either 'assume away' these data problems himself, and knowingly use straightforward Statistical methods which are not entirely adapted to the data he is handling; or, to one degree or another, he can introduce various modifications of Statistical theory devised to deal with the data problems he faces. The daunting complexity of present-day econometric procedure is almost entirely due to the development of such modifications. They are, as it were, a complicated technical superstructure built on the rather simple pattern of reasoning entailed in 'model-building', as it has been described above.

It is fair to say that at times, these technical developments have seemed to become the be-all and end-all of 'advancement' in econometric theory, as it has been viewed by econometricians themselves. At times, perhaps, this preoccupation with technical detail has diverted attention from some more fundamental features of econometric reasoning which might have repaid examination. Given that the Statistical superstructure of econometrics is large, complex, and imposing, how sound are its epistemological foundations?

9.2 The epistemology of econometrics

This description of the model-building process may perhaps have struck a bell of recollection in your mind. We have seen its successive stages: specification of the model, testing against data, further testing against predictions, then either provisional acceptance as 'probably the best model', or rejection and respecification. What this may remind you of is the formulation and testing of a *hypothesis*, a subject we first met in Section 4.1.

And indeed, the fact is that 'model-building', in epistemological terms, is really a specialized form of hypothesis formulation and testing. The original model corresponds to the hypothesis; and you will see that in specifying the model, the econometrician is really giving a lot of effort to formulating this hypothesis in precise detail, expressed algebraically. The 'testing' stage entails checking the model against real-life data, using Statistical criteria to see how well the model and these real-life data correspond. Finally, the stages of respecification and retesting reflect the reformulation and empirical rechecking of hypotheses with which we are already familiar from our discussion of hypothetico-deductive method.

As we know, all testing must entail reasoning in the form of the hypothetical syllogism, and econometric model-testing is no exception. It is instructive to work out just what hypothetical syllogism needs to be used in this particular testing process.

As we saw, the econometrician checks for the existence of a Statistical relationship between the variables he is studying. But why does he do this? Obviously, because he wants to get an idea whether there is a cause-and-effect connection between the economic phenomena represented by these variables. Thus, the hypothetical he starts from can be spelt out in some such way as this, calling the two variables simply X and Y:

1. *If* there is a causal link between variable X and variable Y, *then* the value of X will vary with the value of Y (within acceptable limits of random variation).

The phrase in brackets is added as a reminder that the econometrician does not expect the observed values of his variables to fall into an *exact* relationship one with the other; he accepts that there will be a certain amount of random variation in the observed values, and uses his statistical tests of significance and correlation as a standard of whether the variation is or is not to be regarded as 'acceptable'.

We must be particularly careful not to mix up the antecedent and the consequent of this hypothetical. We say: 'If there is a causal link, then X and Y will vary together'—and *not*: 'If X and Y vary together, then there is a causal link.' It is a matter of common sense to see why this is. To formalize matters a bit more: this hypothetical, like all hypotheticals used in empirical testing, depends for its acceptance on *intersubjective* agreement; and, for rather obvious reasons, the first version is intersubjectively acceptable, while the second is not.

How about the remaining two statements of the syllogism? The econometrician would probably *not* choose to phrase his reasoning in this way:

2. the value of X does vary with the value of Y (within acceptable limits of random variation);
3. therefore there is a causal link between X and Y.

If he were to do so, as we well know, he would be committing the fallacy of affirming the consequent (if you are in doubt why this is so, have a look back at Section 4.4.1). He would probably prefer to take the more formally correct 'falsificationist' approach, and see if he could say:

2. the value of X does *not* vary with value of Y (within acceptable limits of statistical variation);
3. therefore there is no causal link between X and Y.

Texts in Statistics and econometrics, indeed, usually follow this formally more acceptable line, and regard the hypothesis (represented by the model) as being put up for Statistical refutation, rather than for verification.

However, as we saw in Section 4.4.2, when one is working with real-world probabilistic data, this formal distinction between verification and falsification becomes pretty blurred. Because we have allowed for the likely presence of random variation, we admit that we can never say for certain either that X does vary with Y, *or* that it does not; instead we must say that the X and Y *probably* do, or *probably* do not, vary together.

Further, the Statistical criteria of 'acceptability' in random variation are themselves purely arbitrary. Conventionally, we refer to a relationship as 'highly significant', 'significant', or 'not significant', according to the probability figures mentioned above. But these figures, and the phrases used to describe them, are merely convenient intersubjective rules of thumb.

And, as we have noted, the econometrician does not in any case necessarily stop testing and respecifying as soon as he gets a model which gives him 'acceptable' results according to these rules of thumb; often he will respecify and retest until he has several different versions of the model, all of which give him results which fall within the zone of Statistical acceptability. He may then choose between these alternative versions according to his Statistical criterion of 'goodness of fit' to give one version that is regarded as provisionally 'the best', pending the development of any other versions which perform still better according to the criterion chosen. Again this reflects an epistemological concept—that of attaching differing 'degrees of confirmation' to differing hypotheses (Section 4.4.2). This last notion probably gives the most realistic epistemological description of what is actually done in model-building and model-testing.

If all this seems a bit abstract, let us return to our much-simplified model of the relationship between national income and consumption:

$$C_t = a + bY_t + u_t$$

In order to get this into testable form against the statistics available, the econometrician needs to make a deduction along the lines mentioned above, namely: 'If C really is determined by Y, then, over a run of years, the observed values of C and Y should vary with one another, within acceptable limits of random variation.' To deduce this from the original model entails the use of several auxiliary hypotheses (recall Section 4.4.3). You may care to work out for yourself what these are. Some are trivial, as in all scientific hypothesizing; but one auxiliary hypothesis which does have practical relevance is this: 'My data for the value of C and Y can be accepted as appropriate measures of the economic concepts "consumption" and "national income."' In the discussion of error in the previous chapter, we have seen that the material truth of *this* particular auxiliary hypothesis always needs careful examination.

As it happens, in the case of the two variables which come into this particular example—'consumption' and 'national income'—there would be a high degree of intersubjective agreement that the data series available to the econometrician are empirically acceptable. Thus, he will go on to set the data against his model: taking the observed values for consumption and national income over the run of years he was studying, he will solve for the *a* and *b* in his equation. In econometric parlance, these unknowns in the equation are called the *parameters* (or *coefficients*) of the model. Crucially, his Statistical calculations will not only 'fit the line' which expresses the relationship between his plotted data, but will give him a measure of the Statistical significance of the relationship—that is, of how probable it is that this relationship could have arisen by mere chance. The less this probability, as we have seen, the more 'significant' does the econometrician consider his result to be.

The investigator might go on, in the way already described, to try different sets of data or to alter the specification of his model. Finally, having chosen the 'best' version of the model, he might try using it for prediction—whether genuine prediction or 'prediction of the past'—to see whether, given values of national income in unobserved years, the model turned out results for consumption which were acceptably near the observed figures for this variable.

For these particular two variables, C and Y, it turns out that in most developed economies the relationship between the two data sets is very close, with the plotted results for a run of years clustering tightly round a straight line. Thus the investigator can say: 'Yes, there *is* a close Statistical relationship between C and Y.'

It is important, though, to register what he can and cannot conclude on the basis of this Statistical finding. We are well aware that he is *not* able to say: 'Therefore, consumption is determined by national income.' What he can say correctly is a lot more complex and indefinite, and would go something like this:

1. I have shown that there is a close Statistical relationship between C and Y;
2. in other words, I have shown that these variables are related so closely that the relationship could pretty certainly not be caused by pure chance.
3. I recognize that it is still *perhaps* the case that C is *not* determined by Y;
4. but my Statistical results have made this eventuality of 'perhaps not' seem pretty unlikely;
5. therefore I can regard my original hypothesis—namely that C is determined by Y—as having drawn strong support from this Statistical finding.

We may register that no technical developments in analysis can in the least alter the epistemological scheme of things as it has been described in this section. Whatever the mathematical procedures used, model-building remains hypothetico-deductive in nature. The necessary reasoning must be cast in the form of the hypothetical syllogism, with the 'testing' stage attempting to check the material truth of the *consequent* of the hypothetical.

These limitations apply, of course, not only to econometric model-building but to any investigation, in any field of science, which is based on a hypothetico-deductive approach. However, it can be argued that some features of economic investigation make it especially important for the econometrician, as compared, say, to the physicist or biometrician, to be aware of the epistemological limitations of the methods he is using. In later sections of this chapter, some of the reasons for this will be suggested.

9.3. Model-building as 'explanation'

If any dedicated model-builders happen to read the last section, they will almost certainly be indignant at the implied suggestion that a 'best' model would be chosen from several possible versions on the criterion of Statistical 'fit' *alone*. That, they will tell us, is mere line-fitting. The whole point of model-building is that the empirical evidence, as assessed by Statistical procedures, is held to tell only *part* of the story. Just as important, in the model-builder's view, is to reason out his model correctly at the stage of specification, by rigorous deduction from whatever part of economic theory he judges appropriate to his problem, and to make sure that in any subsequent respecification, no slips in this deductive reasoning are allowed to creep in.

What the model-builders are arguing here is that the use of models in econometrics is an aid to *explanation*, in the sense in which we met this word in Section 4.5—that is, the process of tying in empirical observation with the deductive framework of a theory. As we saw, the confidence we place in a hypothesis does not rest only on the strength of the empirical support we have for it, but also on its logical consistency with other propositions in the theory we are using.

On this interpretation, the econometric model plays the role of a low-level statement in economic theory; this statement is compared with observation of the p-domain, via rules of correspondence defined by the Statistical procedures used. Thus, the econometrician will argue, model-building can assist in the development of empirically based theory in economics. Likewise, on this argument, the appraisal of the theoretical correctness of the model chosen can aid interpretation and prediction of the data observed.

Clearly, this is an important argument, and one that deserves close consideration. But I am now about to suggest that, at least in the present state of economic science, the explanatory function of econometric models is, unfortunately, more apparent than real.

The trouble with the econometricians' argument is this: it depends on the presumption that economic theory corresponds to the textbook picture of the ideal theory of general science—that is, a network of statements which are comprehensively linked in a single deductive framework, free of mutual inconsistency or irrelevance. But, as we know from Section 6.3, what we call 'economic theory' is—at least in the present state of the art—not like this at all. Instead, it seems to consist of a conglomeration of 'models'—in the *epistemologist's* sense this time—some of which may be irrelevant or contradictory to others, and which are deductively linked only very tenuously or not at all. As we have seen, it is often difficult to decide what 'low-level statements' can be worked out to provide acceptable tests of these models, because the *applicability* of the models can be viewed as inadequately specified or else non-ascertainable (Section 6.3.5). Viewed in this light, the model-builders' claim to be using 'theory as an aid to explanation' must be viewed with a certain scepticism.

One of the greatest unsolved problems of empirical economics today, as several writers have pointed out, is that econometric model-building has not made any noticeable headway in weeding out 'conflicting hypotheses' in the economic c-domain. Once we accept that the higher levels of economic 'theory' are in any case 'models' (in the epistemologist's sense), then this failure becomes unsurprising. It clearly may be the case that an econometric model which lends support to a given set of higher-level statements in one set of applicability conditions may fail to do so in another, and vice versa.

And, of course, in so far as this *is* the reason why econometric model-building has not succeeded in 'weeding out less sound hypotheses' from the higher-level statements of economics, then to that same extent it becomes pointless to suggest that one can appraise an econometric model on the criterion of its consistency *with* these higher-level statements.

I close this section by adding another sceptical note on whether model-building, as carried out in actual practice, really does go very far towards 'using theory to aid explanation'. (An econometrician who vetted a draft of this chapter added a marginal note beside the coming paragraph, saying: 'This is not a criticism of econometrics—it is a criticism of *bad* econometrics.' Having thought over his comment, I am going to go ahead and make the criticism anyway, replying first: 'Granted that what I am going to talk about *is* bad econometrics, then it seems as though a very great deal of the econometrics that actually gets done is bad econometrics.')

The criticism is this: in practice, the specification of econometric models is often only vaguely linked to the propositions of 'economic theory'. Certainly, the econometrician may start with an equation, the form of which is set by mathematical economic theorizing. But in testing and respecification, he will usually just add and take away variables on an *ad hoc* basis, using his intuition and prior knowledge of the situation under study. (Alarming as the notion may be to empirically minded econometricians, this procedure brings the model-builder close to the introspective economists of the analytical school, even though the latter have usually not tried to add Statistical figuring to their common sense.) And, despite the scruples of these econometricians who see their procedure as drawing support from economic theory, the real-life model-builder will usually choose between various possible versions of his model solely on the criterion mentioned in Section 9.2—that is, he will favour the model which maximizes his measure of Statistical 'significance'.

9.4 Application

9.4.1 Causation

In this and the following sections, we look at some of the problems which arise when econometric method is applied to the analysis of economic policy questions. Most of these problems relate back, in some measure, to the epistemological limitations which we have noted in the earlier sections of this chapter.

We may as well enter a reminder of what we have chosen as the hoped-for objective of any kind of economic analysis—that is, to aid the policy-maker by proffering an *explanation* of economic events. The term 'explanation' is to be interpreted in the more lax of its two possible definitions: we shall say we have 'explained' an economic event in so far as our explanation helps us to exercise control over future economic occurrences of the same type. Finally, let us recall that *prediction* may or may not accompany explanation in this sense: you may come across prediction which gives very little assistance in control, and you may achieve control while not being able to make any specific prediction.

With these notions as our starting-point, then, let us examine some of the practical problems of applying econometric methods. The first problem to consider is that of establishing *causation*.

As we are by now well aware, correlation can never show causation. All that can be shown is that a causal link between variables is at least possible—or, to put it in falsificationist language, that the existence of the causal link has at least not been ruled out.

Now, this picture, as we have also seen, applies not only to econometrics, but to *any* form of scientific investigation that entails the testing of hypotheses against observed data. Why, then, do we especially need to bear it in mind when looking at econometrics?

Here we come back to a point we first met in Section 5.3, namely, that in trying to tie up correlation and causality, the social scientist has a much harder job to do than the physical (or biological) scientist. As we saw, in the physical sciences it is usually possible to set up *controlled* experiments, in which two versions of the experimental set-up are used, identical but for the vital difference that in the 'control' the scientist does *not* introduce the factor whose effect he is trying to gauge. Then, if he can establish that an effect follows in the version where he does introduce the change, he is intersubjectively reckoned to be safe in saying that this effect has been caused by the change he introduced.

The social scientist, we saw, is usually not so lucky. He cannot normally conduct experiments, nor use 'controls'. In other words, he almost always has to face situations in which it is likely that not just one possible cause of events, but several, may be operating at the same time. Thus, even if Statistical methods show a close correlation between a set of *possible* causal factors and the observed events, the investigator will usually have great difficulty in establishing (intersubjectively) the existence of a causal link.

Every textbook of econometrics points out that 'correlation does not demonstrate causation'. Unfortunately, this does not seem to have prevented many econometric studies being done on the apparent assumption that correlation—if it can only be shown to be close enough—*does* demonstrate causation. The error of this view can perhaps be underlined in this way: the textbooks are fond of talking about 'nonsense correlations'—that is, close correlations between sets of data between which there could not, by any sane reasoning, be a causal connection. One text points out a close correlation between the number of storks in Sweden and the birth-rate there; while another writer has recently drawn attention to an almost perfect relationship between the rise in the number of economists employed by the UK government and the fall in the purchasing power of the pound. In Statistical terms, correlations like these may work out to be highly 'significant'; but clearly, say the books, it would be nonsense to read any causal connection into this.

And, of course, so it would.* But the econometrics texts seldom go on to draw a further, and important, epistemological conclusion. The fact is: *all correlations, in themselves, are nonsense correlations*. Looking back at these two examples: on what grounds do we say the correlations are 'nonsense'? Not because of any lack of Statistical 'significance'. Rather, it is because we have realized the need to consider commonsense evidence *in addition to* the Statistical results. Since it is this reasoning that enables us to identify some correlations as being nonsense, we must conclude—correctly—that we use the same kind of evidence to identify 'non-nonsense' correlations. Thus we are led back to the conclusion: Statistical evidence, on its own, can never allow us to appraise the strength of a causal link, *no matter how close the correlation between the observed variables*. A close correlation, of course, helps support the hypothesis that there *may* be a causal link. It encourages the investigator to examine the background data to try to arrive at a common-sense assessment of what the causal link or links may be. But it can never, in itself, tell us anything about the nature of cause-and-effect relationships.

There is a feature of model-building which accentuates the problem still further. If a model is simple, i.e., has relatively few variables, it will call for relatively simple computations, and will be capable of giving relatively clear-cut Statistical results; but at the same time it will often be too simple to give a useful portrayal of the reality of an economic situation. If, however, the econometrician elaborates his model by adding more and more variables, he may get nearer and nearer to a full portrayal of the workings of the real-life economy, but at the same time the results of his analysis become more and more difficult to interpret, and the calculations required become more costly.

As a tailpiece to this section, some complex econometric procedures, still being elaborated, claim that they *do* demonstrate causality. At first sight, it seems difficult to understand how this can be possible, since it would indicate that the econometricians involved had somehow found a way to evade the fundamental epistemological arguments which have just been sketched out.

On examination, though, it turns out that nothing of the kind has taken place. What these econometric techniques actually do is this: given two sets of data $X_1, X_2, \ldots, X_n$ and $Y_1, Y_2, \ldots, Y_n$, the analysis does not only work out the correlation between the X's and Y's; it establishes also whether each X

---

* A colleague who read this chapter in draft commented here: 'But would it?' I leave this question to your judgement.

happened before the Y it corresponds to, or after. If the X happened first, then the investigator will state that X 'caused' Y; if the Y happened first, then Y is held to have 'caused' X.

I hope that, if any econometricians chance to read this, they will excuse this drastic simplification of a very ingenious mathematical technique. But I hope also that they will admit that its epistemological foundations are, to say the very least, shaky. Probably, common sense will already have told you why. But the point can be brought home by considering this proposition: 'In the Western economies, there is typically a large upsurge in the amount of currency in circulation in the few weeks before Christmas. Therefore, the occurrence of Christmas is caused by the rise in currency circulation.'*

Obviously, of course, it is reasonable to suggest that this kind of reversed time-order in causation is unusual, and that *if* X causes Y, *then*, as a rule, X will happen before Y. But suppose even that events do happen in this more normal time order, and that we do observe a series of X's happening before a series of Y's. Quite clearly still, this does not allow us to conclude that, in any normal sense of the word, the X's have 'caused' the Y's. If we tried to argue this, we would be falling into the elementary trap of the *post hoc ergo propter hoc* fallacy—and so are the econometricians who say that this particular procedure can 'demonstrate causation'.

9.4.2 *Motivation*

The next point is really a special instance of the previous one. It turns on the particular nature of the 'causation' we are most concerned with in economics and the other social sciences. As we know, in these sciences we are concerned with *people*. (In economics, we must say 'with people *as well as* with things'.) And, when it comes down to it, economics must be concerned, not just with the actions of people, but with the actions of *individual* people. Admittedly, it is very often convenient, in studying economic questions, to talk about aggregated groups *as if they were* individual beings. We talk about 'the reactions of the economy' to a certain policy, or the 'objectives of the firm' as regards profit maximization, to give just two examples. But in the economic *p*-domain, there is in reality no such thing as 'the economy'; no such thing as a 'sector' or an 'industry'; no such thing as a 'firm'; indeed no such thing as a 'household'. All these things are *constructs*, which we use as useful devices in our economic reasoning. What we are really observing, in all these cases, is the mass result of the actions of individuals. And if, as investigators, we are trying to get an idea of the causes behind economic events, we may land in trouble if we forget that these events are dictated by the motivations, knowledge, and reactions of individual people.

One problem of econometric techniques—as indeed of all styles of investigation that use aggregate data—is that they can never look directly at

* This splendid example, I must ruefully admit, is not my own: it was coined by Joseph P. McKenna.

motivation. Instead, the user of these methods can only hypothesize motivations, and then see how far his hypothesis is supported by the aggregate figures he is examining. This remains equally true, whether the method in use is simple 'eyeballing' or the most elaborate econometric analysis.

Some writers have suggested that this suggested limitation of aggregate approaches is more apparent than real. The line taken by these writers is that motivations are bound to be pretty obscure anyway, and that therefore the economist should deliberately turn away from trying to find out what these motivations are; his objective should simply be to find a method that predicts accurately what is going to happen in the economy at mass level, and then to proceed straight from this prediction to the recommendation of policy.

Whether, in fact, one can claim that econometric methods *do* aid in 'prediction' is a question which I shall take up in a later section. For now, we may bring back to mind the epistemological objections to the viewpoint that 'prediction is all that matters' (Section 4.5). Prediction, we saw, may help in explanation, or it may not. In fact, in the specific context of applied economics, we can be more precise about the reasons for this. The point is that economic *policy* measures must have their effect at the level of the individual in the first instance, irrespective of what the aggregate results may turn out to be. Groups—such as firms, sectors, households—cannot themselves 'react' to policy, or indeed to anything, except in terms of the total reactions of all the individuals in the group. Clearly, then, since the investigator is trying to give advice which will help with control of these actions, it is important for him to know how individuals react to various policy measures, why they react as they do, how they may react in the future, and indeed, whether they know anything about the policy measure in the first place! Any investigational method using aggregate data can do no more than guess at these questions, whether or not the guesses are accompanied by Statistical analysis.

9.4.3 Intangibles

An 'intangible', roughly defined, is some feature of an economic situation which the economist believes to be relevant to the problem under analysis, but which cannot readily be expressed in quantitative terms (monetary or otherwise)—things like amenity, nuisance, noise, pollution, and so on. With these features also, econometric and other aggregate methods of analysis have problems. The reason for this will be plain from what we know about the nature of model-building and econometric methods in general —namely, that their essence consists in finding relationships between sets of quantitative variables and arguing back from the Statistical links to possible causal links. Therefore, when the econometrician meets a likely causal factor that cannot readily be put into quantitative terms, he has several possible ways to proceed—none of which is very satisfactory. He can simply ignore the factor altogether. Alternatively, he can give it a verbal mention in the text accompanying his figuring, without attempting to attach any quantitative importance to it. While this practice necessarily comes into a lot of economic problem-solving, not just into econometrics, it is rather obvious why it is more of a relative shortcoming when econometric methods are being used: the main objective of these methods is to produce a detailed *quantitative* analysis of a situation, rather than looking at things qualitatively.

As a final alternative—and perhaps the most potentially dangerous one of all—the econometrician can cast around for some quantitative figure which he can use to 'stand in' for the intangible in question—the sort of figure which economists call a *proxy measure*.* To give two well-known examples: to quantify the concept 'economic activity'—which cannot be directly identified with any one series of economic statistics—it is usual to use the proxy of unemployment percentage (the looked-for relationship, of course, being negative). Or, to mention a more difficult case, some econometricians have used statistics of 'days lost in disputes' as a proxy for the concept 'union wage-bargaining pressure'.

You may be able to work out by common sense why I have suggested that this is 'potentially the most dangerous' course to choose in dealing with intangibles; the point will be taken up again in Section 9.4.5.

9.4.4 Prediction

In Chapter 5, we looked in some detail at the question of inductive-statistical prediction and the limitations which it meets in the social sciences. At this point, therefore, all we need do is to enter a brief reminder of these limitations, and to register how they apply to the particular kind of inductive reasoning which is used in econometrics.

We noted that the economist could not predict the behaviour of people in anything like the same way that the physicist can predict, say, the 'behaviour' of gas molecules. As we saw, this may or may not be because people have 'free will' in reality; what concerns us as economists is not the truth or otherwise of that psychological-philosophical proposition—but the empirical fact that, in the present 'state of the art' at least, we *cannot* predict the behaviour of people with systematic quantitative accuracy.

We saw that, in economic studies using Statistical techniques predictively, the implied reasoning was that while people's behaviour could not be predicted at individual level, it could be predicted in the mass within Statistical limits of probability. And our final realization was that this

---

* As an epistemological aside, it may be added that *any* empirical statistic must to some extent be a 'stand-in' for the concept which it is being used to express; in other words, *all* measures are proxy measures, but some are more proxy than others. In reality, of course, there is a large degree of intersubjective agreement on what statistics are to be regarded as 'proxy measures' and what others are to be regarded as straightforward quantification of the concepts concerned.

implied reasoning had never been shown to be correct; on the contrary, there were strong arguments to suggest that it was incorrect. In trying to predict human behaviour, we faced not just statistical *uncertainty*, but also *ignorance*; we could never know in advance how probable it was that a Statistical relationship worked out from past observation would continue to apply during the period of prediction.

In the context of econometrics, it is worth while to mention yet again a point which was stressed in our general discussion in Chapter 5. That is, these limitations of inductive prediction in economics are an epistemological fact of life which *cannot be evaded by any Statistical computation, no matter how sophisticated.*

Some econometricians, in writing about the methodology of their discipline, have explicitly recognized this limitation. For instance, L. R. Klein has pointed out that:

> . . . econometrics is a way of studying history—a very systematic way. We never know what economic behaviour will be like in future, unobserved situations, but we try to make as strong a statement as possible about this unknown area on the basis of past history . . . a sensible method of extrapolation is not naive or mechanical, and the econometrician is no less flexible than any other historian who tries to evaluate the future on the basis of the past.

This underlines the real usefulness of econometric method in economic analysis: it enables the analyst to make a very explicit examination of the degree of relation between features of an economic situation which he sees as possibly being causally important, and thus gives him the material on which he can base his overall appraisal—aided essentially by his qualitative assessment of the meaning of the variables whose interrelationships he has demonstrated. Without this commonsense back-up, as we have seen, correlation in itself is meaningless.

In the same way, though Statistical computation is in itself not predictive, it can *aid* prediction: by laying bare the relationships between observed variables, it can help the analyst to make his commonsense appraisal of the causal links which may be involved, and hence to try to assess how likely it is that these causal relationships will persist into the period of prediction.

Unfortunately, the perceptiveness of writers like Klein has not always been matched by other practitioners of econometrics, or by the bodies who commission econometric studies. The superstition still persists that, somehow, the computations of econometric method provide a 'crystal ball' which can attach quantitative values to the unknown future courses of economic variables. It is easy to see why policy-makers in official circles feel the lure of a method which seems to promise a spy-hole into the future; and easy, also, to see why some economists, seeking sources of funds to back research, are ready to attempt to supply this need. But, as we know, there are fundamental epistemological arguments which make it pretty clear that econometric analysis cannot supply the systematic prediction which is called for by policy-makers. And indeed, the track record of econometric work—as compared to other, cheaper and simpler means of prediction—seems no more impressive than these epistemological arguments would lead one to expect. This point will be taken up again in Section 9.5.

9.4.5 Sources of error

You will recall the formidable list of 'sources of observational error' which we went through briefly in Section 8.2.2. Now, there is no conceivable method of economic investigation that is immune to these sources of error: all methods—eyeballing, survey method, econometrics—are bound to be affected to some extent by the various kinds of human error that we listed, and, where applicable, by machine error as well. However, where econometric method is in the picture, there are certain kinds of error which need to be watched for with special care.

One of the most obvious is that the econometrician, probably more than the user of any other kind of investigative method, is 'distanced' from the possible human errors in collection and analysis which may affect his raw data. The danger is that this 'distancing', together with the reassuringly complex nature of the computerized calculations carried out, may make econometric results especially liable to spurious accuracy.

The fact is, of course, that no Statistical method, however sophisticated, can give final results which are more accurate than the raw data. This point, like one or two others we have come across, is made by every textbook of econometrics, but seems not to have stopped some econometricians from going ahead with investigations in which very complex methods of analysis are applied to raw data in which the margin of observational error may potentially be large.

Another type of error we mentioned, *machine error*, is clearly a more severe pitfall in econometrics than in less complex styles of investigation, simply because almost all econometric studies entail the use of the computer. Here, we can bring back to mind the point that computer error is not by any means always tied up with actual *faults* in the computer; it can arise from various features of rounding and calculation which themselves are built into the computer, and therefore may be extremely difficult to detect.

It can be suggested that in econometric work we have to pay special attention to one further source of error, though the nature of the 'error' is more subtle, and perhaps even more difficult to quantify, than were the sources mentioned in Section 8.2.2. This is the error which may arise from the use of *proxy measures* in econometric studies (recall page 203). The statistics thus used may be judged 'acceptably' accurate as measures of the economic variable for which they are 'standing in'; but a familiar problem arises—it is never possible to tell quantitatively how 'inaccurate' a proxy measure is in this sense. All the economist can do is to keep in his own mind the fact that such inaccuracy is built into his results; and, more important, to make sure those results are presented in such a way as to keep this fact in the reader's mind also.

Here again, this is a problem which is not confined to econometrics—it must be borne in mind by anyone who is using any kind of proxy measure—but which calls for extra caution in econometric work because of the complex nature of the calculations that are carried out. A computer, as we know, will churn out results to a degree of 'accuracy' which may on occasion be spurious. This is always a matter for commonsense judgement on the part of the investigator. If, for instance, a model entails the use of 'days lost in disputes' as a proxy for union wage-bargaining pressure, then, no matter how many decimal places appear in the results nor how high the correlation coefficient, the model's results only have meaning in so far as the proxy actually *does* give a meaningful measure of union wage-bargaining pressure.

As the final point to be covered in this section: where, you may ask, does the 'error term'—the u which we first met on page 190—come into all this?

Again, texts in econometrics give a range of different answers to this question. At a very simple level of exposition, the error term is portrayed as merely expressing the amount by which an actual observation differs from what it might have been expected to be on the basis of the deterministic version of whatever model is being used; in this simple version, the error term is put in just to take account of the fact that empirical observation is probabilistic, or in other words, the error term is there to signal the presence of *sampling error* (which we discussed in Section 8.2.1).

All the books, in fact, agree that this is one role of the error term. When it comes to the treatment of *observational error*, however, opinions differ widely among econometric writers. Some books (such as the one from which I took the quotation on page 184) simply 'assume away' the presence of observational error. Other writers say that observational error (*as well as* sampling error) is one of the justifications of the error term, without saying anything more about why this should be so; and still other writers, while also lumping observational error into the error term, justify this by making the assumption that observational error is random. On page 184 we have already had cause to criticize this assumption in the context of economic data.

But even these tasks do not complete the role of the error term as it is described in many books on econometric method: at least two more jobs are often assigned to it. One is that the error term is supposed to take care of mis-specification of the model, in the sense that the functional form of the model may have been mistaken or that it may have missed out some variables which should really have been put in. The other is that the econometrician may have (indeed, almost certainly *has*) missed out some equations about the working of the economy which have some degree of relevance to the economic situation he is setting out to investigate; again, any disturbance caused by this is viewed as showing itself in the error term.

We see, then, that this small and unobtrusive letter u is a very busy character indeed. And our final realization is that any kind of econometric estimation is only possible if the econometrician makes certain *assumptions* about the probability characteristics of u (in econometric jargon, these are the 'stochastic assumptions'). Some of these assumptions can be checked by empirical means from samples: others cannot. The details of what the assumptions entail would take us too far into the technicalities of econometric method, and you should turn to econometrics texts for this information. From these, you will note that, as with some other aspects of econometrics, the practitioner has the choice of making relatively simple assumptions which enable easy calculation but fail to allow for the Statistical peculiarities of economic data; or alternatively, making more realistic assumptions which make computation and interpretation more complex.

9.5 Summing-up

In Section 7.3, we suggested that the methodologist-economist may appraise different methods in the same way as he would appraise any economic question: that is, rather than attempting to assess the 'value' of a given method in isolation, he would *compare* different methods on what was essentially a cost–benefit approach.

Thus, in evaluating econometric method, we need to compare it with something. With what? Following through our economic reasoning, we should in theory compare it with the next-best alternative. In practice, needless to say, there is no agreement on what this 'next-best' is. Of the possible comparisons we can make, that between econometrics and survey method is given the next chapter to itself. Here, let us compare econometrics with simpler methods of aggregate analysis, which do not involve the regression techniques of econometrics, but rely instead on a more common-sense 'eyeballing' approach.

When you use econometrics, you are introducing into your analysis something *additional* to the more simple styles of investigation you could otherwise have used; and so the methodologist's question is: given that you do something extra, is it the case that you *get* something extra in return? If so, what form does this 'something extra' take? And, most important of all: does the value of this 'something extra' at least repay the extra costs of using econometric methods?

As always, we find ourselves unable to quantify the cost–benefit equation in this comparison. We have to use qualitative common sense, and the final answer will always to some extent be a matter of individual interpretation. But we may get some clues if we sum up the features of econometric method which have been covered in this chapter.

Despite all epistemological criticisms, it is still probably true to say that the biggest 'selling point' of econometric method, in relation to other possible methods of economic investigation, is its supposed ability to aid quantitative *prediction*. We have already examined the epistemologist's reasons for casting severe doubt on this ability. But how about the practical side of things? Does econometric prediction 'just happen to work' in practice, even though abstract arguments say it should not?

This sensible question is one which is extremely difficult to answer convincingly. The trouble is that an empirically acceptable answer could only be given if someone were able to make a systematic study of the predictive success of econometric work, not just in one area of economic investigation, but over the whole sweep of the subject; and this study would have to look at the success of predictions, not just in a few instances—because, of course, predictions can be right or wrong by pure chance—but over a Statistically reliable sample of cases. Needless to say, no one has ever carried out this mammoth task. Apart from the obvious problems of time and resources, there are other difficulties in the way of such a project. For a start, the investigator would have to find a way of making comparable all the diverse kinds of subject matter which may be covered in economic prediction.

Some exercises of this kind have been done for various very restricted areas of economic investigation, and, for what it is worth, the balance of findings seems to be that econometric methods do not have any more success in predicting events, taking one instance with another, than do other and simpler approaches. The reading guide at the end of this chapter will lead you to the results of some relevant studies.

Here in particular, it is important to realize that comparisons of predictive power need to be with the *next-best* alternative—or at least, with an alternative that can convincingly be argued to be the 'next-best'—and not just with any arbitrary alternative. When econometricians are trying to appraise predictive success, they very commonly compare the predictions of their models with predictions generated by what are called 'naïve' means. An example of 'naïve' prediction would be the assumption that past values would simply continue unchanged into the future; or that past trends would likewise continue exactly as in the past, with no variation from the observed trend line.

The trouble with this comparison is that, in practice, such 'naïve' methods are pretty certainly *not* the 'next-best' to econometric analysis. If we look at how practical economists, outside the econometric field, actually try to predict events, we see that they seldom are so unwary as to think that the past will just repeat itself in the future, or to make any other such naïve assumption. What they do, much more often, is to use their accumulated knowledge of the situations they are studying. They make a qualitative, commonsense appraisal of the cause-and-effect relations which have typically operated in these situations, then take into account their knowledge and guesses about future events which may react on this pattern, finally coming up with suggestions about the outcome of these events. These suggestions may be purely qualitative, or they may be quantitative, without the formal statement of Statistical 'confidence' that would be attached to econometric predictions. Virtually no systematic empirical work has been done in comparing such 'informed predictions'—as we might call them —with corresponding econometric predictions; but it would seem to be common sense that the econometric methods might emerge from the comparison with even less relative credit than they do from the comparison with 'naïve' methods.

Econometric methods, then, have not been shown to contribute systematically to the success of prediction in economics. And when it comes to the more general objective of *explanation* (or, we may say, control) of economic events, we see also that the potential 'something extra' contributed by econometrics must be pretty limited. Despite the Statistical analysis used, econometric analysis is no more able to look directly at *causation* than is any other aggregate approach to economic investigation. In particular, econometric method is 'distanced' from the individual *motivations* which must be so important in determining the responses to economic policy measures. Problems over the treatment of *intangibles* may further hamper the contribution which econometrics can make to explanation; and some sources of *error* in analysis may affect econometric results more severely than they do simpler approaches.

In reading through this section, you may have felt that I have emphasized the shortcomings and difficulties of the econometric approach, rather than its good points. In this impression you would be correct, and the choice of emphasis is deliberate. Textbooks on econometrics, perhaps understandably, seldom give much space to discussion of its epistemological and practical limitations.

There is, in fact, little doubt that econometrics has been 'oversold' in recent decades as a method of analysis. This development has been closely connected with the arrival of the computer, which has made it practical to carry out the complex calculations called for by econometric analysis. As Professor Kuhn has pointed out, there are fashions in science as in everything else, and econometrics is perhaps the most notable fashion ever to have emerged on the empirical side of economic science. Not too many years ago, it seemed almost as though econometrics was destined to take over the entire discipline of economics: the few methodologists who continued to contest its epistemological value were widely dismissed as out-of-date reactionaries.

But fashions change. Over the last few years, it has been noticeable that a certain disenchantment with econometrics has crept into the economic scene. This disenchantment has been expressed, not only by diehard analytical economists, but also by many empiricists, many of whom had previously been impressed by the seeming potential of econometrics. Some writers have pointed out that exaggerated claims have sometimes been made about the capabilities of econometric analysis, present or potential. It may perhaps be a growing scepticism about the ability of econometricians to 'deliver the goods' in line with these claims—even at some unspecified time in the future, when they have developed their procedures to a higher technical level—that lies at the root of the current change in attitudes to econometrics.

Reading guide: Chapter 9

There are so many textbooks available on econometrics, at every level, that it is almost superfluous to make recommendations. But here are three: as a basic introduction, R. J. Allard, *An Approach to Econometrics;*[1] from a more applied point of view, R. F. Wynn and K. Holden, *An Introduction to Applied Econometric Analysis;*[83] and for more advanced theory, R. and T. H. Wonnacott, *Econometrics.*[82]

More than most econometricians, L. R. Klein has been willing to discuss the epistemological problems of predictability and observational error; see his book *Econometrics.*[39]

A journal article which gives a good introduction to the process of 'model-building', in non-specialist language, is L. D. McClements, 'Some Aspects of Model-Building'.[55] Despite the journal in which it appears, its relevance is not confined to agricultural economics. In Krupp, *The Structure of Economic Science,*[42] read the essay by Gerhard Tintner.

An excellent monograph by Erich W. Streissler, *Pitfalls in Econometric Forecasting,*[79] discusses the 'problem of prediction' in the context of econometric work in greater technical depth than I have been able to do here.

For some empirical results on how econometric forecasting works in practice, try R. L. Cooper, 'The Predictive Performance of Quarterly Econometric Models of the United States'.[19] This is criticized in E. P. Howrey, L. R. Klein, and M. D. McCarthy, 'Notes on Testing the Predictive Performance of Econometric Models'.[29] Try also the article by C. F. Christ, 'Judging the Performance of Econometric Models of the US Economy'.[14]

For support of my assertion that 'a certain disenchantment' is arising over econometric method, turn again to D. P. O'Brien's article, 'Whither economics?',[63] mentioned in the reading guide to Chapter 6.

10

Survey method

Here, for a change, is a topic that must be familiar to everyone—economist or not—from everyday experience. Hardly a day goes by without the results of some 'opinion poll' or 'attitude survey' being reported in the news media. There is a fair chance that you yourself, at your door or on your way along the street, may have been invited by an interviewer to answer questions on anything from your political leanings to your preferences for different brands of tinned beans. We need no introduction, therefore, to the investigational approach known as *survey method*.

10.1 Basic detail

This mental picture of the interviewer with his questionnaire and clipboard is the one that will usually be conjured up in our mind by the mention of survey enquiries, and indeed this particular means of data collection—the face-to-face interview—is an important method of survey investigation. However, also very often used is the postal enquiry, in which questionnaires are sent through the post to be filled in by the respondents and returned; and sometimes interviews are carried out by telephone rather than by face-to-face encounter.

All these styles of data collection are typically carried out on samples of respondents, though sometimes it is practicable to make a 100 per cent enumeration of the group under study. There are some other kinds of enquiry which are closely related to these, but which may nor may not entail the use of formal sampling procedures; whether you count them as instances of 'survey method' or not is merely a matter of your choice of definitions. Among these are the *group discussion*, the name of which describes its nature; and *direct observation*, which implies a group of methods in which, instead of being asked what they do, people are actually observed doing it (for instance, the investigator might stand by the check-out in a supermarket and look at the relative frequency with which different brands of a given product turned up in the trolleys). The term *depth interviewing*—another that is probably quite familiar to you, if not this time from personal experience—is a catch-all phrase, indicating procedures which may range all the way from a full-scale psychiatrist's couch set-up, to the mere use of an ordinary interview in which the questions are left open to discussion and 'talking around', and not precisely phrased in advance.

Thus, of the four stages of the advisory process, that of data collection is the one which delineates the everyday image of survey work. But the survey researcher, like any other investigator, has all four stages of the process to carry out. The stage of problem formulation is as important here as in any other style of enquiry; and the survey researcher has available a formal means of aiding this process, the *pilot enquiry*. By this is meant a preliminary round of interviews (or whatever method of data collection is being used)—a 'dummy run', as it were, which serves to direct the investigator's mind to the important aspects of the topic and to the kinds of questions which will need to be asked to throw most light on these aspects. Often, there will be not just one but several rounds of pilot enquiry before the main enquiry is run. The survey researcher may start off with a very vague investigational brief, and an equally vague notion of the kinds of questions he will need to ask. After the first round of pilot interviews, in which he will simply 'talk around' the subject with a number of respondents, his ideas will probably crystallize sufficiently to let him draw out a specific set of interview questions in draft form; in the next (and perhaps subsequent) rounds of pilot study he will revise the questionnaire into its final form. Importantly, piloting will also help in revealing ambiguous or badly phrased questions.

We have already noted the range of methods which the survey researcher has available for the stage of data collection, and part of his task at this stage lies in working out which of these methods (or which combination of them) to use, a question which will be determined jointly by the question of cost and the objectives of the study. Very importantly also, he will pay great attention to the design of the questionnaire. Should the questions be 'pre-coded' or 'open'?—that is, should a set of predetermined answers be set out for checking by the interviewer, or should the answer given by the respondent be taken down in just the way it is expressed? Exactly how should the questions be worded so as to make quite clear what is being asked, without getting so verbose as to confuse or bore the respondent? Texts on survey method will give you full detail on this fascinating process of questionnaire design, a process which is still just as much an art as a science.

Also at the stage of data collection, the size and design of the sample have to be decided. Some texts give methods of working out 'optimum' sample size according to the cost of interviewing and the Statistical characteristics of the data, but more often than not in real-life enquiries the size of the sample is decided quite arbitrarily, in accordance with the total resources and the total time available for the carrying out of the survey.

For some enquiries, the sample may be purposively chosen, with no attempt at randomization; more often, a random method of selection is used. For many reasons of economy and practicability, it is seldom that a simple random sample will be employed (that is, the kind you would get just by tossing coins or throwing dice). Instead, various modifications are made which will lower the cost of selecting the sample and make for greater usefulness of the data, while preserving the unbiased nature of true random sampling as far as possible. For instance, a 'systematic random sample' is one in which, from the list of names from which the sample is to be drawn, you choose the *first* one at random; you then take every *n*th name, counting from that first randomly chosen one. Say, for instance, you had a total list of 5000 names, and wanted a final sample of 500; you would, of course, want to pick one name in ten. Thus for your 'random start' you would use random number tables to pick a number between 1 and 10; say it happened to be 3, then you would pick names 3, 13, 23, and so on. As you will see, this is a vast deal simpler than, say, throwing a set of dice 500 times.

Again, a sample is very often *stratified*. Say you are studying a certain industrial sector. As we have noted, the size distribution of firms is typically 'skewed'—that is, there are a few very big firms that account for a large proportion of the sector's business activity, and a long 'tail' of relatively very small firms. For many purposes, you will want to give a higher representation to the views and actions of the big firms than to those of the small (though not for all purposes, of course—it depends on the subject matter of the enquiry). To do this, you can divide your population into a number of size classes, and sample in such a way that proportionately more of the big firms than of the small are included in the sample. For chapter and verse on these and many other sampling devices, you can turn to the text cited in the reading guide at the end of the chapter.

Even before selecting the sample, the important question has to be settled: what should the sample be picked *from*? It is all very well being briefed to carry out your enquiry among a given population—but how do you translate these requirements into a real-life list of names which include the whole of the population you are supposed to be studying? In technical terms, this is the problem of establishing a *sampling frame*. There are many devices by which this can be done, varying from the ingenious and exact to the hit-and-miss. Quite often, the survey researcher will have reason to believe that the sampling frame does not quite succeed in representing the entire population which he is supposed to be sampling. Say, for instance, you were briefed to carry out a survey among 'wholesale coal and coke merchants'. You might get a list of current members of the wholesale coal and coke merchants' trade association and use that as your sampling frame, while having strong reason to believe that there were a few merchants about who did not belong to the trade association. When the sampling frame is known, or suspected, to deviate from the ideal in this way, then the researcher has to bear in mind that his sample results can only be generalized Statistically to the 'population' represented by the sampling frame, not to the ideal population. This may or may not have any practical effect on the results—and whether it does or does not must normally be a matter of guesswork.

The data having been collected, the survey researcher goes on to the stage of analysis. This can range all the way from qualitative assessment of the verbal answers given by respondents, through simple averaging and graphing of numerical answers, all the way to highly complex Statistical testing, according to the subject matter of the study in hand and the professional leanings of the researcher. The last stage, recommendation, follows as usual; though where survey studies are concerned, the adviser's task may rather often be simply to describe the situation revealed by the enquiry, leaving the job of deciding action to those who have commissioned the study.

This description of survey method, like the description of econometric method in the preceding chapter, has been simplified down to its barest essentials, and is designed purely and simply to provide a basis for further discussion for anyone who has not come across any details of survey practice before.

In the following sections, survey method will be compared, in its role as a means of economic investigation, with aggregate methods in general and econometric method in particular. You may ask: what is the real difference—if any—between survey method and aggregate methods? After all, as we know, almost all the data used in economic study have to be collected from individuals in the first place, and so must depend on the use of survey method, even if it is sometimes of a very routine kind—for instance, the periodic collection of trade returns on a sample or 100 per cent enumeration basis, the use of population censuses or agricultural censuses, and all the numerous other kinds of information which are collected by government and other official bodies in the present-day economy. And indeed, it is the case that almost all the information used in economic enquiry, even in econometric analysis, is collected by survey means in the first instance.

(To digress for a moment: we have to say 'almost all', not 'all'. There are some kinds of economic information which are purely technical—for instance, the way in which crops respond to fertilizer, the length of life of a machine—and this information will be collected by the appropriate technical means. Importantly also, as we noted in Section 7.4.2, institutional and legal detail can be got by looking it up in the appropriate books or by direct once-off enquiry. Finally, and more contentiously, if we admit the views of some schools of economic method, we need to add introspection as a source of information.)

In fact, we meet a familiar problem of exposition here: everybody knows what the difference is between an econometric study and a study using survey method, but it is very difficult to work out a cut-and-dried definition of the difference. Rather than try to do so, it is more useful to set out the main contrasts between the approach of survey method and that of aggregate methods. The latter go straight to existing aggregate data, which will usually have been collected for some purpose other than that of the study in question; they are concerned with picking out the relationships between these aggregates; and if they seek to say anything specific about the actions or motivations of individuals underlying these aggregate relationships, then they do so only at second hand, by putting forward hypotheses which cannot be checked directly against the data which are being used. The emphasis in aggregate methods is thus on the analysis of data more than on the initial collection of these data.

In survey methods, on the other hand, the emphasis is on the data-collection stage as much as, or more than, the analysis stage. In a survey study, the data collected and the means of collecting them are purpose-built to suit the question which is being examined or the hypothesis which is being tested. The data collected may be aggregated at the analysis stage, but this is simply for the purpose of more readily interpreting the data—'the orderly loss of information in order to gain knowledge'—rather than because the relations between the aggregates *per se* are considered of prime interest. The emphasis is on viewing the actions of individuals (or individual economic units constructed for analysis, such as firms and households), even though for the purposes of interpretation, these individual actions may be expressed 'on average'.

With these basic details in mind, we can go on to look at the capabilities of survey method as a means of economic investigation, under the same headings as we have done in Chapter 9 for econometric method. Because that chapter's discussion examined the relevant epistemological concepts in some detail, the coming sections can be brief.

10.2 Application

10.2.1 Causation and motivation

There is little doubt that the most important capability of survey method as compared to aggregate approaches in economics is its ability to look directly at the kind of causation that is all-important in social science, namely, motivation. To stress this notion in simple terms: in everyday life, when we want to find out why people do something, what they know, or what they intend doing, we go and *ask* them; why not do the same in economic studies?

One of the most astonishing features of the 'positivist' school in economic methodology (Section 6.2.4) has been their seeming rejection of the idea that human motivations ever *can* be directly investigated. This idea, like very many other ideas of this school, finds its most famous expression in Professor Friedman's essay, 'The Methodology of Positive Economics'. Survey interview questioning of businessmen about the factors influencing their business decisions, says Friedman, constitutes:

> . . . a procedure for testing economic theories that is about on a par with testing theories of longevity by asking octogenarians how they account for their long life . . .

and he affirms that

> . . . questionnaire studies of businessmen's or others' motives or beliefs

about the forces affecting their behaviour . . . seem to me almost entirely useless as a means of *testing* the validity of economic hypotheses.

As with so many other features of Friedman's methodological approach, one can only guess at the reason for this vehement rejection of survey method. Perhaps it is an overflow from his initial adoption of the 'positivist' viewpoint itself: he argues that higher-level statements are inaccessible to direct observation, and so, since very many higher-level statements in economics concern motivation, the only logically consistent attitude for him to take up is that survey method *must* be worthless.

Alternatively, perhaps the positivist opposition to survey method has come from a vague feeling that the survey approach—and particularly anything which might be labelled 'motivational research'—is unscientific mumbo-jumbo. Visions arise in these economists' minds of bearded gentlemen with Austrian accents, quizzing respondents on the psychiatrist's couch, and then making up the conclusions to suit the researcher's own preconceptions. These critics would suggest that when you ask someone why he does something, what he knows, or what he intends, you have no way of knowing whether the answer you get is correct, a rationalization, or just a deliberate lie. Thus, they argue, you are better advised to avoid all such questioning altogether, and rely on the 'hard figures', as the aggregate analyst does. In so far as this view is still held by some economists, it does scant justice to the abilities of present-day survey method and motivational research.

Of course survey results—whether relating to motivations, intentions, or more straightforward factual data—are open to error from all the sources we discussed in Chapter 8. But equally obviously, any other investigational approach is open to these errors. To dismiss survey results because they are not perfect implies the rejection of *all* investigational methods, including econometrics. Here again, in the context of applied economics, the most relevant question to ask is, simply, does it *work*? That is, do survey studies give the policy-maker the kind of information which systematically allows him to improve his control of economic events? The empirical evidence available to check out this question, as in the case of econometrics, is so difficult to assemble that no universal answer has been produced, or is ever likely to be. But we know enough to be able to say objectively that the positivists' out-of-hand dismissal of survey method in economics is quite unjustified.

One may add a final guess about the sources of this positivist misconception: when you are working with aggregate data all the time, and devoting all your intellectual effort to detecting the relationships between these aggregates, it is perhaps not at all surprising if you tend to acquire the feeling that the changes in these relationships are somehow self-propelling; and that the economy works like a vast machine (a model?) with moving parts that slide around in automatic interaction one with the other. The government is the mechanic, pressing policy buttons to make the parts slide in various directions. Press the button labelled 'tax', and down goes the consumption function; depress the lever labelled 'interest rate', and up slides the investment schedule. If one does fall into this frame of mind, it is clear that issues of individual motivation, knowledge, and intention will rather easily be relegated to the sidelines.

These positivist attitudes, if they were stated in the bald form in which they have just been spelled out here, would scarcely be admitted by the majority of working economists. But they nevertheless find their way, diluted or not, into a great deal of economic writing and analysis; they affect the choice of investigational method, and most unfortunately of all, they sometimes colour the views put forward in the teaching of economics.

A realization of the true capabilities of survey method in investigating motivations, intentions, and knowledge of economic events is invaluable to the student, even if only to dispel the comforting idea that the economy *is* a machine, responding automatically to policy push-buttons. Go out on the street, on to the shop-floor or farm, and do some survey questioning about economic events and policy. When you discover how many people have never heard of the policy measures concerned, let alone meaning to respond to them in any way whatever; how many people react to events in a way that theory would call 'irrational'; how many people have weird and wonderful interpretations of the nature and meaning of economic policy and economic figures—then you will be permanently cured of any temptation to think that economic policy can be made to work mechanically.

10.2.2. Intangibles

After the discussion of the last section, we can deal with intangibles in short order. We see that, here again, the survey approach has clear advantages over aggregate investigation. The direct questioning of the survey approach enables the investigator to examine respondents' attitudes to issues of amenity, nuisance value, and so on, in a way that is quite impossible when events are being studied in aggregate.

Here again, since the survey researcher is dealing in what people *say*, it is clear that there is room for argument about the interpretation of whatever answers he gets. But equally clearly, it is erroneous to dismiss survey answers on these topics as worthless simply for this reason. The test, as always, lies in the empirical usefulness of the results gained.

The survey researcher, far more than the user of aggregate analysis methods, is able to deal with qualitative data: his 'raw data' come to him in words as well as in figures, and his analysis, if he likes, can be verbal in whole or in part. And if the survey worker wants to try to quantify, he again has a wider choice of procedure than the econometrician. He can express his results quantitatively in either or both of two ways: he can say how commonly held a certain view is (that is, what proportion of his sample hold that view); or he can try to measure the strength of a view as it is held by individual respondents, using various kinds of 'scaling' procedures. These, of course, entail quantification which must be to some extent arbitrary: but it seems clear that they still allow the survey researcher a more direct look at attitudes than the user of aggregate data can get by such secondhand means as the use of proxy measures.

10.2.3 Prediction

Here, once again, the most obvious difference between survey method and aggregate approaches is that the survey researcher can *ask* people what they intend to do; and many survey studies—like the famed or dreaded pre-election opinion polls—have typically had prediction as their main aim.

It is clear that this capability to make direct enquiry about future action is a genuine epistemological difference as between survey method and econometrics—since, for example, you certainly cannot 'ask' aggregate national income what it intends doing next year. However, what is doubtful is the empirical ability of such direct survey questioning to give a *correct* prediction of what actually happens. Any method of empirical enquiry cannot help but run up against the barrier between present and future. As we have seen, econometric method is prevented from penetrating this barrier by the fact that past Statistical patterns may change in future, and we are ignorant about the possibility of such change. But the corresponding difficulty in survey research is that *intentions* may likewise change between the period of enquiry and the period of prediction—as the well-publicized failure of some election predictions has shown—and, again, we are ignorant about the likelihood of this happening. (Interestingly, the survey researchers who carry out pre-election polls now go to some length to stress that the results are *not* to be regarded as predictive.)

The fairest assessment is probably that neither survey method nor econometric analysis have yet shown that they add systematically to our quantitative ability to look into the unknown future of economic events. But, in making our qualitative appraisal of patterns as the basis for an informed prediction (recall Section 9.5), it may often be useful to have survey results which tell us declared intentions—just as it may help to have econometric results which tell us the quantitative shape of past patterns.

10.2.4 Sources of error

Here, survey method shows one notable advantage as compared with aggregate investigation: the researcher on survey work, far from being 'distanced' from his raw data, comes into direct contact with them. As the researcher collects his information from respondents at interview, or looks at the returns which come to him in a postal enquiry, he can hardly help but be alerted to the possible ambiguities, recording errors, and nuances of meaning which will influence his interpretation of the data. This is particularly so if the researcher himself does the 'piloting' of his questionnaire.

This, of course, does not mean that survey results are proof against error, any more than the results of any other kind of investigation. But it must be judged likely that the survey researcher will be more conscious than the user of aggregate methods of the nature and possible seriousness of the observational errors in his data. A fair amount of empirical work has been done by survey-research methodologists on the incidence of various kinds of bias and recording error, and the references in the reading guide to this chapter will lead you to this information.

Self-evidently, the potential danger of machine error in survey results will depend on the complexity of the analysis that is done; but in most instances, this will be less than in econometric analysis. And, since proxy measures are not needed in survey investigation, then error arising from questionable choice of proxies will not enter the picture.

10.3 Summing-up

Summing up the capabilities of survey method, in the same way as we did for econometric method in the previous chapter, we see that in many ways the survey approach seems better adapted to economic investigation than do aggregate methods. Survey research can throw direct light on some aspects of *causation* which are of vital importance to the understanding of economic questions—namely those connected with individual motivation, actions, and knowledge. *Intangibles*, likewise, can usually be dealt with more meaningfully by survey studies than they can be by aggregate methods. Some of the specific sources of *error* which beset aggregate data and analysis are less of a problem in survey work. Finally, survey method is no more and no less limited than econometric method in its ability to help us in *prediction*.

Since survey method thus appears to score over aggregate methods in some important respects, we may ask why survey method is not much more often used than other methods in economic studies. The answer lies largely on the cost side of the cost–benefit equation. Survey method entails costs—not only in the form of salaries for interviewers and clerical staff, but also in the time taken to carry out a study and arrive at results—which are often greater than the costs entailed if the same problem is investigated using aggregate methods. In this connection, one of the features already suggested as a strength of survey method must be regarded as a weakness: namely, that while econometrics and other aggregate approaches can rely on virtually any kind of information that can be expressed in figures and is available from some published source, the survey investigator collects his data 'from the ground up'. The results thus produced will often be more meaningful than those produced by aggregate investigation, for all the reasons that have been suggested in this chapter—but they will also often be more costly.

Further, there are certain economic problems which specifically require us to look at events in the aggregate, and not at individual level. This will be the case in situations where the fallacy of composition may enter the picture (recall Section 2.5.3); for instance, if we were investigating the pattern of saving in the economy, there would be obvious dangers in founding our recommendations solely on a study of individual saving intentions. In an ideal investigational world, all problems like these would be studied by a combination of survey *and* aggregate approaches. In reality, while this combined approach is sometimes possible, lack of resources makes it most uncommon.

All this having been said, it is probably fair to suggest that survey method is not used in economic investigation to as great an extent as an objective cost–benefit appraisal of methods would warrant. Just as the econometric approach seems to have been more fashionable in recent decades than its actual usefulness has justified, so survey method seems to have been rather much the 'poor relation' as regards prestige among academic economists and research-sponsoring bodies. Perhaps the positivist bias against survey investigation, expressed as it was by some influential figures in the academic world, helped initially to bring about this state of affairs.

Here again, there are signs that in the last few years the balance has begun to swing. As attitudes towards econometric work have become more critical, so the feeling has grown that economists could profitably turn back to look empirically, not just at aggregates, but at the individual actors on the economic scene, and that the obvious means of doing so is by survey investigation.

Perhaps this swing in methodological emphasis, like many phases of change in economics, is a response to changes in the *problems* which present themselves to the economist for solution. We hear a great deal nowadays about the 'crisis in economics', or the 'plight' of economic science. As previously familiar economic situations have changed in the last few years, so old predictions have been falsified, old policies made powerless to deal with current problems. Some economists hope for a new Keynes who, wizard-like, will produce a new body of theory to tackle these present-day conundrums. But until such a genius arrives on the scene, one way ahead is perhaps to recognize that the 'crisis' may be one of observation and analysis, rather than of deficiency in theory. It has become clear that the change currently taking place in the economic environment is primarily a change in motivations, reactions, and intentions. Aggregate investigation can tell us *what* these changes do to the economy, but not *why* they do it—and it is the latter question that is of desperate importance to the policy-maker. As the emphasis in empirical economic method shifts back towards individual and qualitative studies, we may perhaps find that economics regains its power to perform the only task which justifies the existence of our science: that is, to provide *useful* guidance on how to control economic events.

Reading guide: Chapter 10

A well-established and comprehensive text on survey method is C. A. Moser and G. Kalton, *Survey Methods in Social Investigation.*[62] You will find that some of its chapters discuss general problems of data collection and analysis with which we have been concerned in earlier chapters of this book, e.g., sources of error (the chapter cited in the reading guide to Chapter 8), the nature of accuracy, and problems of establishing causality. To get some idea of how the incidence of observational error in survey work is empirically investigated, skim the monumental book *Interviewing in Social Research*, by H. H. Hyman *et al.*[33]

For concrete instances of the way survey method can be used to attack problems in economic research, see the book edited by L. R. Klein, *Contributions of Survey Methods to Economics.*[40] My remarks in this chapter about the usefulness of survey method in revealing policy knowledge and attitudes were based on personal experience: see Part VI, Chapter 5, of my book, *Information in the Cereals Market.*[77]

To get the feel of some of the economic survey data used by UK policymakers, have a look at the annual volumes of results of the Family Expenditure Survey and the National Food Survey (both published by HMSO, London; to find the latter in the catalogues, you need to look up 'Household Food Consumption and Expenditure').

Glossary

I have tried to include in this Glossary all the main philosophical terms which you may come across in reading about economic methodology. I have kept the definitions as brief as possible, and have phrased them in the way which seemed to convey most clearly the sense of their usage by *economic* philosophers. In no way have I tried to give the full range of confused and overlapping meanings which apply to many of these terms when they are used in other philosophical fields; for this, you should turn to a philosophical dictionary.

AD HOC HYPOTHESIS   Hypothesis arbitrarily added to a theory in order to account for an otherwise unexplained observation.

AFFIRMING THE CONSEQUENT   Formally fallacious reasoning which runs: '1. If *A*, then *B*;
>2. *B*;
>3. therefore *A*.'

ANALYTIC(AL) (of statements)   Derived purely within the confines of a deductive argument, rather than from real-world observation. (Contrast SYNTHETIC.)

ANALYTICAL SCHOOL (used in this book to mean)   School of economic methodologists who see economic theory as being reasoned out from starting statements the *material* truth of which is obvious at a common-sense level.

ANTECEDENT   The 'if . . .' clause of a hypothetical.

ANTHROPOMORPHISM   Reasoning as though inanimate objects were really people.

APODICTIC (of statements)   Necessary, in the sense of being unambiguously demonstrable.

A POSTERIORI (of the truth or falsity of statements)   Based on observation of the real world. (Contrast *A PRIORI*.)

A PRIORI (of the truth or falsity of statements)   Known without reference to real-world experience, i.e., inherent in the structure of our thinking. (Contrast *A POSTERIORI*.)

APPEAL TO AUTHORITY   Attempt to support an argument by appealing to the statements of some esteemed individual, the principles of an ideology or religion, etc.

APRIORISM (in economic methodology)   Viewpoint which sees economic theory as being reasoned out from starting statement(s), the *material* truth of which is known *a priori*.

ARGUMENT BY ANALOGY   Reasoning which suggests that because two things are alike in certain particulars, they are also alike in (some or all) other particulars.

ARGUMENTUM AD HOMINEM   Attempt to support one's argument by criticizing personal characteristics of one's opponent.

ASSUMPTION (*Note*: usage of this term in economic methodology is very confused, and you should consult Section 6.3.2.) In brief:
1. Alternative name for the ANTECEDENT of a HYPOTHETICAL used in scientific testing.
2. Starting statement used in theoretical reasoning in economics.

ATOMISM   Alternative term for METHODOLOGICAL INDIVIDUAL-ISM.

AUXILIARY HYPOTHESIS   Statement about experimental conditions, modes of interpretation, etc., used together with a substantive hypothesis in a theory when deducing predictions from that hypothesis.

AXIOM (alternative term for)   Highest-level statement in a theory. (BUT N.B. sometimes also carries confusing overtones of 'being true *a priori*'.)

AXIOMATIZATION   Ascertaining the set of highest-level statements from which all the other statements in a theory can be deduced.

BEGGING THE QUESTION   Argument based on an unstated contentious premise.

CALCULUS (in epistemology)   Set of deductively linked symbolic statements: by replacing these symbolic statements with specific constructs, one arrives at a theory which is an 'interpretation' of the calculus.

CASUAL EMPIRICISM   Observation of the real world which does not make use of instrumentation.

CATALLACTICS   The study of market exchange.

CATEGORICAL   Any statement of the form: 'such-and-such is the case' (or 'such-and-such is not the case').

CATEGORY OF ACTION   View of *any* human action as being aimed at substituting a 'better' for a 'worse' state of affairs, in the view of the actor.

CAUSAL EXPLANATION   Explanation of the form: 'Event B happened because event A had happened previously.' (Contrast TELEOLOGICAL EXPLANATION.)

c-DOMAIN   The domain of constructs, i.e., the 'world of theory' as opposed to the 'real world'. (Contrast p-DOMAIN.)

CIRCULAR REASONING   Reasoning which uses as a premise the very proposition which the arguer sets out to prove.

CONDITIONAL (noun)   Alternative term for HYPOTHETICAL.

CONFIRMATION (usually used in phrase 'degree of confirmation')

Amount of confidence we can place in the material truth of a hypothesis, as judged by empirical testing.

CONSEQUENT   The '. . . then . . .' clause of a hypothetical.

CONSTRUCT   Notion put together by the scientist's own imagination and incorporated in a theory.

CONTINGENT STATEMENT   Able to be falsified by observation of the real world. (Contrast TAUTOLOGY.)

CONTROL
1. Ability to influence the course of events in the real world.
2. (in scientific experimentation)   A duplicated experimental set-up in which one experiment does *not* introduce the factor whose effect the scientist is setting out to judge.

CONVENTIONALISM   Doctrine that, since all testing must be carried out on *sets* of linked hypotheses, it is a matter of choice which of these hypotheses we regard as having gained support (or lost support) as a result of testing.

DEDUCTION   Reasoning which starts from given statements to reach a conclusion.

DETERMINISM   Doctrine that human action is predetermined, and that 'free will' is therefore illusory.

DETERMINISTIC
1. (of hypotheses)   Making an assertion about *all* the members of the group under study. (Contrast STATISTICAL.)
2. (of reasoning)   Not designed to allow for the chancy nature of real-world events. (Contrast PROBABILISTIC.)

EMPIRICAL   Relying on observation of the real world.

ENTHYMEME   Omission of one of the statements in a syllogism.

ENUMERATION, 100 PER CENT   Empirical investigation which covers all the members of the group under study.

EPISTEMOLOGY   The study of knowledge.

EXACT SCIENCES   Sometimes used to mean the same as PHYSICAL SCIENCES; but alternatively may indicate wholly deductive disciplines like mathematics or formal logic.

EXPERIMENT   Investigational situation set up deliberately by the scientist (rather than being thrown up by chance).

FALLACY   Any argument in which the reasoning used does not lead *necessarily* to the conclusion.

FALLACY OF COMPOSITION   Reasoning which assumes that whatever is true of the part must also be true of the whole.

FALSIFICATION   Attempt to show, by empirical testing, that a hypothesis is materially false. (Contrast VERIFICATION.)

224

FALSIFICATIONISM   Doctrine that proper scientific reasoning must be founded on attempts to falsify (and not verify) hypotheses.

HEURISTIC   Concerned with discovery rather than proof. ('Discovery' often implies here the discovery of new hypotheses.)

HIGH-LEVEL (of statements in a theory)   Of relatively great generality, thus, often remote from real-world observability.

HISTORICISM   Doctrine that history evolves according to ascertainable patterns.

HOLISM   Doctrine that the explanation of the behaviour of groups cannot be achieved merely by explaining the actions of the individuals making up these groups. (Contrast ATOMISM.)

HYPOSTATIZATION (in epistemology)   Giving substance to a metaphysical principle by transforming it into a methodological rule.

HYPOTHESIS (*Note*: usage of this term in economics is very confused. Consult Section 4.3.1.) In brief:
1. The 'informed guess' from which the scientist starts hypothetico-deductive investigation.
2. Any statement forming part of a theory.
3. High-level statement in a theory, partly or wholly inaccessible to direct observation.

HYPOTHETICAL (noun)   An 'if–then' statement.

HYPOTHETICO-DEDUCTIVE METHOD   Method of scientific investigation consisting of repeated sequences of: deduction of predictions from hypotheses; empirical testing of predictions; revision of hypotheses as necessary; deduction and testing of further predictions.

IGNORANCE   Departure from certainty, the extent of which cannot be expressed in terms of statistical probability.

INDUCTION   Reasoning which draws a general conclusion from observing a number of individual cases.

INSTRUMENTALISM   Doctrine that scientific theories are instruments for predicting observable phenomena, and are therefore to be judged by their usefulness in this role.

INSTRUMENTATION   The use of instruments (rather than the unaided human senses) in empirical observation.

INTERSUBJECTIVITY   Agreement among scientists on how empirical observations should be carried out and interpreted.

INTROSPECTION   Examining one's own reactions (actual or potential) to a given situation.

LAW (in science)   Empirical assertion of the form: 'If X happens, then Y (always) happens.'

LAW OF LARGE NUMBERS   Doctrine that, over a large number of observations, individual variations from a norm will tend to cancel each other out.

LOGIC   The study of (correct) reasoning.

LOGICAL FALLACY   Fallacy which arises from faulty construction of a syllogism.

LOGICAL 'TRUTH' (of statements)   Quality of being accepted as 'true' purely for the purpose of a deductive argument, without any reference to real-world observation. (Contrast MATERIAL TRUTH.)

LOGIC-IN-USE   What scientists actually do (as opposed to what they say they do). (Contrast RECONSTRUCTED LOGIC.)

LOW-LEVEL (of statements in a theory)   Of relatively restricted generality, thus, usually close to real-world observability.

MAJOR PREMISE   The premise in a syllogism which runs: 'All A's are B.' (Compare MINOR PREMISE.)

MATERIAL FALLACY   Name used to describe various kinds of faulty reasoning which are not classed as logical nor verbal fallacies.

MATERIAL TRUTH (of statements)   Quality of being true of the real world. (Contrast LOGICAL 'TRUTH'.)

MECHANISTIC EXPLANATION   Alternative term for CAUSAL EXPLANATION.

METAPHYSICAL   Concerned with speculations about the world which science (currently at least) has no means of investigating.

META-THEORY   The theory of theory.

METHODOLOGICAL INDIVIDUALISM   Doctrine that the behaviour of groups can only be understood in terms of the actions of the individuals making up these groups.

METHODOLOGY   The study of method.

MINOR PREMISE   The premise in a syllogism which runs: 'C is an A.' (Compare MAJOR PREMISE.)

MISPLACED CONCRETENESS, FALLACY OF   Mistake of thinking that a construct necessarily has an exact, directly observable counterpart in the p-domain.

MODEL   1. (in epistemology)   Set of deductively-linked statements, the applicability conditions of which are not fully specified.

   2. (in econometrics)   Algebraic statement of an economic hypothesis, set up for empirical testing by statistical means.

MODUS PONENS   Correct reasoning which runs:
   '1. If A, then B;
   2. A;
   3. therefore B.'

MODUS TOLLENS   Correct reasoning which runs:
   '1. If A, then B;
   2. not B;
   3. therefore not A.'

MONISM   Doctrine that different kinds of phenomena (e.g., those of the physical and social sciences) can be explained in essentially the same ways. (Contrast PLURALISM.)

NATURALISM   Alternative term for PHYSICALISM.
NATURAL SCIENCES   Alternative term for PHYSICAL SCIENCES.
NOMOLOGICAL   Concerned with the discovery of scientific 'laws'.
NORMATIVE (of statements)   Based purely on the personal tastes of whoever is making the statement. (Contrast POSITIVE.)

OCCAM'S RAZOR   Doctrine that, of any two explanations of an event, the more simple is to be preferred to the less simple.
OPERATIONISM (OPERATIONALISM)   Doctrine that the scientist should admit to his c-domain only such constructs as can be defined in terms of operations of measurement.

PANPHYSICALISM   Alternative term for PHYSICALISM.
p-DOMAIN   The domain of protocols, i.e., the 'real world' as opposed to the 'world of theory'. (Contrast c-DOMAIN.)
PERFECT INDUCTION (used by some philosophers to mean)   Conclusion arrived at by observing all the members of the group under study.
PETITIO PRINCIPII   Alternative term for BEGGING THE QUESTION.
PHYSICALISM   Doctrine that the phenomena of social science are (actually or potentially) explicable in the same terms as those of physical science.
PHYSICAL SCIENCES   Sciences which deal with things rather than people.
PLURALISM   Doctrine that different kinds of phenomena (e.g., those of the physical and social sciences) need to be explained in different ways. (Contrast MONISM.)
PLURALITY OF CAUSES (usually in phrase 'principle of . . .')   Doctrine that any observed event may have more than one cause.
POSITIVE   (*Note*: usage of this term in economics is very confused. See Sections 5.2.1 and 6.2.4.) In brief:
  1. (of statements)   Concerned with matters of fact rather than with the personal tastes of whoever is making the statement. (Contrast NORMATIVE.)
  2. (used by economic positivists to mean)   Relying on the empirical testing of predictions.
POSITIVISM   (*Note*: usage of this term, in economics and science generally, is very confused. See Section 6.2.4.) In brief:
  1. (in philosophy)   Doctrine that unless a statement is testable in practice, it has no meaning.
  2. (in economics)   Doctrine that competing hypotheses should be judged by their predictions, not by the realism of their assumptions.

POSSIBILITY   Chance of an event happening, not expressible in terms of statistical probability.

POST HOC ERGO PROPTER HOC   Fallacious reasoning which runs: 'Event *B* happened after event *A*; therefore, event *B* was caused by event *A*.'

POSTULATE   High-level statement in a theory (sometimes used as alternative term for AXIOM.)

PRAGMATIC   Concerned with practical application. (*Note*: philosophers give this word a variety of more technical meanings.)

PRAXEOLOGY (used by apriorists to mean)   Wide-ranging social science based on the 'category of action', having economics as one of its sub-disciplines.

PREDICTION
1. Lowest-level statement in a theory.
2. Alternative term for the CONSEQUENT of a hypothetical.
3. Statement of future outcomes (quantitative or qualitative).

PREMISE (PREMISS)   One of the statements in a syllogism that, taken together, lead to the conclusion.

PROBABILISTIC (of observational method)   Taking account of the chancy nature of real-world observation.

PROBABILITY (*Note*: a brief definition of this term cannot adequately be given. Consult Section 4.4.4).

PROPOSITION OF REGULARITY (UNIFORMITY)   Proposition which states: 'What is true of observed cases is also true of unobserved cases.'

PROTOCOL (in epistemology)   An event observed happening in the real world.

PROTOCOL STATEMENT (*Note*: this term is given the following two confused meanings by different writers:)
1. Alternative term for PROTOCOL.
2. Lowest-level statement in a theory.

RATIONALISM   Doctrine that (some or all) scientific conclusions can be arrived at by pure deductive reasoning, unaided by real-world observation.

RECONSTRUCTED LOGIC   What scientists say they do (as opposed to what they actually do). (Contrast LOGIC-IN-USE.)

REDUCTIONISM   Doctrine that concepts should be spoken of in the most empirically accessible terms possible. (In economic methodology, often used as alternative term for PHYSICALISM.)

RULES OF CORRESPONDENCE
1. (used in this book to mean)   Intersubjectively agreed rules by which the lowest-level statements of a theory are to be compared with protocols.
2. (used by some other writers to mean)   Rules by which a calculus is to be related to its interpretation in the form of a specific theory.

SOCIAL SCIENCES   Sciences which deal with people rather than (or as well as) with things.

STATISTICAL (of hypotheses)   Making an assertion about *some* of the members of the group under study.

SUBJECTIVISM   Doctrine that the meaning of an action can be judged only by the person carrying out that action.

SYLLOGISM   Form of deductive reasoning in which two statements, taken together, lead to a conclusion.

SYNTHETIC (of statements)   Derived from premises, some at least of which are assertions about the real world. (Contrast ANALYTIC.)

TAUTOLOGY   A statement which consists in defining one thing in terms of another, and hence is true irrespective of anything which may happen in the real world. (Contrast CONTINGENT STATEMENT.)

TAXONOMIC   Concerned with classification (of objects, events etc.).

TELEOLOGICAL EXPLANATION   Explanation which runs: 'Event *A* happened because it was aimed at making event *B* happen.' (Contrast CAUSAL EXPLANATION.)

TERM (in syllogistic reasoning)   Any of the entities spoken of in the syllogism.

TESTING   Process of setting low-level statements in a theory against observations of the real world.

THEOREM
1. (used by some epistemologists to mean)   High-level statement in a theory, though of lower level than an axiom.
2. (used by the analytical school to mean)   Set of theoretical statements in economics which can be used in policy recommendation, in so far as that set of statements is judged applicable to the particular situation under study.

THEORY   Set of deductively linked statements in the *c*-domain (ideally, with applicability conditions fully specified and containing no mutually contradictory nor irrelevant statements).

UNCERTAINTY   Departure from certainty, the extent of which can be expressed in terms of statistical probability.

UNIVERSAL (of statements)   Asserted as being materially true of all times and places.

VALIDATION   Process of judging the strength of hypotheses (hence of theories) against the probabilistic results of real-world observation.

VALUE-JUDGEMENT   Alternative term for NORMATIVE judgement.

VERBAL FALLACY   Faulty reasoning in which the syllogism seems at first sight to be correctly constructed, but (on closer inspection of its wording) turns out not to be.

VERIFICATION Attempt to show, by empirical testing, that a hypothesis is materially true. (Contrast FALSIFICATION.)

VERSTEHEN Approach to explanation of social events which entails 'getting inside the thoughts' of the actors concerned.

References

The sources cited in the end-of-chapter reading guides are numbered below in alphabetical order by author.

1. ALLARD R. J., *An Approach to Econometrics*, Philip Allan, Oxford, 1974.
2. BAUMOL W. J., 'Economic Models and Mathematics' in S. R. Krupp (ed.), *The Structure of Economic Science, q.v.*
3. BEAR, D. V. T., and D. ORR 'Logic and expediency in economic theorizing', *Journal of Political Economy* **75**, 188–96, April 1967.
4. BLAUG, M., 'Kuhn versus Lakatos or paradigms versus research programmes in the history of economics' in S. J. Latsis (ed.), *Method and Appraisal in Economics, q.v.*
5. BOULDING, K., *The Skills of the Economist*, Howard Allen, Cleveland, 1958.
6. ———, 'The verifiability of economic images' in S. R. Krupp (ed.), *The Structure of Economic Science, q.v.*
7. ———, *Economics as a Science*, McGraw-Hill, New York, 1970.
8. BRANDT, R. B., 'The concept of welfare' in S. R. Krupp (ed.), *The Structure of Economic Science, q.v.*
9. BRONFENBRENNER, M., 'A middlebrow introduction to economic methodology' in S. R. Krupp (ed.), *The Structure of Economic Science, q.v.*
10. CAWS, P., *The Philosophy of Science*, van Nostrand, Princeton, 1965.
11. CENTRAL STATISTICAL OFFICE, *Economic Trends*, HMSO, London, monthly.
12. ———, *National Income and Expenditure*, HMSO, London, annual.
13. ———, *Studies in Official Statistics*, HMSO, London, annual/occasional.
14. CHRIST, C. F., 'Judging the performance of econometric models of the US economy', *International Economic Review*, **16**, 1, 54–74, February 1975.
15. CHUNG, A., *Linear Programming*, Merrill, Columbus, 1963.
16. COATS, A. W., 'Economics and psychology: the death and resurrection of a research programme' in S. J. Latsis (ed.), *Method and Appraisal in Economics, q.v.*
17. CODDINGTON, A., 'Are statistics vital?', *The Listener*, 11 December 1969, p. 823.
18. ———, 'Economists and policy', *National Westminster Bank Quarterly Review*, February 1973, 59–68.
19. COOPER, R. L., 'The predictive performance of quarterly economic

models of the United States' in B. G. Hickman (ed.). *Econometric Models of Cyclical Behavior*, Columbia University Press, New York, 1972.

20. COPI, I. M., *An Introduction to Logic*, 3rd edn, Macmillan, New York, 1968.

21. DASGUPTA, A. K., and D. W. PEARCE, *Cost-Benefit Analysis: Theory and Practice*, Macmillan, London, 1972.

22. DAVIES, J. T., *The Scientific Approach*, Academic Press, London, 1973.

23. DEPARTMENT OF EMPLOYMENT, *Family Expenditure Survey*, HMSO, London, annual.

24. DEVONS, E., *Essays in Economics*, Allen and Unwin, London, 1961.

25. DORFMAN, R., P. A. SAMUELSON, and R. M. SOLOW, *Linear Programming and Economic Analysis*, McGraw-Hill, New York, 1958.

26. ECONOMIST, THE, 'Charts for every occasion', December 27 1958, p. 1171.

27. FRIEDMAN, M., 'The methodology of positive economics' in his *Essays in Positive Economics*, University of Chicago Press, Chicago, 1953.

28. HOUGH, R., *What Economists Do*, Harper and Row, London, 1972.

29. HOWREY, E. P., L. R. KLEIN, and M. D. McCARTHY, 'Notes on testing the predictive performance of econometric models', *International Economic Review*, **15**, 2, 366–83, June 1974.

30. HUFF, D., *How to Lie with Statistics*, Gollancz, London, 1969.

31. HUTCHISON, T. W., *'Positive' Economics and Policy Objectives*, Allen and Unwin, London, 1964.

32. ———, *Knowledge and Ignorance in Economics*, Blackwell, Oxford, 1977.

33. HYMAN, H. H., *et al.*, *Interviewing in Social Research*, University of Chicago Press, Chicago, 1965.

34. JAY, P., 'Putting a new face on things', *The Times*, 4 September 1970, p. 23.

35. JÖHR, W. A., and H. W. SINGER, *The Role of the Economist as Official Adviser*, Allen and Unwin, London, 1955.

36. KAPLAN, A., *The Conduct of Inquiry*, Chandler, Scranton, 1964.

37. KENNEDY, M. C., 'The economy as a whole' in A. R. Prest and D. J. Coppock (eds), *The UK Economy*, 7th edn, Weidenfeld and Nicolson, London, 1978.

38. KEYNES, J. M., *The General Theory of Employment, Interest and Money*, Macmillan, London, 1936.

39. KLEIN, L. R., *Econometrics*, Row Peterson, Evanston, 1953.

40. ——— (ed.), *Contributions of Survey Methods to Economics*, Columbia University Press, New York, 1954.

41. KNIGHT, F. H., '"What is truth" in economics?' in his *On the History and Method of Economics*, University of Chicago Press, Chicago, 1956.

42. KRUPP, S. R. (ed.), *The Structure of Economic Science*, Prentice-Hall, Englewood Cliffs, 1966.

43. KUHN, T. S., *The Structure of Scientific Revolutions*, 2nd edn, University of Chicago Press, Chicago, 1970.

44. LATSIS, S. J., 'A research programme in economics', in S. J. Latsis (ed.), *Method and Appraisal in Economics, q.v.*

45. —— (ed.), *Method and Appraisal in Economics,* Cambridge University Press, Cambridge, 1976.

46. LIPSEY, R. G., *An Introduction to Positive Economics*, 4th edn, Weidenfeld and Nicolson, London, 1977.

47. LOASBY, B. J., 'Hypothesis and paradigm in the theory of the firm', *Economic Journal,* **81**, 863–85, December 1971.

48. ——, *Choice, Complexity and Ignorance,* Cambridge University Press, 1976.

49. MACHLUP, F., 'The problem of verification in economics', *Southern Economic Journal,* **22**, 1, 1–21, July 1955.

50. ——, 'Are the social sciences really inferior?', *Southern Economic Journal,* **27**, 173–84, January 1961.

51. ——, 'Operationalism and pure theory in economics' in S. R. Krupp (ed.), *The Structure of Economic Science, q.v.*

52. ——, 'Theories of the firm: marginalist, behavioral, managerial', *American Economic Review,* **57**, 1, 1–33, March 1967.

53. MANSFIELD, E., *Microeconomics,* 2nd edn, Norton, New York, 1970.

54. MARGENAU, H., 'What is a theory?' in S. R. Krupp (ed.), *The Structure of Economic Science, q.v.*

55. McCLEMENTS, L. D., 'Some aspects of model-building', *Journal of Agricultural Economics,* **24**, 1, 103–20, January 1973.

56. MINISTRY OF AGRICULTURE, FISHERIES AND FOOD, *Household Food Consumption and Expenditure,* HMSO, London, annual.

57. MISES, L. von, *Epistemological Problems of Economics,* van Nostrand, Princeton, 1960.

58. ——, *The Ultimate Foundation of Economic Science,* van Nostrand, Princeton, 1962.

59. MORGENSTERN, O., *On the Accuracy of Economic Observations,* 2nd edn, Princeton University Press, Princeton, 1963.

60. MORLEY, R., *Mathematics for Modern Economics,* Fontana/Collins, London, 1974.

61. MORONEY, M. J., *Facts from Figures,* 3rd edn, Penguin, Harmondsworth, 1970.

62. MOSER, C. A., and G. KALTON, *Survey Methods in Social Investigation,* 2nd edn, Heinemann, London, 1971.

63. O'BRIEN, D. P., 'Whither economics?' *Economics,* **11**, 2, 75–98, Summer 1975.

64. PAPANDREOU, A., *Economics as a Science,* Lippincott, Philadelphia, 1958.

65. PHILLIPS, A. W., 'The relationship between unemployment and the rate of change of money wage rates in the United Kingdom, 1861–1957', *Economica,* **25**, 283–99, 1958.

66. POPPER, K., *The Poverty of Historicism,* 2nd edn, Routledge and Kegan Paul, London, 1961.

67. ———, *The Logic of Scientific Discovery*, rev. edn, Hutchinson, London, 1972.
68. PREST, A. R., and R. TURVEY, 'Cost-benefit analysis: a survey', *Economic Journal*, **75**, 683–735, December 1965.
69. 'RADCLIFFE REPORT': *Report of the Committee on the Working of the Monetary System*, HMSO, London, Cmnd. 827, 1969.
70. ROBBINS, L., *An Essay on the Nature and Significance of Economic Science*, 2nd edn, Macmillan, London, 1935.
71. 'ROSKILL REPORT': *Report of the Commission on the Third London Airport*, HMSO, London, 1971.
72. ROTWEIN, E., 'On "The methodology of positive economics"', *Quarterly Journal of Economics*, **73**, 4, 554–75, November 1959.
73. ———, 'Mathematical economics: the empirical view and an appeal for pluralism', in S. R. Krupp (ed.), *The Structure of Economic Science, q.v.*
74. ——, 'Empiricism and economic method: several views considered', *Journal of Economic Issues*, **7**, 3, 361–82, September 1973.
75. RYAN, A., *The Philosophy of the Social Sciences*, Macmillan, London, 1970.
76. SHAPIRO, E., *Macroeconomic Analysis*, 4th edn, Harcourt Brace Jovanovich, New York, 1978.
77. STEWART, I. M. T., *Information in the Cereals Market*, Hutchinson, London, 1970.
78. STILWELL, F. J. B., *Normative Economics*, Pergamon, Sydney, 1975.
79. STREISSLER, E. W., *Pitfalls in Econometric Forecasting*, Institute of Economic Affairs, London, 1970.
80. TINTNER, G., 'Some thoughts about the state of econometrics' in S. R. Krupp (ed.), *The Structure of Economic Science, q.v.*
81. 'VERDON-SMITH REPORT': *Report of the Committee of Inquiry into Fatstock and Carcase Meat Marketing and Distribution*, HMSO, London, Cmnd. 2282, 1964.
82. WONNACOTT, R., and T. H. WONNACOTT, *Econometrics*, Wiley, New York, 1970.
83. WYNN, R. F., and K. HOLDEN, *An Introduction to Applied Econometric Analysis*, Macmillan, London, 1974.

Index

Accounting, 131, 161, 171
Accuracy, 164, 168
  nature of, 1, 174–176, 178, 183–185
  spurious, 176–177, 186, 206
Ad hoc enquiry, 168–169, 172
Advisory function, 158–162, 177, 212–214
Affirming the consequent, 21
  and apriorist account, 120
  in hypothetico-deductive testing, 51–56, 194
Aggregated data, 167–168, 171, 182
  and motivation, 201–202
  v. survey data, 214–220
Algebra, 48, 124, 139
  use in economics, 113–117
Analysis, nature of, 159–161
Analytical school:
  and econometrics, 198, 209
  and models, 147–150
  nature of, 118, 121–127
  and validation, 135, 138–141, 150–153
Anthropomorphism, 109
Appeal to authority, 27
Applicability:
  in analytical account, 123–125, 147–150
  and models, 145–152, 162, 197–198
A priori statements, 118–121
  (*see also* Apriorism)
Apriorism, 118–123, 126–127, 135, 138–141, 150–151
Argument by analogy, 26–27, 104
  as between economics and physical science, 86–87, 91, 97
Argumentum ad hominem, 27–28
Arithmetic, 49, 121
'As-if' reasoning, 129–131
Assumptions:
  and algebraic reasoning, 115–116
  in economic theory, 118
  in hypothetical statements, 18
  'realism of', 118, 127–136, 150–151
  simplifying (*see* Simplification)
Astronomy, 66, 68, 104
Attitudes, 180, 217–218
Auxiliary hypotheses:
  and applicability, 124, 149, 151
  nature of, 59–61
  and 'testing by predictions', 129–131, 145, 163, 195

Axiomatisation, 137
Axioms, 73

Basis of compilation, 175–176
Begging the question, 28, 66, 86
Bias:
  and observational error, 180
  in official submissions, 170
  in sampling, 180–181
Boulding, K. E., 161

'Casual empiricism', 168
Categorical statements, 15
Categorical syllogism, 14–15
'Category of action' (*see* Human action)
Causation, 24–26, 73, 108–109
  v. correlation, 66–67
  and econometrics, 193–204, 209
  and experimental control, 104–106, 140
  and prediction, 65–69, 208
  and survey method, 215–217, 219
Caws, P., 74n
Census, 161, 214
c-Domain:
  in economic theory, 134–139, 141–142, 148, 198
  nature of, 70–75, 116
Certainty, 61–64, 71, 120
Choice, 6–7, 102, 119
Circular reasoning, 28–29
Coddington, A., 176–177, 183
Comparability, in economic statistics, 175
Composition, fallacy of, 22–24, 220
Computer, 4–5, 166–167, 186
  and econometrics, 205–206, 209
  and machine error, 181, 205
Confidence:
  and accuracy, 177
  in statistical analysis, 88–89, 92, 184, 208
Confirmation, 56, 195
Constructs, 70, 135, 201
  (*see also c*-Domain)
Consumption function, 3, 121–122, 190–191, 217
Contingent statements, 48
Control, experimental, 104–106, 139–140, 199
Control, of real-world events, 68–69, 113, 131, 199

Control—*contd.*
 and policy advice, 158, 202, 216, 220
Correlation, 46
 v. causation, 67–68, 199–201, 204
 'nonsense', 199–200
 tests of, 45, 59, 194
Cost-benefit analysis, 7, 101, 160, 166–167
 used in appraising investigational method,
 162–172, 207, 219–220

Deduction:
 in analytical account, 123–125, 152
 in apriorism, 119–121
 as basis of induction, 35–37
 and certainty, 62
 in hypothetico-deductive method, 40–43,
 58–75, 141, 195, 197
 in structure of theory, 72
Definitional statements, 46–48, 99
'Desk study', 167
Disaggregated data, 167–168, 182, 215, 219
 (*see also* Survey method)
Disproof, 32–35, 41, 46
 'logic of', 53–56
 (*see also* Falsification)

Econometrics, 3, 163, 166, 188–210
 and economic prediction (*see* Prediction,
 econometric)
 and error, 182, 184–185, 205–207
 v. survey method, 214–220
'Economic man', 133, 135, 143
Economics:
 definitions of, 6–7
 as a science, 2–8
Einstein, A., 61
Empirical basis, 4, 39
Epistemology, 13
 of econometrics, 193–196
 of testing, 56–64
Error, 174, 177–186
 in econometrics, 182, 184–185, 205–207, 209
 observational, 59, 141–143, 179–186,
 205–206
 sampling, 178–184, 206
 and statistical analysis, 177–186
 and survey method, 218–219
Error term, 178, 188, 190, 206–207
Experiment, 18, 40, 104–106
 'crucial', 57
 (*see also* Control, experimental)
Explanation, 71, 113, 150–151, 158
 causal v. teleological, 107–109, 139
 and model-building, 196–199, 209
 v. prediction, 65–69, 131
Explanatory power, 112, 114, 133–134
Extrapolation, 92, 96, 204
'Eyeballing', 88, 171–172, 185, 202, 205

Facts, 4, 74, 126–127, 135, 180
 (*see also* Positive statements)
Fallacies, deductive, 20–29
Falsification, 53–56, 61, 123, 137, 148, 194
Fashion, in economic method, 2, 209, 220
Firm, theory of, 64, 115–116, 131, 134, 171
Forecasting (*see* Prediction)
Free will, 85–86, 140, 203
Friedman, M., 100, 122n., 126–133, 215–216

Generality, (*see* Level)
Geometry, 48–49, 121

Historicism, 153
Human action, 6, 92, 119–121
Hypotheses, 43–50, 65–67, 69, 71
 auxiliary (*see* Auxiliary hypotheses)
 competing, 3, 126, 130, 146–147, 197–198
 deterministic v. statistical, 45–46, 54
 and problem formulation, 165–172
 (*see also* Hypothetico-deductive method;
 Testing)
Hypothetical statements, 16–19, 80–81
 with compound antecedent, 59–61, 129–
 130, 145–146
 (*see also* Hypothetical syllogism)
Hypothetical syllogism, 15–19, 21–22
 and econometrics, 193–196
 in hypothetico-deductive testing, 50–56,
 196
 in 'testing by predictions', 129–130, 146
Hypothetico-deductive method, 39–76
 in econometrics, 193–196
 and economic reasoning, 123–125,
 128–130, 135–141, 147–153
 and 'Phillips Curve' (*see* 'Phillips Curve')

Identities (*see* Definitional statements)
Ignorance, 61–64, 71, 140
 and economic prediction, 96–97, 149,
 152–153, 204, 218
 and error, 182–186
Impossibility, 62–63
Induction, 31–37
 and explanation, 67–69
 logical problem of, 36–37
 and prediction (*see* Prediction, inductive)
 and sampling error, 178, 181
 and testing, 41–42, 122–124, 149
 and uncertainty, 57, 63–64
Instrumentation, 4, 123
Intangibles, 3, 101, 166
 and econometrics, 202–203, 209
 and survey method, 217–219
Intelligibility, 164–165
Intentions, 216–218, 220
Intersubjectivity, 58–61, 74–75, 105, 123, 183
 and econometrics, 194–195, 199
 and economic application, 163–164

Intersubjectivity—*contd.*
  and 'testing by predictions', 129–131, 140, 146
Interviewing, 180, 184, 211–212, 219
Introspection, 122–125, 135, 198, 214

Joad, C. E. M., 9
Judgement, 24–26

Kaplan, A., 66, 117
Keynes, J. M., 3, 24, 26, 29, 121–122, 125
Klein, L. R., 185, 204
Knowledge, 13–14, 161, 189, 215, 219
  of policy, 217
Kuhn, T. S., 153, 209

Lakatos, I., 153
'Law of large numbers', 90–92
'Laws', scientific, 90, 136
Level, of statements in theory, 73, 133–134
Linear programming, 166–167
'Line-fitting', 189, 197
Lipsey, R. G., 82–83, 151
Loasby, B. J., 64
Logic, 1, 13, 48, 124, 139
Logical 'truth' (*see* Material truth, v. logical 'truth')

Machlup, F., 108, 127, 132, 137, 163
McKenna, J. P., 201n
Margenan, H., 70n, 74n, 75, 141
Marginality, 114
Marxian economics, 27, 102–103, 153
Material truth:
  v. logical 'truth', 19–21, 48, 53, 62, 71, 119–121
  and 'realism', 133–136
'Mathematical economics', 113–117, 188–189, 198
Mathematics, 48
Mises, L. von, 109, 119–121
Models:
  in econometrics, 142, 188–200
  in economics, 13, 142–152, 197–198
  and policy advice, 158, 163, 168, 172
  in science generally, 26, 142
Moderate empiricism, 127–128, 135, 140–141, 147–153, 209
Monetarists, 68–69
Morgenstern, O., 182
Motives, 109, 143
  and econometrics, 201–202, 209
  and 'positive economics', 129, 131–132
  and survey method, 214–217, 219–220

National income, theory of, 3, 44, 122
Neo-Keynesians, 68–69
Non-rejection, 41–42, 50
Normative statements, 47, 97–104, 126–127, 139, 169–170

Objectivity, 99–100
  (*see also* Intersubjectivity)
O'Brien, D. P., 150
Observability, 40–43, 71, 116, 133
  of motives, 131, 216
100 per cent numeration, 33, 178, 183, 211, 214

Paradox of thrift, 23
p-Domain, 70–75, 134–142, 149, 197, 201
Perfect competition, 128–129, 132, 135
Phillips, A. W. (*see* 'Phillips curve')
'Phillips curve', 42–43, 50–51, 58–61, 71, 93, 189, 192
Phlogiston theory, 68
Physical science, 5–6
  (*Note*: for comparisons of physical science with economics as regards aspects of method, *see* the aspect concerned, e.g., Control, Experiment, Prediction).
Pilot enquiry, 212, 219
Plurality of causes, 105–106
Policy:
  and analytical view, 124–125, 148
  and economic advice, 158–165, 168, 182, 209, 220
  and economic explanation, 67, 105, 112, 131
  and fallacy of composition, 23–25, 201–202
  and positive/normative distinction, 102–103
  and prediction, 83–84
'Positive economics', 100, 118, 126–136, 150–151
  and survey method, 215–216, 220
  and validation of economic theory, 138–141, 147, 182
Positive statements, 97–104, 126–127, 170
Positivists, in philosophy of science, 126
Possibility, 54, 63–64
Post hoc ergo propter hoc, 24–26, 65, 105, 201
Postulates, 48, 73, 136
Prediction:
  econometric, 3, 191, 196, 203–205, 208–209
  (*see also* Prediction, inductive-statistical)
  in economics, 13, 79–97
  v. explanation, 65–69, 199, 202
  in hypothetical statements, 19
  in hypothetico-deductive method, 42–43, 58–64, 72–73
  inductive-statistical, 33, 69, 83–97, 107, 138, 140, 150–153
  'naive', 208–209
  'of the past', 42, 81, 192, 196
  qualitative v. quantitative, 80–81
  and survey method, 218–219
  'testing by' (*see* Testing, 'by predictions')
Premises, in syllogism, 14, 19
Probability, 54, 62–64, 179, 191
  and prediction, 86, 89, 96, 203
Problem formulation, 159–160, 165, 172, 177–178, 212

Problem-solving, 159–165, 168, 171–172, 177, 202
Proof, 32–35, 41–43
(*see also* Verification)
Proposition of regularity, 36–37, 69, 73, 87–96
Protocols, 70–75, 131, 183
(*see also* *p*-Domain)
Proxy measures, 203, 205–206, 218–219

'Rational consumer', 128, 133, 135, 143
'Realism' (*see* Assumptions, 'realism of')
Regression analysis, 189, 191, 207
Robbins, L., 6–7, 82–83, 126, 149
'Royal Commission' method, 169–170
Rules of correspondence, 74–75, 123, 139, 152, 197

Sample, 31, 178–180, 185–186
random selection of, 180–181, 212–213
in survey method, 211–214
Sample surveys (*see* Survey Method)
Samuelson, P. A., 22
Science:
development of, 136–137
nature of, 4–6, 39
Significance tests, 45, 191, 194–195, 200
Simplification, 116, 128
and models, 142–146
Social science, nature of, 5–6
Statistical analysis, 45, 213
and causality, 106, 140
and error, 177–179, 182–186
and validation of theory, 51–56, 122, 128, 136–137
(*see also* Correlation; Econometrics; Prediction, inductive-statistical; Regression analysis; Significance tests)
Subjectivity, 99
Supply-and-demand theory, 3, 124, 143–144
Survey method, 5, 163, 166, 169–171, 211–220
and error, 182–185, 205
and 'positive economics', 131, 215–217
Syllogism, 14–22, 28
hypothetical (*see* Hypothetical syllogism)
in induction, 35–37, 87–90

Tastes, 3–4, 47
(*see also* Normative statements)

Tautology, 47–49, 99, 122n
and analytical approach, 124
and apriorism, 121
Terms, in syllogism, 14
Testability, 46–50, 98–100, 107
and 'mathematical economics', 116
Testing:
in econometrics, 189–198
of economic theory, 13, 109, 119, 124–152, 163
in hypothetico-deductive method, 40–65, 74–75
and models, 145–150
'by predictions', 100, 125–135, 138–142, 148–151, 182
of significance (*see* Significance tests)
statistical (*see* Statistical analysis)
and survey method, 215–216
'by usefulness', 125, 163, 168
Theory, in economics, 8, 20, 102, 112–153, 220
v. application, 158
and econometrics, 189–198
and economic prediction, 84, 87, 197
'inductive', 136–139
predictions of, 80, 120
(*see also* *c*-Domain; Testing)
Theory, in science generally:
and explanation, 67–69, 107, 113
nature of, 3–4, 39
structure of, 70–75, 129, 197
(*see also* *c*-Domain; Testing)
'Third London airport', 102, 160
Time-series analysis, 92, 200–201
Trend, 31, 88, 208
breaks in, 92, 96
projection (*see* Extrapolation)

Uncertainty, 61–64, 71, 96–97, 149, 204
and error, 184–186

Validation, of theory, 56
(*see also* Testing, of economic theory; Testing, in hypothetico-deductive method)
Value-judgements (*see* Normative statements)
Verification, 53–56, 61, 123, 137, 148, 194
Viner, J., 7

Welfare, 6–7, 49, 101, 103, 107, 115

PRINTED AND BOUND IN GREAT BRITAIN
BY W & J MACKAY LIMITED, CHATHAM